T0287393

RON
GREENWOOD

Mike Miles

RON GREENWOOD

A Biography of Football's Forgotten Manager

First published by Pitch Publishing, 2021

Pitch Publishing
A2 Yeoman Gate
Yeoman Way
Worthing
Sussex
BN13 3QZ
www.pitchpublishing.co.uk
info@pitchpublishing.co.uk

ISBN 978 1 78531 868 9

Typesetting and origination by Pitch Publishing
Printed and bound in Great Britain by TJ Books, Padstow

Contents

Preface

I AM a West Ham fan and have been since the mid-1960s. I have often asked myself why.

I have no known family connection with the East End of London, and if I knew the grief and anguish the Hammers would cause me over the years I would have gone for a safer, and dare I say, more successful, option.

I was born and grew up in Hereford and cut my football-watching teeth at the local team, Hereford United (who would play their own distinctive part in Hammers history), playing in the Southern League at their Edgar Street ground. The great John Charles was their player-manager. The 1964 FA Cup Final came along at just the right time. If that was the aperitif, then the European Cup Winners' Cup Final a year later was the main course. And West Ham 'winning' the World Cup that memorable summer of 1966 made an indelible impression on this 14-year-old.

I saw my first live West Ham match in September 1967. We didn't have a car, and somehow I must have persuaded my father to undertake the long, tedious coach journey from Hereford to London. They were playing bottom club Wolves at Upton Park. West Ham had won their previous two matches 5-1 away from home. So of course, they lost that day! But by then it was too late. I was hooked.

'It's hard to explain what the club is, but I do know that it's *my* club. I've been brought up with it all my life. One thing's for sure – it's something that has always been there. You can't explain it.'

* Colin Green, a West Ham supporter, quoted in Charles Korr's book *West Ham United*.

'West Ham United. Those three words have meant so much to literally millions of people over the past 120 years. To many, following West Ham is a way of life, tantamount to a religion. Across the world it is a team that people recognise and admire for what it has brought to the beautiful game over the decades.'

* Iain Dale, in his introduction to *West Ham – A Nostalgic Look at a Century of the Club*.

As Brian Williams says in his ode to West Ham, *Nearly Reach the Sky*, written after the move to Stratford, 'There are people who consider football to be a religion, but I don't see it that way. Religious faith offers certainty, salvation and in some cases virgins. I've never found any of these while watching West Ham United, and I've been following them for 50 years. If it's not a religion, it's certainly an addiction. I've seen all the great players who have turned out in claret and blue since the late 1960s, and rather too many of the not-so-great as well. I've been there when we've triumphed and when we've been humiliated. I've rejoiced at cup final wins, despaired at relegation, celebrated promotion, savoured the sweet and sour pleasure of unlikely escapes, and looked on powerlessly as the club has been taken to the brink of financial disaster more than once. Who in their right mind would willingly become a football supporter, and choose to support a club like mine?'

Now if only I knew the answer to that.

I moved to college near London in 1970, and that season saw every West Ham home game bar one. Typically, they did not win a league match until October – at the 11th attempt. Things reached a nadir later that season with Ron Greenwood suspending Bobby Moore, Jimmy Greaves and two others for nightclubbing on the eve of a 4-0 FA Cup defeat at Blackpool.

Even this loyal fan was becoming aware that Greenwood, the Hammers' manager, was different to many of his contemporaries, especially the title-winning Matt Busby, Don Revie and Bill Shankly – and not just because he didn't win the number of trophies they did.

After the cup-winning exploits of the early 1960s, Greenwood's tenure at West Ham became increasingly fraught as his team became regular relegation strugglers and increasingly prone to early cup exits in the late 1960s and early '70s.

However, the passing years lend a better perspective, not least on football managers, and I feel now is the right time for a full biography of a man who is not just probably West Ham's greatest-ever boss, but one who contributed immensely to the wider footballing landscape in the 1960s and '70s.

When I set out to write this book, I was surprised to find there was no biography of Ron Greenwood. I hope I have been able to rectify that gap in football's literature.

Mike Miles

Introduction

'I WANTED to see pleasure on the pitch and pleasure on the terraces … football is a battle of wits or nothing at all.'

'Football is a simple game. The hard part is making it look simple.'

The words are those of former West Ham and England manager Ron Greenwood and they sum up, with characteristic simplicity, the sporting creed of one of the most imaginative, idealistic and downright decent men to have made their living as a manager in English football since the Second World War.

After Greenwood's death in February 2006, the acclaimed sportswriter Hugh McIlvanney wrote, 'Obituarists rightly emphasise his distinction as an innovative coach whose advanced thinking and purist philosophy enabled West Ham United to supply three key players to England's World Cup-winning team of 1966. But above all Greenwood was a lover of the game, of the beauties implicit in its fluid geometry.

'He was immensely proud of England's triumph, and of the part played by Bobby Moore, Geoff Hurst and Martin Peters, but it was characteristic that when we discussed those 1966 finals, he rhapsodised about a goal scored for Hungary by János Farkas.

'It happened to be the best goal of the tournament and Ron wanted to celebrate excellence.'

Greenwood's playing career from 1945 to 1956 took in over 300 appearances for the likes of Bradford Park Avenue, Brentford, Chelsea and Fulham (and one England B appearance). A cool, constructive defender, he captained both Bradford and Brentford. By the time he joined Fulham he was 33, at the end of his playing career, and becoming captivated by coaching.

He had fallen under the spell of the England coach Walter Winterbottom, and while still playing he had already coached several amateur teams, including Oxford University and Walthamstow Avenue. He was already a holder of an FA full coaching badge. Both men had witnessed the Hungarian destruction of England at Wembley in November 1953, and the influence of that game was with Greenwood throughout his coaching career.

He would write, 'I sometimes think I have a little insight into how Paul felt on the road to Damascus. My own moment came at Wembley on a misty November day in 1953, when Hungary beat England by six goals to three – and proved to me beyond all doubt that football can be a game of beauty and intelligence, a lovely art as well as a muscular science.

'Perhaps, without realising it, I was waiting for someone to show me the way. My ideas on the game were firm; but proof – undeniable, public proof – was needed that football had more to offer than the average league club's performance on a Saturday afternoon. When the proof came, on 25 November in Coronation year, it was as if someone had removed scales from my eyes. All my basic ideas on the game suddenly came together. Hungary's victory was written up like a national disaster but for me it was a fresh start.'

In 1956 Greenwood became boss of non-league Eastbourne United, as well as assuming responsibility for the England youth side, which included a certain Bobby Moore.

In November 1957 he was appointed coach of Arsenal, a job he combined with supervision of the England under-23 team. In April 1961 he was asked to manage their First Division rivals, West Ham United, a club whose 61-year existence had only a cursory meeting with on-field success. Indeed, it was only in 1958 that they had been promoted back to the First Division, having been Second Division occupants since before the war.

Greenwood was the first manager to be appointed from outside the West Ham 'family', and only the fourth person to take the role in the club's history. Since Greenwood became general manager in 1974 there have been 18, including caretakers and two spells for David Moyes.

Greenwood lacked the ruthlessness of more feted contemporaries like Bill Shankly and Don Revie, with whom his success rate, in terms of winning trophies, did not compare. But his West Ham team of the mid-1960s had its own moments of heady triumph including an FA Cup win in 1964, the club's first, and a European Cup Winners' Cup triumph in 1965, only the second European win by an English club, but, crucially, the side was invariably easy on the eye, even in defeat.

Then there was the little matter of supplying three members to England's World Cup victory in 1966, a tournament in which their perfection of Greenwood's near-post cross ploy proved so devastating.

The club years after 1966 brought no more silverware, and by the early '70s the 'Greenwood Out' banners were appearing at

Upton Park. By 1974 he had had enough and moved upstairs while handing the managerial reins to his protégé John Lyall.

In 1977, he was asked by the FA to restore the fortunes and dignity of the England national side after Revie had absconded to the Middle East. Greenwood, even at the age of 55, remained faithful to his belief that footballers must set out to create rather than to destroy. However, results were largely disappointing in view of the outstanding players available. Aged 60 he took the decision to stand down after comparative failure at the 1982 World Cup, having done an honourable and competent job without ever perhaps capturing the imagination of the public. It was his final active role in football.

Greenwood was inducted into the English Football Hall of Fame in 2006, as recognition of his achievements. He is also a member of the FA and LMA Halls of Fame, as well as having been awarded a CBE in 1981.

Football historian and author David Goldblatt wrote in *The Ball is Round*, his 2006 history of global football, 'The key English managers [of the 1960s] were Bill Nicholson at Spurs, Ron Greenwood at West Ham United, and Alf Ramsey at Ipswich Town and England. The leading Scots were Matt Busby at Manchester United, Jock Stein at Celtic and Bill Shankly at Liverpool. Between them this cohort of coaches remade British football and in the mid-1960s returned it to the very pinnacle of the world game.'

There have been biographies written of all these managers, with the exception of Greenwood.

Greenwood was born on 11 November 1921 and now, a century after his birth, is an appropriate time for a full biography of a man who had been a strong and positive influence on English football.

An impeccable sportsman, he deplored the greed and hostility, the cynicism and win-at-all-costs mentality which had become pervasive by the mid-1970s. He was a deep thinker and skilled communicator who painted pictures with words on the training ground, believing simplicity was beauty. He was no shouter of odds, no conventional hard man, treating players as adults and expecting them to impose their own self-discipline. He was a noble servant to football; with more men like him, the game would be much the richer.

The first chapter in Greenwood's 1984 autobiography *Yours Sincerely* was entitled 'Footballing Philosophy'. These footballing principles were not the result of hindsight but something he had held to throughout his playing and managerial career and were to have the decisive effect on how he approached the game throughout his life.

He wrote, 'I spent my whole career as a manager trying to stop this devaluation of the game. I cared more about the purity and finer values of football than I did about winning for winning's sake – and if that is a sin, I am a sinner. Football should be a game of risks. When I was manager of West Ham, I sent out teams that were prepared to gamble, whatever the dangers, because I believed strongly that this was the secret of football's appeal. We gambled with intelligence and skill, otherwise we would have been committing suicide, but I wanted to see pleasure on the pitch and pleasure on the terraces. I took on a different, heavier responsibility when I became manager of England, but my philosophy did not change – even when time and circumstance clipped our wings. There are people who will write me off as an idealist. That is fine with me.'

Perhaps the crucial flaw in Greenwood's make-up was his man-management. Bobby Moore claimed that he never received a 'well done' from his boss. Many regarded Greenwood as cold and aloof. Even his integrity caused him to miss out on signing Gordon Banks in 1967 because he already had a gentlemen's agreement to buy Bobby Ferguson from Kilmarnock.

Also, while Greenwood's ideas were perfect in theory, West Ham lacked the players to implement them, and they could literally be kicked off the park. Moore once said, 'I couldn't deny his brilliance. The man is the encyclopaedia of football. He sees things that were beyond the comprehension of many coaches and players. But he talked about the game at such a high level that sometimes it went over the head of the average player.'

Greenwood would admit, 'Indeed, if there was a weakness in our make-up during my years at West Ham it was that we did not always have the players to counter the bright ideas of others. We were good at doing our thing but not so hot at stopping others doing theirs.'

And he was not a style 'snob', adding, 'There are a thousand ways to play football and the trick is always in playing to your strengths. The British way works very well at its best. There was enormous and even vitriolic criticism of the way Watford played in their climb from the Fourth Division to becoming runners-up in the First Division in the 1980s. Yet I thought they were brilliant. The long ball was the basis of their game and quick, constant pressure was their object. It was not a style I would employ by choice nor would I like to see every team using it. But in the league there is room – and a need – for individual styles. We should be grateful to Watford's manager, Graham Taylor, for trying something different. His side made people think, and it is variety that gives football its appeal. Those managers who don't like Watford's style should do their darndest to find ways of proving it wrong.'

He would tell author Brian Belton, 'You have to see what the rest of the world is doing. I've always believed football is a developing game – it constantly changes, and the possibilities are endless. That's part of its fascination. But if you don't see new and different things, how others do things differently, it's hard to be inventive and you get into a rut; everyone likes best to do what they know – what's hard to learn is that you don't know and then do it better than what you learnt. There's not a great deal of point in anything if you are just going to repeat yourself over and over. Apart from getting found out eventually, people will know what to expect and counter what it is you do, it's unrewarding.'

1

Early Life: 1921–1940

RON GREENWOOD was born on 11 November 1921. He always maintained that making an entrance into the world on Armistice Day meant there was no excuse for forgetting his birthday. His birthplace, 18 Ormerod Street in the Lancashire village of Worsthorne, was less than three miles from the town of Burnley.

An early football memory was his father carrying him as a five-year-old down the hill to Turf Moor, where he would be perched on a barrier to watch his heroes, Burnley FC, who were a First Division club in the 1920s and Football League champions in 1921.

Greenwood would describe Worsthorne as a, 'Quiet, pretty, rather rural place in those days, with a church and a school, a big obelisk in the centre, a little row of shops and a post office. It had a couple of mills, one big, one small – the economic pillars of our community. Worsthorne was a friendly place above all.'

The entry for Burnley in Wikipedia lists some 16 sportspeople associated with the town. This list includes England and Lancashire cricketer James Anderson, former England international footballers Jimmy Crabtree and Billy Bannister, as well as current

Premier League striker Jay Rodriguez. Fabián Coulthard, second cousin of Formula One driver David Coulthard, also gets a mention.

But there is no inclusion for Ron Greenwood. I have called this book *A Biography of England's Forgotten Manager* and it is a shame this applies even to his home town as much as to his coaching record.

The start of the 20th century saw Burnley's textile industry at the height of its prosperity. By 1910 there were approximately 99,000 power looms in the town, and by 1920, the Burnley and District Weavers, Winders and Beamers Association had more than 20,000 members. However, the First World War heralded the beginning of the collapse of the English textiles industry and the start of a steady decline in the town's population.

The war was followed by a short period of prosperity, but then came the slump of the 1920s and 1930s, which led to short-time working, unemployment, and the collapse of many firms.

In *The Rise and Fall of the British Nation*, David Edgerton wrote, 'The pre-Great War cotton industry was an expanding and world-dominating industry, and most people would have expected it to continue to be so. But in the inter-war years, apart from a short-lived boom the markets for British cottons did not resume their growth. Countries put up tariff barriers against British goods and a major competitor appeared – Japan. By the 1930s the British national industry was no longer the leading exporter of textiles, even though textiles still accounted for a quarter of its exports. The result was that the industry never retained the output of 1913 and was in perpetual trouble. Investment dried up, and most companies continued to use the equipment they had in 1921 – most of it pre-1914, until the firms closed in the 1930s.'

English Journey is an account by the writer J.B. Priestley of his travels around England in 1933. Priestley did not visit Burnley, but he did spend a little time 11 miles away in Blackburn – which he described as a 'sad-looking' town – which had a similar industrial, cotton-based industry to Burnley. 'The whole district had been tied to prosperity, to its very existence, with threads of cotton, and you could hear then snapping all the time,' Priestley wrote.

'That very day, a mill, a fine big building that had cost a hundred thousand pounds or so not 20 years ago, was put up for auction, with no reserve: there was not a single bid. There hardly ever is. Nobody has any money to buy, rent, or run mills anymore. The entire district has been sliding towards complete bankruptcy for years.'

He found wastelands; industrial decline had been so bad that it made him question whether the whole 19th-century industrial revolution had been worth it.

Greenwood's father Sam was a stocky fellow, about five feet tall, a painter and decorator as well as a useful footballer. 'He was a kind and sympathetic man who did not anger easily. He never pushed or gushed but his helping hand was always there. He enjoyed life but did not have any illusions about it. His feet were always firmly on the ground,' wrote Ron. When the Depression hit, he moved alone to London, where he had a sister, to establish a new home. That left his wife to run the home at Worsthorne and she worked around the clock. She had a job at the big mill, where she ran six looms and would be out of the house at 6.30am. She would be back in time to get Ron and his sister Ivy off to school and then she'd return to work.

Money was short in the Greenwood household, and Ivy had a nasty accident so had to spend nearly four years in hospital, much of that time in Liverpool. Even so the children were always well-scrubbed and decently clothed. Young Ron was in the local choir, which meant church three days a week as well as Sunday school, and these were the only occasions on which he wore shoes. For the rest of the week he wore clogs with leather tops and wooden soles. He wore these out so quickly playing football that his mother had a standing order at the cobblers. 'The oddest feature of life when we moved down south was to find that I wore shoes every day instead of only on Sundays,' Greenwood would recall. He wasn't alone in his choice of footwear; most people in the village wore clogs.

Football was an early obsession with Ron. He went to the local school, and by the time he was eight he was playing with 14-year-olds in the first XI. There just weren't many boys of his age in the village. Classes were unwelcome interludes between games, with teachers telling him that if he devoted half as much time and energy to his lessons as he did to football, he'd go a long way. Their remonstrations fell on deaf ears.

Greenwood got his first job in the sport aged only six. The village had two major sides, church teams but deadly rivals, who played in the Burnley Sunday League: Wesleyan, and Church of England. Ron was appointed official ball boy to both. Describing himself as simply a retriever, it was a job he did with enormous pride. Most of the players worked at the big mill, and the only time they really got on together was when they played for the mill's own side. It was a good team and they won the Burnley Hospitals Cup – the knockout tournament which mattered most locally – with the final played at Turf Moor itself. At the age of seven,

Ron was appointed mascot for his first role at a league ground. Worsthorne won 4-1.

Greenwood had an early association with Wembley Stadium. He had an uncle who managed a decorating firm with a base in London and he used to visit him at his big house in Shepherd's Bush. Ron made his first visit to Wembley in 1925 to see the British Empire Exhibition; he was three years old and Wembley just two.

The Greenwood family followed their father to London in 1931 when Ron was ten. Their new home was in Alperton, only a mile or so from Wembley. 'Our house had a real luxury. It had a bathroom,' Ron wrote. His new school was Alperton Secondary Modern School. He described himself as 'academically average'.

But the move south posed special problems for him. 'Changing schools was difficult,' he said. 'I had a broad Lancashire accent and had to endure quite a bit of mickey-taking.' Again, he became the youngest and smallest member of another first XI. He played at left-half and went on to captain the school as well as Wembley Boys at under-13 and under-14 levels. He was also picked for a trial with Middlesex Boys but, with a rotten sense of timing, he broke an arm beforehand and could not play.

Ron left school at the age of 14. His father used his connections in the decorating business to get him a job in 1937 with a firm of sign and glass writers run by a Preston man, a Mr Westby. In return for £30 he launched Ron on a five-year apprenticeship on five shillings a week.

His new employers happened to be the contracted sign writers for Wembley, as well as the Olympia and, later on, the Earl's Court exhibition centres. This gave Ron a free seat for some of the best sport and entertainment in the country.

One of the firm's jobs, in the days before big electronic scoreboards, was writing out the team changes for the various cup finals. They had to be written quickly and legibly and were then wheeled around the stadium on a sort of mobile sandwich board. Fred White, the foreman, always did the writing for finals and nobody envied him more than Greenwood, as this was the most prestigious job of all. Eventually he was given rugby league's Challenge Cup Final, seemingly because nobody else wanted it, and finally he was given the 'big one' – the 1938 FA Cup Final between Preston North End and Huddersfield Town.

Sometimes Ron worked at Wembley for months on end, doing the signs for the dressing rooms, and later – after the war – much of the work for the 1948 Olympic Games. His dad eventually became maintenance manager on the painting side at Wembley, while Ron became so involved with the stadium that he thought of himself as part of the scenery.

Greenwood was turning out for a variety of football teams, among them Ealing Road Methodists and Alperton Old Boys, of which he was a founder member, and which his father Sam helped train. It was around this time that one or two league clubs decided they might see a future professional footballer in him.

He was picked to play for a representative side, the Wembley Juvenile Organisation Committee League, and the goalkeeper Harry Brown told Greenwood he was going for a trial with Queens Park Rangers. 'Why not go with me?' Harry asked. It seemed a good idea but when they got there they found an army of kids kicking a ball round among themselves. There did not seem to be much organisation, but they joined in. Eventually a man called Alec Farmer approached Ron and asked him what position he played.

'Centre-half,' was the reply.

'Right,' said Farmer. 'You're in the next game.'

Afterwards Rangers invited Ron to sign for them, but he'd heard Chelsea were coming to Alperton and told Rangers he wanted to wait before making a decision. It was Chelsea's trainer, Norman Smith, who invited Ron to sign for them in 1940. Chelsea's traditions and style appealed more to the aspiring professional who knew that because of the war they were forming an under-19 side, instead of the usual reserve team mixture, to play in the London Combination. That was the start of the Chelsea youth scheme, and Ron could lay claim to being one of its first products.

2

Wartime Playing Career: 1940–1945

JUST AFTER Christmas 1940, Ron Greenwood was at Fulham with Chelsea's reserves when he received a message to say that the first team were a man short for their home game with Aldershot, and he was wanted to fill in. As the home of the British Army, Aldershot was able to call on many footballers in uniform, and their half-back line that day included Joe Mercer, Stan Cullis and Cliff Britton.

Chelsea star Dicky Spence, still at Stamford Bridge helping with the youth teams, took Greenwood to one side and said, 'If you are in trouble at any time son, kick the ball to me.' Greenwood celebrated his first-team debut with a 6-1 win and would later write in his autobiography that the score was 6-0, perhaps taking a defender's pride in a clean sheet! He also wrote that the 'papers were very kind to me'.

Chelsea's manager was Billy Birrell. He would become one of the major influences on Greenwood's career, teaching the young player that football at its best was a thinking game as much as a physical one. He encouraged players to be true to their own ability, and this was a philosophy his pupil could agree with, then, and for the rest of his playing and managerial career. Birrell turned the raw youngster into a student of the game. Ron recalled, 'He used to talk to me for hours about football, and first made me conscious that this was a thinking game. He taught me the basic things and opened the door for me. I went on from there until I reached the point where nobody else agreed with my thoughts on the game and for five years, I found nobody with whom I could discuss football.' Birrell allegedly told the Chelsea players, 'That boy Greenwood has the best football brain I've ever encountered.'

It was in the early days of the Second World War that Ron met his future wife, Lucy. His father was a warden and one night a bomb failed to explode after hitting a house just up the road from the Greenwoods. It was the home of Lucy's family, who had moved there about six months before. His father decided that Lucy's family would have to spend the night elsewhere but did not like the idea of them sleeping in one of the local air raid shelters. So, at two in the morning he brought them to stay with his own brood. It was not exactly 'love at first sight'. Lucy even referred to her future husband as that 'stuck-up boy Ron Greenwood'. When his name came up again a few days later, a boy told her, 'You don't want to worry about him. All he cares about is football.'

Nevertheless, they were married in 1941 during his first leave after he had joined the RAF and been posted to Northern Ireland as part of a mobile radio unit.

Greenwood was stationed in an old vicarage in Maghera, and on hearing of his albeit modest Chelsea connections, a local publican put him in touch with Belfast Celtic. He turned out for them regularly and was the only Englishman on their books. Other internationals in the Celtic side included Billy McMillan, who would later become West Ham's representative in Ireland.

Greenwood would win a runners-up medal with the Green Hoops in 1941 when his adopted team lost to Larne Olympic in the County Antrim Steel Cup Final.

To ensure he could be free to play on Saturdays, he made himself competent at cooking, preparing the meals for the rest of the week. Lucy later said, 'He is a very good cook, and often does the Sunday lunch for the family at home.' Mrs Greenwood underlined her husband's competence around the house by recalling one of his finest achievements, keeping their son Neil clean when he was a 15-month-old baby. Lucy and her daughter were away so for a fortnight Ron maintained the house, looked after Neil and conquered the nappy-changing chore.

On the pitch, he had decided centre-half was his best position. As a boy he had fancied himself as an inside-forward, largely because he was too small to play elsewhere, but as he grew his options increased, and the central defensive position better suited his ability and temperament.

Greenwood had several other short-term postings, including one at Goodwood racecourse. He had also been based for a period in Ghent in Belgium and would enjoy the idea of going back to the country when West Ham were drawn against La Gantoise (today known as KAA Gent) in the first round of the European Cup Winners' Cup in 1964.

Eventually he found himself back in London where he signed as a professional for Billy Birrell's Chelsea in 1943.

Wembley entered Greenwood's life again when, in 1944, Chelsea reached the War Cup Final. He was named as a reserve but in those days before substitutes did not get on the pitch.

Ron was sent overseas in 1944 but was returned home after contracting appendicitis. The Greenwoods now had their first child, a daughter, Carole, and she and her mother moved north to stay with relatives in Bradford to escape the doodlebugs then falling on London. After convalescence Ron asked to be nearer his family and was moved to Lissett, near Hull. Many northern clubs invited him to guest for them, and he settled on Bradford Park Avenue, for whom he played as a guest until the end of the war.

At Bradford the regular centre-half was Alan Brown. He was a policeman and when his job saw him posted elsewhere Greenwood was asked to fill his position.

Greenwood was still registered with Chelsea, but by 1945 John Harris had established himself at centre-half. Greenwood could see no future for himself with the Blues and persuaded them to let him go permanently to Bradford Park Avenue in December 1945. The fee was £3,500, the most the Yorkshire side had ever paid for a player.

3

Bradford Park Avenue

THE MANAGER at Valley Parade was Fred Emery, described by Greenwood as 'an honest soul', though hardly a manager in the modern sense. He doubled as the club's secretary and the team would only see him just before kick-off on Saturdays. No one talked tactics; the players worked things out as the game went along.

Tactics, coaching and thoughtful preparation were still new concepts for most teams and totally alien to many more. English football had barely progressed over the previous half-century. Until the Second World War, most Football League teams had been overseen by a 'secretary-manager' who was often regarded as little more than an office boy by the club directors. His administrative duties were frequently considered more important than getting the players ready to win games.

Even the concept of the manager having sole responsibility for picking the team was considered newfangled. Dave Sexton, a one-time West Ham player himself and someone who would become a respected coach, said, 'Managers at that time were not used to bringing in fresh ideas. It was like they were forbidden to do anything new.'

As well as at centre-half, Greenwood played in various positions at first. He didn't mind, believing that experience in more than one role gave a player a much greater appreciation of all that was happening around him on the pitch.

A key member of that early Bradford side, before being transferred to Newcastle for £14,000 in October 1946, was Len Shackleton, the 'Clown Prince of Soccer'. Greenwood described Shackleton as a 'player with lovely, almost unbelievable skills, and tremendous confidence in himself'. He played right-half behind the star for a while but never got much help from Shackleton when it came to defending.

A lot of Bradford's goals were scored by Jack Gibbons. He would later move to Brentford, becoming their manager. Greenwood would be his first signing for the west London club.

Later on, Bradford's attack would be led by George Ainsley, who Greenwood credited with awakening his interest in coaching when he found the boot of Ainsley's car full of footballs which he was utilising at local schools.

While Bradford Park Avenue comfortably held their own in the Second Division they never threatened to set it alight, but they could be a handful in the FA Cup. All rounds in the 1945/46 competition were held over two legs.

In the fourth round Bradford lost 3-1 at home to Manchester City in the first leg then for the return at Maine Road the team coach arrived only 20 minutes before kick-off after being stuck in snow crossing the Pennines. Nevertheless, the Yorkshire side triumphed 8-2. The club reached the quarter-finals that season, eventually succumbing to Birmingham City 8-2 on aggregate.

In the third round during 1947/48 Bradford were drawn away to Arsenal, the First Division leaders and subsequent champions. Captained by Greenwood, Bradford came away from Highbury with a 1-0 win under their belt in front of a crowd of 47,738. According to one newspaper report, 'Towering like a giant over the whole fantastic and fanatical game was the figure of Bradford's centre-half Greenwood. Every Bradford player was a hero, but Greenwood was the greatest of them all.'

Bradford were favourites for the fourth-round tie away to Colchester United (managed by Greenwood's predecessor at West Ham, Ted Fenton) but lost 3-2.

The next season a crowd of 82,771 saw them draw 1-1 with Manchester United at Maine Road – used because Old Trafford was undergoing repairs – in a tie which went to a second replay, Bradford eventually losing 5-0.

Despite these occasional successes, and being made captain, Greenwood conceded that he could not 'pretend life was always perfect at Bradford. Very few people there tried to lift their colleagues' spirits or confidence. It was a case of "if you don't do it, you're out".'

So when the chance came to join Brentford in March 1949, he took it. Coincidentally, he moved on the same day that Alf Ramsey transferred from Southampton to Tottenham Hotspur. Greenwood's timing was opportune as 1949/50 saw Bradford relegated, heralding the onset of the club's decline.

4

Brentford

WHEN THE chance came to join Brentford and return to London just before the transfer deadline in March 1949, Greenwood took it gladly. Jack Gibbons, who had moved from Bradford to Brentford as a player 18 months before, was now the west London club's manager and Greenwood was his first purchase. For a fee of £9,000 he was signed to shore up the Bees' defence, replacing Jack Chisholm who had gone to Sheffield United.

Greenwood enjoyed 'three wonderful years' at Griffin Park, where he would become captain and persuade a young wing-half called Jimmy Hill to take over as the players' union representative. 'You're an intelligent lad,' Greenwood wrote of his conversation with Hill. 'You can be the players' union representative and collect the subs. Nobody else wants the job!' It is now a matter of history, of course, that Jimmy became chairman of the union – later the Professional Footballers' Association – and successfully led the campaign for the abolition of the maximum wage and the old retain-and-transfer system.

Hill wrote in his autobiography about how much he enjoyed playing alongside Greenwood, who became a good friend, 'With his experience he was able to help me tremendously in mastering the defensive arts which were in short supply on my CV. It was also Ron's influence which persuade me to attend an FA coaching course at Lilleshall. I had never thought about it before, but it did seem to make sense to do everything I could to learn about the profession I had just entered.'

The forthright Hill left for Fulham in March 1952 after a row with the manager, in which he had supported Greenwood but had too much to say about it to the press, a subject we will return to shortly.

Greenwood claimed to be instrumental in Brentford signing Tommy Lawton, then in his early 30s but still a 'name' player. Brentford were playing Notts County at Meadow Lane and Lawton, an old friend, said to him that he was fed up with the Magpies. Greenwood 'pricked up my ears and after the game reported what he'd said to [manager] Jack Gibbons, who was not enthusiastic. But soon after I mentioned Lawton's words to a Brentford director and his response was very different. The board decided to go for Lawton. Brentford paid more than they had anticipated but the move received tremendous publicity.'

While at Brentford, Greenwood considered himself fortunate to be involved with Malcolm MacDonald, the club's player-coach, a Glaswegian who had learnt the game with Celtic during the 1930s. MacDonald, like Greenwood, was a football thinker and helped to restore some of the confidence Greenwood claimed to have lost during his latter days at Bradford. Greenwood wrote, 'He [MacDonald] had a lot of ability and self-belief himself and more than once I saw him put his foot on the ball on his own goal line. Malcy would say to me, "Look Ronnie, if you want to do something, and you've got the confidence, then do it. If you haven't, don't! It's your judgement that matters."'

Greenwood made 12 appearances for his new club during the 1948/49 season, with his debut coming in a 1-0 home win on 19 March against, ironically, Bradford Park Avenue.

In 1949/50, his first full Brentford season, Greenwood was the only ever-present, being described as an inspiration at centre-half by one historian of the club.

The six goals scored by Spurs and QPR early in the campaign accounted for exactly half the total Greenwood and co. were to concede at home all season, with no fewer than 14 visiting sides failing to score at Griffin Park. With only 12 goals conceded, Brentford's against column was the best in the top two divisions.

Greenwood took over as captain the following season, against West Ham, in his 60th consecutive appearance. He also scored his first goal in a 3-0 win at Doncaster Rovers on 3 February 1951.

The home game against Everton, on 27 August 1951, marked his 100th outing in a row. According to the club history, *100 Years of Brentford*, 'The foundation of Brentford's success was built on the Harper, Greenwood, Hill half-back line. In Ron Greenwood, Brentford possessed one of the finest centre-halves in the game, a combination of the classical and competent who refused to get flustered under pressure and made every pass tell. His style of play, one which he later brought to bear as manager of West Ham and England, blended perfectly with the all-action style of Tony Harper and successful chaser of lost causes Jimmy Hill.'

In the early stages of the Christmas morning encounter with Southampton at Griffin Park in 1951, Brentford looked well on their way to a win but when Greenwood and Gaskell went to clear, they left it to each other and in the process allowed Southampton to score.

During the half-time interval the inquest into the goal caused the mother and father of a row between manager Gibbons and Greenwood, which hardly left the team in the right frame of mind for the second half, and they duly went on to lose 2-1.

According to Greenwood, 'Jack Gibbons came storming into the dressing room and "blew his top". Everything we were doing was suddenly wrong, and that included the way the defence played.

'"Hang on a minute," I said. "We've been playing this way all season and I can't remember anyone complaining before. We've lost one game. But one defeat doesn't make it a bad system or us a bad side."' A blistering row developed and in the heat of the moment some damaging things were said on both sides. Greenwood continued, 'I lost my temper and started charging about, and I even shouted, "That's it, I'm going to ask for a transfer." The criticism mattered to me deeply because I believed in what we were doing. I suppose I was a bit idealistic, perhaps I was even the sort some managers might call a troublemaker, but I cared about our side and what we were achieving.'

Twenty-four hours later another mistake by Greenwood in the return fixture gifted Southampton a winner in a 2-1 victory.

The bust-up between Gibbons on one side, and Greenwood and Hill on the other, led to both players demanding a transfer and being dropped for the next game at Birmingham City.

A board meeting was called, and Greenwood was invited to attend and say his piece, along with any of the other players who wanted to support him. But when the moment came only one man stood up to be counted – Hill. The directors backed their manager and the transfer requests were granted.

Nevertheless, Greenwood and Gibbons patched up their differences a few weeks later with the result being that the defender withdrew his transfer request and was reinstated to the side. Sadly, however, the damage had been done and Brentford were never the same force again that season. From challenging for promotion at Christmas, by the end of the season they had slipped to mid-table.

Nine games into the 1952/53 season, on 27 September 1952, Brentford played away to Bury and lost 3-0. For Greenwood it marked the end of his tenure in the Bees' number five shirt. He had another unhappy afternoon which culminated in conceding the penalty from which the Shakers went three goals clear. Greenwood was dropped and transfer-listed again at his own request.

The sports pages were full of speculation concerning his future, which was finally settled when he signed for Chelsea in exchange for Irish international Seamus D'Arcy – more commonly known as Jimmy – and a cash adjustment in Brentford's favour.

The parting was amicable, but there was little doubt that Brentford drew the short straw. Greenwood was a football purist and his style of play was poles apart from the Griffin Park management's idea of how the game should be played.

* * *

Greenwood turned out for various FA representative sides, including in November 1951 when a London FA XI played against a Berlin XI in the Olympic Stadium in Berlin, the first representative match to be played between teams from the two countries since the Second

World War. The half-back line was Greenwood, Jimmy Hill and Bill Nicholson.

However, his only major honour was to be selected as England's captain for a B international against the Netherlands in the Olympic Stadium in Amsterdam on 26 March 1952. England won 1-0 in front of a crowd of 60,000. Bob Paisley was listed as an unused substitute.

Football in the Netherlands was still moving toward full professionalism, and though they put out their strongest international side they were still not considered strong enough to merit the game being recognised as a full international.

Greenwood admitted that, nevertheless, such an honour meant a great deal to him, 'Pulling on a white England shirt for the first time was something I will never forget. It was a moment of deep fulfilment. We won the game squarely by a goal to nil, but as Bernard Joy, the old Arsenal defender, and a respected reporter for the *London Evening Standard*, said to me afterwards, "It was a good performance but the reports won't be much because it was such a cold, miserable day!" I would have given anything to win a full cap for England, but it was not to be.'

Neil Franklin had been England's primary centre-back for some time but his controversial move to sign for Independiente Santa Fe in Bogotá, Colombia, had ended his international career so there was a vacancy for the position. There was the inevitable newspaper speculation surrounding Greenwood and Walter Winterbottom, the England manager, came to watch him at Brentford. Unfortunately, Sheffield Wednesday beat the home side 3-2 with Derek Dooley, the man Greenwood was marking, scoring a hat-trick. Greenwood later claimed, 'The ball went into the net off his knees, even his backside – anything rather than his head or feet.' Dooley himself stated that he found he 'could beat Ron for speed, although I know when it came to playing football, he had me skint'.

* * *

It was while at Brentford that Greenwood's early interest in coaching grew into a passion. The team travelled everywhere by train and there would always be two quite separate groups of players, each in a different compartment. In one they played cards and in the other they talked football. Greenwood and Jimmy Hill were always in the latter, and they listened to players such as goalkeeper Ted Gaskell and outside-right Jackie Goodwin talk with such enthusiasm about the courses they had attended, and how coaches like Walter Winterbottom had opened their eyes.

Professional players were already responding to such courses designed for them in greater numbers. In the 1952/53 season 151 players applied to attend courses at Lilleshall and St Luke's College, Exeter and 107 were accepted. One of the men accepted for the course at Lilleshall was Greenwood, along with Hill, taking part in the first to be held in that splendid, rambling old mansion in Shropshire.

In his autobiography, Greenwood exalted, 'What an exciting, enlightening week it was. Walter [Winterbottom] and his coaches – Walter above all – gripped us with their ideas. They taught us how to teach but, more than that, they seemed to take us right inside the game. Theory and practice were always nicely balanced, and everything was geared to getting the best out of individuals and teams. We [Jimmy Hill, Johnny Paton and Greenwood, the three Brentford players on the course, came to be known as "The Three

Musketeers"] would stay awake until three o'clock in the morning, taking imaginary training sessions, and more than once there was a loud bang on the door followed by a blunt suggestion from one of the staff that we got some sleep. Our enthusiasm was endless, the touchpaper had been well and truly lit, and at the end of the week I remember wishing the course would go on for ever.'

5

Chelsea

GREENWOOD WAS already 30 years old when he signed for Chelsea in October 1952. As at Brentford, he benefited from a new manager. In 1952, former Arsenal and England striker Ted Drake was appointed as Chelsea's boss. Regarded as one of the first 'tracksuit managers', Drake proceeded to modernise the club on and off the field. He improved the training regime, introducing ball work to training sessions – a practice rare in England at the time – the youth and scouting systems begun by his predecessor were extended and he abandoned the club's old recruiting policy of signing often unreliable stars, opting instead for lesser known but more reliable players from the lower divisions.

Drake's first signing was Johnny McNichol, an inside-forward from Brighton. Greenwood was his second. They paid Brentford the equivalent of £16,000 – a part-exchange deal involving Seamus 'Jimmy' D'Arcy – which was a lot of money for someone his age.

Greenwood made his debut at Stamford Bridge against Spurs on 25 October 1952, in a 2-1 win. He played only five games in that early spell, then one more in February, and came back into the team at the end of the campaign, with Chelsea needing to win their last game against Manchester City to stay in the First Division. City were duly beaten 3-1.

Stamford Bridge had a greyhound track running around the pitch, and sometimes footballers and greyhounds would find themselves practising together – and the footballers would have to stop because they were distracting the dogs.

The following season Chelsea finished eighth with Greenwood making 33 appearances. But eighth place meant that for the first time since 1920, Chelsea finished as the top London club. That may well have been the limit of their ambition for the following season, especially after four successive defeats in October. By mid-November Chelsea had won five of the first 17 games and nobody was thinking about the championship, then things began to look up. Losing to Lawton's goal for Arsenal on Christmas Day at Highbury was one of the few setbacks, although it cost Greenwood his place in the side.

Greenwood must have hated playing on Christmas Day as it was a defeat to Southampton on 25 December 1951 that was the catalyst for his eventual departure from Brentford. But the club had signed two promising defenders – Stan Wicks from Reading and Peter Sillett from Southampton – and Greenwood recognised that he was one of the players threatened.

Chelsea had begun the 1954/55 season much as they had finished the last, with four consecutive defeats, including a thrilling 6-5 loss to Manchester United, which left them 12th in November. From there the team went on a remarkable run, losing just three of the next 25 games. They secured the title with a game to spare after a 3-0 win against Sheffield Wednesday on St George's Day, in the club's Golden Jubilee year. Chelsea's points total of 52 for that season remains one of the lowest to have secured the English title since the First World War. Greenwood had played 21 league games so qualified for a winners' medal. Despite his having already left for Fulham, at the end of the season the club invited him to their championship celebrations, a gesture which was very much appreciated by Greenwood.

A month after he had been replaced by Wicks, Fulham made him an offer and Ted Drake advised Greenwood, who by now was 33, to accept it. Nevertheless, he was sorry to leave Chelsea, who he considered had always looked after him.

Over two and a half seasons Greenwood made 66 appearances for the team in blue, yet it's a record that doesn't merit even a mention in Rick Glanville's 2006 400-page history of the club. Another instance of him being one of football's forgotten men.

While at Chelsea, Plymouth Argyle had also made an offer for Greenwood. He visited the club and liked what he saw but turned them down as it would have conflicted with his growing coaching interests as he was already chief coach for the Middlesex FA and coaching Oxford University.

Greenwood was still a decent player while at Chelsea, as evidenced by his winning a place in England's party of 40 for the 1954 World Cup in Switzerland. He missed out on the finals as well as warm-up games – including the 7-1 loss to Hungary in Budapest.

That Hungarian team was to prove such an inspiration to Greenwood's coaching career. On the infamous November 1953 day, when Ferenc Puskás and his Magical Magyars colleagues beat England 6-3 at Wembley – the national team's first home defeat to overseas opposition – Greenwood was in the stands.

The contrast between his morning and afternoon exposed the different attitudes to football in England and on the continent. At 9.30am he was training with the other players at Chelsea – which consisted only of the obligatory laps around the pitch. The club had provided the players with tickets for the match, but only half of them bothered to go. At 3pm Greenwood was in the stand opposite the Royal Box, feeling a flutter of expectation.

He described his impressions of the match in his autobiography, devoting a chapter headed 'Revelation' entirely to the occasion.

6

Fulham

GREENWOOD MOVED the short distance to Craven Cottage in February 1955 on a free transfer. He was made captain immediately and appeared 14 times over the remainder of the 1954/55 season.

Greenwood would claim that he was enthusiastic about the switch to Fulham, despite it being a move from the top tier to the Second Division. He was looking forward to 'playing with a talented bunch of chaps', including his old friend Jimmy Hill.

However, he was subsequently to label the two seasons he spent with the Cottagers among the most distressing and traumatic of his whole career, which when you take into account his later years at West Ham, not to mention the England spotlight, is quite a claim.

There was no discipline, and although the players were excellent the setup was abysmal. There was no doubt that the star player was Johnny Haynes, someone who was always allowed to have his own way. Haynes was a prodigy who made up his own rules as he went along. Other players had to play to his desires and adapt to him. He was 'protected'.

The joint manager and secretary was Frank Osborne, described as a nice enough man but someone who did not have any control over the team. It was alleged he even rarely watched a game due to a superstition.

Greenwood could see that the club was going nowhere and vowed that most of what was going on at Fulham would not be tolerated if ever he got hold of a club.

He made 28 appearances in the 1955/56 season but realised that his playing days were coming to an end. He had kept on his sign-writing business and there were times alongside the Thames when having such an interest was all that kept him sane.

Even Fulham realised that things could not continue as they were so decided to appoint a team manager. Frank Osbourne called Greenwood into his office, where he also encountered the club chairman John Dean, who said, 'We're looking for a manager and they tell me you've got ambitions.'

Greenwood was surprised at the comment but responded that he would be interested in the job, albeit on condition that virtually all the staff be sacked.

Not surprisingly, Greenwood was not offered the role and instead it went to Dugald Livingstone, who had been in charge of the Belgian national team. Nevertheless, it was an early sign of where his ambitions lay.

7

Pre-West Ham: From Ealing Grammar School to Arsenal

RON GREENWOOD considered there to have been three men who were instrumental in shaping his ideas on the game.

The first was Billy Birrell, the manager of Chelsea during and just after the Second World War, a quiet thinker but someone who made an immediate impact on him.

Birrell had arrived at Stamford Bridge in April 1939, bringing with him a reputation as one of the shrewdest and most capable managers in the pre-war game. He was also Chelsea's first recognised 'manager'. Birrell summarily removed the three incumbent trainers while preparing a new vision for the club. Eschewing the big transfers of the past, his big idea was the Chelsea Juniors scheme. Greenwood was one of the first beneficiaries.

Then there was Malcolm MacDonald at Brentford, who gave Greenwood a belief in himself. MacDonald became one of the big influences in Greenwood's life with his advocacy of the simple things in football. He had just been appointed manager of Brentford when he rang Greenwood to offer him the job of trainer.

Greenwood was in the process of winding down his playing career at Fulham. 'I reckon I would have played for another two years if I had gone back to Brentford [then in the Third Division South] under the management of Malcolm,' recalled Greenwood. But he had to turn down the chance as two days before the call he had agreed to join Eastbourne United as manager.

The third, and most important influence, was Walter Winterbottom, who opened his eyes to that brave new world of coaching and, Greenwood would admit, changed the whole direction of his life.

The blue touchpaper for the wannabe coach had been lit during that very first course at Lilleshall while a Brentford player; Winterbottom was the man who struck the match. He convinced the young Greenwood that coaching itself had a big future. In the mid-1950s the majority of professionals, players and 'managers' looked on it in the same way witch doctors once regarded traditional medicine. Coaching was new and therefore to be viewed with suspicion.

But Greenwood saw Winterbottom as nothing less than a visionary. Winterbottom told the aspiring boss that new methods of training were being investigated and that new ways of teaching were coming to the fore. England might have given the game to the world but now the game's founders were in danger of being overtaken. Though Winterbottom's own England side had been trounced twice by Hungary, in 1953 and 1954, this coaching was regarded as revolutionary stuff, and many were not only wary but downright hostile. He believed in learning from the rest of the world. He believed in abroad.

But all of this attracted its share of scorn and in truth Winterbottom's disciples were in the minority. Egged on by the competing ideology of the denial, there were many who found this mania for self-improvement disconcerting, wrong-headed and vaguely irritating.

Winterbottom was faced with a major problem – the reluctance of some major stars to accept any degree of instruction, especially from someone who had never played international football. With a narrowness typical of the period, certain players believed that fitness and ability were all that mattered.

Winterbottom failed to command automatic respect from players. He was too remote, too theoretical to motivate his teams. Unlike his successor, Alf Ramsey, he did not have that natural, intangible aura which incites devotion. Even players who would find success under Ramsey expressed scepticism about his predecessor.

Attending coaching courses and gaining badges was only the beginning of the development of coaches. It was an evolving process. Winterbottom worked behind the scenes as the puppet master, advancing the careers of his brightest proteges and helping to put them into influential positions. Greenwood's career in coaching provided a perfect example.

Winterbottom had convinced Greenwood that coaching was his future. Writer Barney Ronay, in *The Manager: The Absurd Ascent of the Most Important Man in Football*, described how Winterbottom oversaw the first coaching qualification course, 'Through this he began to acquire his own disciples, a small bright-eyed cult, a Dead Poets Society of similarly minded progressives.' Greenwood later recalled, 'Walter was a leader, a messiah, he set everyone's eyes alight.'

There was further biblical imagery in the *Telegraph*'s obituary for Greenwood, describing, 'Both Greenwood and [Jimmy] Hill became disciples of Walter Winterbottom. The first England manager and an evangelist for the importance of coaching.'

In his biography of Winterbottom, *Sir Walter Winterbottom: The Father of English Football*, Graham Morse wrote, 'Walter encouraged young professional players to think of coaching as a career and a cadre of around 20 were appointed as FA staff coaches. They became known as his disciples and spread the message of coaching at local, national, and eventually international level. In this way a new breed of managers emerged which began to change attitudes to coaching in league clubs. Over the years many of his elite group became famous as managers and coaches, including Ron Greenwood.'

Winterbottom was not only the manager of the England team but also the FA's director of coaching, a post which involved the establishment of coaching schools, giving lectures and the production of handbooks. His coaching role was seen by both him and his employers at the FA, as more important than looking after the national team.

Wednesday, 25 November 1953 is a date painfully etched on the heart of English football. It was the day that Hungary, the Mighty Magyars, rode into the hitherto impregnable fortress of England's football empire and rode out with its most coveted treasure: a reputation as the greatest team on the planet. No longer could England, the inventors and rarely masters of the world's most popular game, lay claim to being its finest exponents.

No doubt a modern English manager, faced with such a result, would be obliged to fall on his sword immediately. Yet, in all the thousands of words written in the newspapers in the aftermath of the Wembley defeat to Hungary, there was hardly a significant reference to the coach of the team. Clearly, the idea that a coach could exert any kind of influence over a team was yet to be acknowledged.

In his official history of the FA, Bryon Butler, who would co-operate with Ron Greenwood on his autobiography, wrote, 'The scoreline hurt but the manner of the Hungarian victory wounded deeply. It touched the inner heart of English football because it confirmed, beyond excuse and smokescreen, that the country which had organised the game for the world did not understand its finer points. The "masters" were using old textbooks.'

Winterbottom was enthralled by the wonderful team skills of the Hungarians. He spoke to his pupils at his FA courses the following summer and told the likes of Greenwood that it was like seeing the light when it had been half lit. His protégé had been at the game and did not need much convincing.

Winterbottom died in 2002. Another of his pupils, Jimmy Hill, in a letter responding to the *Daily Telegraph* obituary, wrote, 'Nearly everyone then believed that good players were born and not made. The Hungarians hit such complacency for 6-3 at Wembley. Walter's England, still unappreciated by some, slowly narrowed the professional gap by continuing to lead those who controlled the professional game at Lancaster Gate out of their power-struck wilderness. Ron Greenwood, Bill Nicholson and Don Revie made their own successful way with their own personalities and ambition, but all learnt something from Walter.'

In April 2013, another of Winterbottom's successors, Roy Hodgson, would unveil the FA's tribute to a man he called the 'Godfather of English coaching', a bronze bust which fittingly stands inside the education department of the national football centre at St George's Park in Staffordshire. It is an appropriate place for a schoolteacher who turned coach and led England to four World Cups and jump-started a coaching revolution.

Greenwood's very first coaching experience was in the humble surroundings of Ealing Grammar School. Each session was supposed to last for an hour and a half but the first lasted nearly three hours simply because it was so enjoyable. There were only six sessions in total, but even this short introduction to coaching gave Greenwood both confidence and hope for his future.

He learned from Winterbottom, 'This was the way the Hungarians brought on their coaches, giving them jobs with schools and smaller clubs and then gradually raising the standard.'

Soon afterwards, when Oxford University had a vacancy for a coach, Winterbottom put Greenwood's name forward to the university on a shortlist of three. Greenwood got the job and earned three years' experience coaching the Varsity soccer team. As he was still a Chelsea player, he was unable to see Oxford play as often as he would have liked, although he did watch the Varsity match at Wembley when he was injured (his opposite number that day, coaching Cambridge, was Bill Nicholson). Greenwood felt that Oxford University gave him a perfect introduction to the art of coaching, in particular because he was dealing with intelligent and responsive students who were eager to learn.

But it worried Greenwood, certainly at the beginning, that someone who left school at 14 should be instructing young men who were studying for degrees. Ultimately it did not matter as he discovered that they wanted to be better players as much as he wanted to be a better coach. Malcolm Allison had expressed similar sentiments when he had coached Cambridge University.

Someone who would figure large in Greenwood's life 20 years later was Professor Sir Harold Thompson, who would, as chairman of the Football Association, appoint him as England manager. In the late 1950s he was the dominant force in Oxford University football.

One early piece of advice Greenwood received was, 'Don't let Tommy rule you.' 'Tommy' was Professor Thompson, who had hounded the previous coach out of his job. Greenwood lasted three years in the role, so the relationship with Thompson was clearly a working one. The Oxford position was automatically rotated after three years, and Greenwood would be succeeded by an ex-playing colleague, one Jimmy Hill.

Greenwood followed Oxford University by becoming coach at Walthamstow Avenue, one of the country's leading amateur clubs, where he stayed for two years. This was an FA coaching appointment, and he was paid £3 a session which had to cover his expenses for the long journey from South Harrow by tube and trolley bus. He was still playing for Chelsea, so money was not a major issue. The reward for him was more valuable coaching experience.

Walthamstow won the Isthmian League and the London Senior Cup while Greenwood was coaching them, but nothing gave him greater pleasure than an FA Cup win over QPR of the Third Division South in November 1954. Immediately prior to Greenwood joining Walthamstow, they had drawn with Manchester United in the FA Cup before going down in a replay.

In the late spring of 1956 Eastbourne United offered Greenwood the job of coach, and this time it was a paid position which matched the £1,000 a year he was getting at Fulham.

There was a suggestion he might have taken over at Fulham, but nothing came of it, so he took the plunge and hung up his boots to become a professional coach. He had been recommended for the job by Eastbourne's previous manager, George Smith. At the same time the Sussex County FA appointed Greenwood as their chief coach and in this capacity, he spent a great deal of time at teacher training colleges and schools throughout the county 'generally spreading the gospel'. It was very hard but extremely worthwhile work. Greenwood maintained he learnt humility and discovered the value of the game at this basic level.

Having accepted Eastbourne's offer of a three-year contract, within 24 hours he had a phone call from Malcolm MacDonald, who was becoming manager of Brentford. McDonald wanted Greenwood to be his player-coach, at a club where he had spent his happiest years as a player. Given a straight choice, Greenwood admitted he would have plumped for Brentford. But he had given his word to Eastbourne and would not go back on it as a matter of principle. It would not be the last such decision in his managerial career. Luckily, Fulham agreed to release him from his contract – his playing career was over.

He was now a full-time coach, and to add to his responsibilities, he was picked by Winterbottom to take England's youth team. He had called Greenwood 'the best young coach in the game'. Greenwood had already been involved with England's youth side at Lilleshall while attending courses as a staff coach and found working with the best young players in the country to be exciting. He recalled saying to Winterbottom on one of these occasions, 'Just look at them … the future of English football is no problem.' The players they were working with included Jimmy Greaves and Bobby Charlton.

Greenwood was under no illusions as to why he had been invited by the FA to take over England's youth team. He was considered 'safe'. All the youth team players in those days were ground-staff boys with Football League clubs, and Lancaster Gate probably had a suspicion that if a coach from a professional club took charge of England's youth team, he would soon start enticing the youngsters on to his own staff. As Greenwood was with non-league Eastbourne United, his employers were not considered a magnet for the nation's best.

He saw as much youth football as he could and one spring evening was at Stamford Bridge watching London Grammar Schools play Glasgow Grammar Schools. He noticed a young, blond lad called Bobby Moore playing for the London side at centre-half. He looked a good player.

The following season, Moore turned up at Lilleshall for the usual early selection course where he was playing left-half – his club position. Greenwood made him captain at centre-half.

Greenwood spent nine 'wonderful' months at Eastbourne. The club did not win a significant trophy in his short time there, but he thought he had helped build a solid and durable platform.

He was also offered three other jobs during his spell on the south coast, so his reputation was spreading. Raich Carter wanted him as his youth coach at Leeds United, and it is fascinating to contemplate what would have happened if his path had crossed there with Don Revie. Portsmouth offered him a similar post and Workington wanted him as manager.

Greenwood said that none of these offers tempted him. Perhaps he had wind of something grander, and in late 1957 Greenwood was contacted by Arsenal's Bob Wall, who wanted him to be the club's coach. Eastbourne agreed to release him from his contract without even asking for compensation.

But there was still a complication as Eastbourne had reached the first round proper of the FA Amateur Cup, then a major national competition. The tie was not until January 1958, so Greenwood coached both Arsenal and Eastbourne until the latter were knocked out, 2-1 at Finchley – wearing borrowed Arsenal shirts. But it had meant that for three months Greenwood was coach of First Division Arsenal while unable to actually see them play.

Arsenal had enlisted the FA to help them find a coach and the organisation, as usual, had produced a three-name shortlist, from which Greenwood was selected. He was the first full-time coach Arsenal had appointed but, more than that, the first FA staff coach to be given such a job by any league club. Greenwood was not a manager, but a coach pure and simple. The whole concept of coaching was on trial because the FA felt that if he made a success of it other clubs would follow suit.

Jack Crayston, Arsenal's manager when Greenwood joined the club, told him that he was like 'a breath of fresh air walking down the corridor'. But Greenwood was under no illusions about how some of his own players resented the whole idea of a coach.

He believed that Arsenal were set and stodgy in their playing ways, with the club's methods of training unbelievably traditional. He would later declare himself to be 'utterly horrified with the pedestrian and backward nature of Arsenal's training methods'.

He set out to change things utilising the talent he had to work with. He tried all kinds of coaching techniques and began to feel that the attitude of the players was becoming more positive, though it took six months before he felt he was getting his message across.

One notable match during this period was Arsenal 4 Manchester United 5. Jack Crayston clinging on to his job by his fingertips, Arsenal were trailing 3-0 at half-time in February 1958, before Greenwood reminded his team at the break to put into practice the work they'd completed on overlapping runs in training. 'The side had been quaking in their boots, and reverted to type against United, knocking the ball long, which was meat and drink for United defenders,' explained Greenwood. 'I insisted that they turn this around at the break, and they did.' His players, delivering pinpoint crosses and ripping down the wings, rallied superbly, narrowly losing 5-4 in the Busby Babes' last match before the Munich air crash. Jimmy Bloomfield, who went on to play for West Ham under Greenwood, reckoned, 'If you could bottle what Ron delivered at half-time that day, you'd have the perfect team talk; inspirational and tactically astute.'

Crayston was sacked at the end of the 1957/58 season. Greenwood was in the running for elevation to team manager but the Arsenal board decided he was too young and inexperienced. However, that didn't stop him being offered the Sheffield Wednesday manager's job in the summer of 1958, an offer he turned down.

Arsenal would make George Swindin their new manager. An ex-goalkeeper for the club, he had played when Greenwood's Bradford famously beat Arsenal in the FA Cup. There was not an auspicious start to the two men's relationship as Swindin had openly criticised the way Arsenal had been playing, which Greenwood took as directed at him.

Nevertheless, Greenwood gave the new man the benefit of the doubt, believing that such comments emanated from a deep care for the club. It helped that Swindin did not involve himself in training, restricting his role in preparing the team to a lengthy team talk on Friday mornings. In the coach's opinion, his approach was never deeply tactical, though he was a good motivator. The two men could claim they were not working along different lines, borne out by a third-place finish in 1958/59 after heading the First Division in the early part of the season.

Nevertheless, as the 1959/60 season progressed it was becoming apparent that Swindin and Greenwood were not in a perfect partnership. There was no personal animosity but they were two radically different personalities. Swindin was a flamboyant character who loved publicity featuring himself. Greenwood was not only more down to earth, but a purist and idealist who believed in the arts and skills of the game.

The difference in opinions became so marked that Greenwood suggested he concentrate on the reserves as the first team were suffering under two conflicting sets of advice. This arrangement only lasted as long as a 6-0 defeat to West Ham. But it was increasingly clear that one man had to go. In April 1961 Greenwood accepted an invitation from First Division rivals West Ham United to manage them. Swindin would last another year before being dismissed in May 1962.

Given Arsenal's lack of success in the three years Greenwood was at the club, there have been attempts to portray him as the main reason for Arsenal's failure from 1958 to 1961. A leading witness for the prosecution was ex-Arsenal man Jim Magill, who wrote to the website blog.woolwicharsenal.co.uk/archives/11661, 'I am a little disappointed regarding the negative comments in connection with his [George Swindin's] reign at Highbury. George lived and breathed Arsenal and was always a great support and always was there to help us when necessary.

'Perhaps one of the obstacles he had to deal with was his partnership with Ron Greenwood. They were both each very qualified to manage football clubs, but together as a partnership there were just too many different opinions which very often led to a bit of confusion as to how we should play and therefore had an influence on the results over the time George was at the helm.'

Derek Tapscott played up front for Arsenal and Wales during the 1950s. After he died in June 2008, aged 75, Brian Glanville wrote in his obituary, 'In the 1957/58 season he lost his place in the Arsenal attack. Unlike most of the first team, he had poor relations with the innovative Ron Greenwood, appointed as coach to the manager and former goalkeeper George Swindin, in December 1957. Bill Dodgin, Arsenal's centre half at the time and a keen student of the game, spoke of Swindin and Greenwood and their contrasting methods as "night and day". But Tapscott once told me, speaking of Greenwood and mimicking a punch, "I'd like to hit him."'

The results would seem to add weight to the argument that Greenwood, and his newfangled coaching, had little impact. Crayston had joined the club in October 1956 and guided them to fifth, winning 14 of his games with seven draws and six defeats. The following season, prior to Greenwood's arrival, Arsenal had won nine games, with three draws and eight defeats. After Greenwood they won seven, drew four and lost 11 before the season closed with Arsenal in 12th.

Crayston was replaced by Swindin in June 1958 and in his first season the Gunners came third with 21 wins, eight draws and 13 defeats. But in 1959/60 they were 13th after 15 wins, nine draws and eight losses, then 11th a year later with 15 wins, 11 draws and 16 defeats. Greenwood left Arsenal for West Ham in April 1961.

Under Swindin, results did improve significantly at first and clearly he took the job with the knowledge that Greenwood was there, but then the club faded away from contention. Greenwood had his own ideas, and they were nothing much to do with Arsenal and the Arsenal tradition. He was essentially a purist who believed in developing a new style of playing, seeking to become the man who gave Arsenal a completely new approach.

It has even been suggested that the Arsenal directors, on appointing Greenwood, were trying to live up to the club's aristocratic image. Here was an inexperienced coach who had worked with the social elite at Oxford University and was linked with the FA. That was the sort of image Arsenal wanted, while Crayston was a footballer through and through who had no such pretensions, as was his successor Swindin. And for his part, Swindin, who had been brought up in the 'Arsenal Way' under George Allison, didn't appreciate this radical transformation of the club's style and approach by a man who was supposedly working under him.

Greenwood stands accused of wanting to transform Arsenal without having had a broad experience of getting players to do what he wanted them to do. He was also coaching the England under-23 side, and did get results there, so clearly with good players he could do things. Arsenal, during his time there, did not have a vast array of great players, but had many good and some very good players who could, it is claimed, have become great with the right nurturing.

Trying to bring success to Arsenal throughout the wilderness years of the late 1950s and 1960s was arguably the toughest managerial assignment in football. Swindin would reflect, 'I tried all sorts of new combinations on the pitch, and experimented with new systems, but I was always some way from the right mix.'

The brave new world at Highbury never came to fruition. Geoff Strong, an inside-forward with Arsenal from 1957 to 1964, recalled, 'Ron quickly became too hypothetical. On one occasion he was talking to us about rotating positions and being clever without the ball. It got very, very technical and there just wasn't the quality of player to run with what Ron said. Players kept being switched around too. It was chaos. I turned to young Gerry Ward and asked him if he grasped what Ron was trying to teach us. "Not a bloody clue," came Gerry's response. We switched off when he spoke in the end. We felt that he was trying to change too much. It got awkward. One of the directors told me that Ron "wasn't an Arsenal man" and that his days were numbered.'

It would appear that the final straw for Greenwood was Arsenal's parsimony when they tried to lure Denis Law from Huddersfield. Greenwood said, 'The kind of system that I was aiming for at Arsenal required the purchase of top players, who were willing to think through the issues, and the board decided to be frugal and conservative when they could have landed Denis. It's a decision they came to regret.'

So, was this another in a catalogue of missed opportunities at Arsenal, a club with a historical penchant for advocating retrenchment and caution when a more expansive approach could have paid dividends? Swindin certainly felt aggrieved at the board's reactive approach to a more monied era in the game, and failure to embrace a new approach on the playing side, saying, 'Ron and I wanted a more attractive game, more like Tottenham's. Whenever I approached the board about signing new players who could play that style, they weren't interested. They felt that sticking to tried and tested Arsenal methods was the way. One director told me, "Don't take too much notice of what Tottenham are doing, George. We'll do things the Arsenal way." They were bloody-minded about it.'

The 1960s never swung at all for Arsenal, and the club went from bad to worse under Billy Wright. It wasn't until the arrival of Dave Sexton at Highbury in 1966 as a coach under the new manager Bertie Mee that the club began to lay down the tactical blueprint of the pressing game and zonal marking which suited the group of players they had at the time and, crucially, fitted better with the club ethos of defensive solidity and tradition. Don Howe would later adapt Sexton's system to great success as Arsenal won the Fairs Cup in 1970 and the domestic Double in 1971.

Perhaps Arsenal's dismal decade, which preceded their short burst of glory, could have taken an entirely different course if Greenwood's fascination with space exploration had been treated in a rather more enlightened manner both among players and directors at Highbury in the late 1950s.

* * *

While coaching Arsenal, Greenwood became manager of the England under-23 side in succession to Bill Nicholson, who had joined Spurs. Again, Walter Winterbottom's hand could be detected behind the appointment.

Under Greenwood's stewardship the team played 14 matches, of which they won eight, drew four and lost two. All were friendlies.

He was working with many talented players including the likes of Alan Mullery, Bobby Moore, Joe Baker, Bobby Charlton, Gordon Banks, George Cohen, Jimmy Greaves and Jimmy Armfield. All would go on to have distinguished careers with the full England team.

Something that always worried Greenwood about the under-23 setup was the lack of professional help when the team travelled abroad. The manager was expected not only to supervise the kit and travelling but he also had to carry the sponge and attend to injuries. No doctor or trainer travelled with the team.

8

West Ham Pre-Ron Greenwood

THE EARLIEST incarnation of West Ham United was the founding in 1895 of Thames Ironworks, as the works team of what was then the largest surviving shipbuilder on the River Thames. Thames Ironworks turned professional in 1898 upon entering the Southern League Second Division and were promoted to the First Division at the first attempt. The following year they came second from bottom but had established themselves as a fully fledged competitive team. Following growing disputes over the running and financing of the club, in June 1900 Thames Ironworks was disbanded, then almost immediately relaunched on 5 July 1900 as West Ham United with Syd King as their manager and Charlie Paynter as his assistant.

The reborn club continued to play their games at the Memorial Grounds in Plaistow but moved to a pitch in the Upton Park area in the guise of the Boleyn Ground in 1904. West Ham's first game in their new home was against fierce rivals Millwall, drawing a crowd of 10,000 as they ran out 3-0 winners. In 1919, still under King's leadership, West Ham gained entrance to the Football League Second Division, their first game being a 1-1 draw with Lincoln

City, and were promoted to the First Division in 1923. In the same year they made it to the first FA Cup Final at the newly built Wembley Stadium, losing 2-0 to Bolton Wanderers. The team enjoyed mixed success in the First Division but retained their status for nine years and reached the FA Cup semi-final in 1933.

However, in 1932 the club had been relegated to the Second Division and long-term custodian King was sacked after serving the club in the role of manager for 32 years. He was replaced by his assistant manager Paynter, who himself had been with West Ham in a variety of roles since 1897 and who went on to serve in this position until 1950 for a total of 480 games. The club spent most of the next 30 years in the Second Division, first under Paynter and then later under the leadership of another former player, Ted Fenton.

The arrival of Fenton attracted little coverage during the World Cup summer of 1950. He was regarded as a safe, conservative appointment, who would make few significant changes. He also inherited a team that had narrowly avoided relegation the previous season due in no small part to containing too many players already past their best. The Hammers were in a paradoxical situation. They needed an injection of new players to shake them out of their Second Division slumber but there was no money available for transfers. So, if the club were to succeed, they would need to establish a proper structured youth development programme.

The Hammers' youth scheme began to take shape and by 1953 the club's colts would progress to the semi-finals of the FA Youth Cup for the first time. Much was made by Ron Greenwood of how England losing to Hungary that year was his 'road to Damascus' moment. Yet Fenton had also become an instant convert to the

Hungarian methods and immediately set about introducing their style of football at Upton Park. The boss claimed to have watched the film of the England v Hungary match five times and declared in his autobiography that he was 'determined to milk that match dry of every possible lesson'.

Fenton had made 163 league and 13 cup appearances for West Ham before becoming player-manager of Colchester United in 1946/47. There his biggest achievement was to take the club to the fifth round of the FA Cup in 1947/48, when one of their victims was a Bradford Park Avenue side captained by Greenwood.

Appointed as only West Ham's third manager in August 1950, he eventually got the club promoted back to the First Division in 1958 after an absence of 26 years.

West Ham changed dramatically under Fenton, becoming one of the most innovative, go-ahead British clubs in the second half of the 1950s. In April 1953 they became the first Second Division club to install floodlights. Over the next seven years the publicity-conscious Fenton would arrange the visits of numerous continental teams, including AC Milan, to play in floodlit midweek friendlies.

Revolutionary training and fitness methods, lightweight playing strips and boots, new dietary regimes and an enforced emphasis on youth development all radically changed the club for good.

However, by March 1961, the team's previously excellent home form began to falter and after losing at home to West Bromwich Albion on 4 March, and 4-0 to second-bottom Preston a week later, Fenton was granted sick leave in mysterious circumstances.

On 13 March 1961, two days after the defeat at Deepdale, chairman Reg Pratt issued the following statement, 'For some time

Mr Fenton had been working under quite a strain and it was agreed he should go on sick leave. For the time being we shall carry on by making certain adjustments in our internal administration,' adding that the decision to take over the team 'was made after a great deal of thought'.

The first public indication that Fenton's days were numbered came three days later when the *Ilford Recorder* ran the intriguing headline 'What's Going On?' and its sports editor Trevor Smith broke the story that Fenton had 'disappeared from the ground'.

The *Recorder* reminded its readers, 'The Upton Park Club are proud of their tradition of never having sacked a manager. The present position gives a distinct impression that a compromise has been attempted to preserve that tradition.' That wasn't quite true, as their first manager Syd King had been dismissed back in 1932.

Chairman Pratt subsequently issued another press statement, saying the club had no new manager in mind and, until such time as they appointed a replacement for Fenton, West Ham would continue to be run by the board with help from trainer Albert Walker and captain Noel Cantwell.

It was subsequently reported that Fenton had 'resigned' after a meeting with Pratt – a notion that appeared to suit both the club and the outgoing manager. Reasons why the board got rid of Fenton after having given the matter 'a great deal of thought' have never been published. And unusually, given the enormity of the decision, no notes about the matter were recorded in the board minutes. Incredibly, Fenton's departure did not even merit a mention in West Ham's programme. It was as if he had never existed, neatly airbrushed out of Hammers history.

In his book *West Ham United: The Making of a Football Club*, published in 1986, author Charles Korr suggested the decision to dismiss Fenton was probably taken by chairman Pratt alone. He wrote, 'The logical inference from the method of Fenton's removal and the role played by Pratt was that the manager violated sensibilities of the chairman that had nothing to do with the every-day operations of the club. The worst offence against the club was doing something that gave the appearance of cutting corners or using the club as a vehicle for self-aggrandisement.'

The possible reasons why Fenton was axed range from the ridiculous to the bizarre. The most commonly touted theory is that the board sacked him for financial misdemeanours – fiddling his expenses is a favourite. Another is that he allegedly received a backhander from the sports company that supplied the West Ham players' boots and equipment.

There were even whispers from within the club that he'd been having a relationship with a woman from East Ham.

Malcolm Allison was quoted in the book *Days of Iron,* published in 1999, as saying that his old manager had been taking bricks and tins of paint from the club while building work had been going on!

A much simpler explanation would be that Fenton paid the price for the team's steady decline and a poor run of just two wins in the previous ten games, seven of them ending in defeats.

In his book *At Home with the Hammers*, published in 1960, Fenton tactfully perpetuated the most prevalent of all myths surrounding West Ham – that they don't sack managers – when the truth is, with the exception of Charlie Paynter and Ron Greenwood, they had sacked and would continue to sack every manager they had ever employed. In his book Fenton wrote, 'Some clubs seem to treat their managers as a species of faith healer. The club has a bad spell, the fans and the shareholders start howling – and out goes the manager. A new man takes his place and if he's lucky things will improve, simply because a long-term policy set in motion some two or three managers back starts to pay off.'

Under the headline 'They gave me no money and sacked me – Fenton', West Ham's promotion-winning manager gave his first public interview on the events surrounding his sacking to Jason Thomas in the *Evening Standard* London football series on 17 October 1970, saying he 'couldn't get tuppence' out of the directors for new players. 'I have always wondered why capital became available to Ron Greenwood but not me. For example, I wanted [goalkeeper Lawrie] Leslie six months before and could have got him for only £6,000. Had I been able to sign some experienced players to back up youngsters coming through from the reserves at the time like Bobby Moore, Geoff Hurst and Martin Peters, I might still have been manager today.

'I was amazed when I got the sack ... Unfortunately, the directors panicked. It was a hell of a strain getting into the First Division and some of our older players were over the hill. Unfortunately, the West Ham directors opposed my idea of promoting Bobby Moore and co. from the reserves and they also said there wasn't any money available to buy from other clubs. I was in an impossible position.'

Despite the fact that chairman Pratt had intimated a week after the sacking of Fenton that 'the board had no plans to name a new manager' and that the team 'would be managed by the board with advice from their trainer Albert Walker and Noel Cantwell', less than a month after Fenton's dismissal, on 13 April 1961 Greenwood was appointed.

Greenwood had been sounded out about the West Ham job by his great mentor Walter Winterbottom, who'd taken his full England team for a behind-closed-doors practice match at Upton Park on the very day that Fenton was given his marching orders. West Ham beat England 1-0, with the only goal being scored by Geoff Hurst, then an unheralded wing-half.

In his own version of the events that took him from north to east London, Greenwood claimed that he was reluctant to leave Arsenal and had doubts about taking on West Ham, a club he knew little about. Of course, his feeling may have had something to do with a hope that he might be made Arsenal manager if and when George Swindin was let go.

The first hint that his career was about to take an abrupt change in direction came in March 1961. England were playing West Germany in an under-23 international at Tottenham on the Tuesday but, the night before, Winterbottom took the senior team to Upton Park for a practice match. That same evening, by sheer coincidence, Fenton left West Ham suddenly and without explanation. Greenwood said he had read the reports of Fenton's departure but did not feel involved.

Then the next day, as they were setting off for the under-23 match, Winterbottom, who just happened to be sitting next to Greenwood on the coach, started talking about the game at Upton Park the previous evening. Suddenly, he asked, 'Would you be interested in the job at West Ham?'

'I'm happy at Arsenal,' Greenwood replied. 'In any case, if they're going to sack people like they did last night it's obviously not a happy club.' Greenwood claimed he then promptly forgot all about this exchange.

Then at Easter, Arsenal's Bob Wall approached him, asking, 'Mr Pratt, the West Ham chairman, has been on, and he's wondering if he can approach you with a view to you becoming their manager.' Greenwood told him he thought his future was with Arsenal and asked him if Swindin knew about the offer. 'Well, yes,' Wall replied, and then he added, 'You know, I think this job may be of interest to you.' Greenwood got the message 'loud and clear'. 'All right,' he said. 'I'll pop across and see him.'

So he drove across to West Ham on the Tuesday morning and met Reg Pratt and his vice-chairman Len Cearns. Even at this stage he claimed still not to have any firm notions about the job or the club. The two directors came straight to the point and said they wanted him to be West Ham's manager-coach. 'But if I do take the job,' Greenwood replied, 'I would want full control of all team matters and no interference.' They assured him he would have complete charge. He was getting £1,500 a year at Arsenal, and they offered £2,000.

Still Greenwood played for time, telling them he would let them know after the following weekend and went home to talk things over with wife Lucy. They were living in west London, in Twickenham, with their daughter Carole taking a secretarial course at a local technical school. Continuing to live in Twickenham and driving across London to West Ham every day meant two and a half hours against the traffic.

Greenwood later said his reluctance to leave Arsenal was changed by a single comment by chairman Sir Bracewell Smith, who said to him, 'I hear you might be leaving us.'

'Well, there a possibility,' was the reply, 'but I haven't made up my mind yet.'

His answer was not what was hoped for, 'Well, never mind. If you leave us, we might eventually come to you and say we want you back here.'

According to Greenwood that was one of the most disappointing things ever said to him, causing him to mutter under his breath, 'Over my dead body.' And, having almost made up his mind to join West Ham, he was furious that Arsenal made no attempt to keep him. He felt, in his innocence, that instead of letting him go the chairman should have talked about the continuing challenge at Highbury. But he didn't – and Greenwood told West Ham he would be delighted to be their new manager.

Any lingering doubts Greenwood may have harboured were dispelled within a few short weeks of joining the West Ham family, when he realised the goldmine of talent he'd inherited.

Fenton's departure from Upton Park may have given some of the old guard at West Ham a nightmare or two, but it was one sign that football was moving into a new era. Fenton, a white-collar, pipe-smoking leader with a military background, had done all he could in 11 years of loyal service. The younger members of the team were sad, but not distraught, to see him go. Even in his tenderfoot years Bobby Moore's creative football brain had queried Fenton's tactics and his rigid policies about the playing of 4-2-4. As an England under-23 player, Moore already knew a lot about the new manager's coaching abilities. Being young, he may have thought there was a bit of the schoolmaster about Greenwood, but he welcomed his new boss to the club with enthusiasm. 'From then on,' Moore noted, 'life began to change for the Hammers.'

* * *

Ted Fenton's first signing had been 22-year-old centre-half Malcolm Allison from Charlton Athletic for £7,000 in February 1951. The next season, Allison replaced Dick Walker as captain of West Ham.

The new defender was a hugely confident figure who was a keen student of modern continental football and a man impatient for success. Despite their contrasting personalities, Allison and Fenton were united by ambition, and this unlikely combination would prove the driving force throughout a decade of great change at Upton Park.

Another take on this period is that Allison had a turbulent relationship with Fenton that clearly affected the attitudes of the players, as demonstrated by a series of poor end-of-season finishes. Allison eventually took over the coaching of the club and implemented a controlled regime, also acting as a mentor to younger players, in particular Bobby Moore.

The future England captain later said, 'I'd been a professional for two and a half months and Malcolm had taught me everything I know ... When Malcolm was coaching schoolboys, he took a liking to me when I don't think anyone else at West Ham saw anything special in me. I looked up to the man. It's not too strong to say I loved him.'

Future Hammers manager John Lyall observed, 'Malcolm Allison was a strong man ... He battled for what he wanted ... He had an open-mindedness to try things.'

So an ongoing area of debate has been the influence of Allison, the argument being that though while only a player he was the man, rather than manager Fenton, responsible for the coaching changes at the club during the 1950s. And, so the argument goes, Greenwood could tap into this and become the beneficiary when he joined the club in April 1961.

One of the main proponents of this line of reasoning was Malcolm Allison himself.

After the war the Hammers were a happy-go-lucky club who placed more emphasis on fun than professionalism. Irishman Frank O'Farrell, who had arrived from Cork in 1948, said, 'It was a laid-back family club. They hadn't been anywhere in football terms for years, but it was a nice club to play for, full of nice people.'

According to his biographer David Tossell, Allison discovered that West Ham was even more backward than Charlton. Training had no more purpose than at The Valley and being even shorter, necessitated even less effort from the players.

Allison began to draw up his own practice schedules for the team, finding allies for his methods among the other players. Fenton, who Allison felt had been promoted out of his depth, might not have been much of a tactician but his wheeler-dealing in the transfer market meant there was a steady influx of new players throughout Allison's time at West Ham even if there wasn't much money to spend. It was his good fortune that so many of them responded to his football philosophies and the force with which he indoctrinated them. The list of ex-Hammers who went on to managerial and coaching careers at the highest level – men such as John Bond, O'Farrell, Noel Cantwell, Ken Brown and Dave Sexton – is the most obvious testament to Allison's influence and the open-minded atmosphere that pervaded the Upton Park dressing room during the 1950s.

O'Farrell remembered most players being in tune with the mood of self-improvement, 'We would talk mostly about how

English football could change. But we put into practice the things we spoke about. We trained with a ball more, varied the time at which we trained. We were trying to improve the game and we were maturing as people as well as players.'

They loved nothing more than to gather after training in Cassettari's, a Barking Road café just around the corner from the stadium, where they would talk long and often about the game.

Allison would be back at the club a couple of evenings every week to coach the schoolboys and junior players. John Cartwright, later a coach of some distinction, claimed, 'When we left school all of us could have gone anywhere but we picked West Ham, even though they were in the Second Division, because of Malcolm Allison – including Bobby Moore.'

Like Greenwood, Allison would describe the England v Hungary match in November 1953 as his own 'Eureka' moment. 'The Hungarians were so bright, so brilliant, that even the walls of complacency in English football began to crumble,' was his view on the aftermath.

He, like Greenwood, was a devotee of the FA coaching courses at Lilleshall. 'I had abandoned any hope of getting any meaningful help from the club,' he said. Once there, he devoured every piece of information offered by the likes of Walter Winterbottom. 'In that atmosphere, I sensed that I could make an impact.'

One wonders whether Greenwood encountered Allison on one of these FA coaching courses.

However, not every West Ham player was as enamoured about coaching as Allison. Striker John Dick always maintained he liked to play without referral to tactics. He would later fall out with

Greenwood, something not unconnected to absenting himself from a Greenwood-led coaching course at Lilleshall early in his Upton Park reign.

Player Eddie Lewis would maintain that there were two camps at West Ham, and provided you were in Allison's, the latter would look out for you and use his influence with Fenton to get you in the first team.

Noel Cantwell, though very much part of Allison's band, agreed that he wasn't popular with everybody, 'A lot of players simply did not like change, and he did a lot of things that were not popular with the manager.'

Which brings us back to the obvious question about this period in West Ham history. Who was running the team – Malcolm Allison or Ted Fenton?

'Eventually I began to run the team, with his tacit agreement,' is Allison's description of the arrangement with his boss. Allison described the relationship with his manager as 'scarcely satisfactory'. Manager and captain could hardly be called bosom buddies.

Allison felt that the club directors' loyalty in appointing an old Hammers stalwart proved that they 'had no sense of how to achieve anything or to be successful'. He believed that they would rather appoint someone unsuitable than bring in a thrusting, forward-thinking outsider who might show up their own lack of football knowledge. The might of Allison's personality inevitably caused friction with Fenton, but the manager at least appeared to appreciate that those issues were born of a desire to see the club's progress. And as long as Allison's influence was dragging the club in the right direction it seems that Fenton was happy to indulge such a brazen show of player power.

According to Dave Sexton, another West Ham player who would go on to a successful managerial career, 'Ted didn't interfere. He was very in love with football and so were we. If it was going to make us better, then Ted let us do it. Coaching was a new scene for most people, but we were lucky to have Ted because he could have put the boot in, as some managers would have. He was as keen as us.'

John Cartwright agreed, 'Ted was really nothing in comparison to Malcolm. Ted used to turn up for training and then go off.'

Jimmy Andrews said, 'Ted would occasionally go on about tactics and you'd see Mal looking at him, as if to say, "Oh, shut up Ted." But in his own way Ted was a good influence – just in a totally different way from Malcolm. And between the two of them they did a great job. If it's good for the club the players let him get on with it.'

O'Farrell added, 'I felt Fenton bridged the gap between the old-fashioned manager who ruled with an iron hand and the newer generation of manager-coaches who thought hard about the game.' Allison's criticism of the players made them more 'self-sufficient and turned us into managers' according to O'Farrell, who continued, 'If we'd had a strong manager, we wouldn't have blossomed the way we did. That's why so many of us succeeded.'

Another great hope in the junior ranks was George Fenn. He was a member of the West Ham team that lost in the FA Youth Cup Final of 1957 but never fulfilled the promise of his teenage years. Nevertheless, he would claim, 'Allison's ideas and knowledge were ten years ahead of anybody else's. The stylish football West Ham became famous for was all started by Malcolm. He kept Bobby Moore at the club.'

In Fenton's 1960 book *At Home with the Hammers*, the only mention of Allison in its 160 pages is a somewhat dismissive six paragraphs. There is no acknowledgement of his tactical input and no reference to Allison in the chapter entitled 'Styling the Hammers'. 'Apart from being a good player, Malcolm was fantastically keen and enthusiastic. He was a fitness fanatic and inspired the others. Because of that I made him skipper,' Fenton wrote. It's hardly a ringing endorsement, much less acknowledgement, of Allison's wider contribution.

Putting aside the claims of both men, there is no doubt that the 1950s at West Ham was a period of inventiveness, neatly topped off by promotion to the First Division in 1957/58. Major European and South American sides travelled to Upton Park for friendlies under the newly installed floodlights, itself a relative rarity at this time. A youth policy was introduced, and it was Greenwood who would be the beneficiary. The team's tactics, shirts and boots illustrated the European influence on this middling club in the East End of London before he turned up.

In his 11 years as manager of West Ham, Fenton presided over the birth of a small revolution in British football at the Boleyn Ground even if this was mainly instigated by Allison. At the same time, he was one of the old school. He was a white-collar leader, wielding a pipe rather than wearing a tracksuit. Perhaps in the end he knew what was needed and understood that he was not the man for the job. He brought something of the modern world to the club, particularly in his relationship with the press and the fans but he was a man made in the English Second Division of the 1930s and 40s.

By the mid-50s it was apparent that player power was becoming increasingly influential at Upton Park, and no doubt many managers would not have tolerated it, but Fenton, to his credit, made little effort to curtail the influence of his senior pros on the training ground.

In Fenton's time Upton Park had already been nicknamed the 'Academy of Football'. Contrary to popular opinion, the Academy was neither a product of the 1960s nor the work of Greenwood. It was a title which owed most to the foresight of Allison, the tolerance of Fenton – and a café on the Barking Road.

9

1961–1965: Success

1960-61

When Ted Fenton was dismissed in March 1961, West Ham's board of directors insisted they would not be rushed into appointing a successor. With no obvious internal candidate to fill the vacancy, the board decided that they would wait until the end of the season before resolving the situation. However, a 4-1 defeat against Blackburn Rovers at Ewood Park left the Hammers on the fringe of the relegation battle and, suddenly, finding a full-time manager became an urgent priority.

On 13 April 1961 the club announced that Arsenal's head coach Ron Greenwood had been appointed and would take sole charge of the playing staff. To provide him with full scope in that direction he would be freed of administrative duties, which would be shouldered by the club secretary, Eddie Chapman. He would be 'concerned solely with coaching and training', the West Ham board told the press.

Greenwood had insisted on control over the football side of the club, which meant a free hand with preparations for matches as well as training and control of the players. He also obtained a commitment from chairman Reg Pratt that West Ham would go into the transfer market. Greenwood was also the first manager to be brought in without having any previous ties to the club. He was even a northerner. Even after a decade at the helm Greenwood still described himself as 'the new boy over here'.

England manager Walter Winterbottom had, once again, been instrumental in guiding his protégé's career. As he explained in his foreword to Greenwood's autobiography, 'It also fell upon me to play a part in Ron's appointment as manager-coach at West Ham. My opinion was sought and Ron, as one of a new type of managers coming through, seemed admirably equipped for the post. He found full opportunity to apply his ideas about positive football at Upton Park.'

The decision to employ Greenwood may have been accomplished quickly, but it was not a snap development by Pratt. According to author Charles Korr, 'The board was making a statement about how it wanted the club to develop. Greenwood's qualities and beliefs coincided with the direction the board wanted to take. The appointment surprised most of the supporters but came as less of a shock to the leading players. West Ham was in transition. No one already there could step into the position [although there were suspicions that Phil Woosnam had his eye on the job], and none of its former players was a likely candidate.'

When he first arrived, Greenwood 'didn't know anything about West Ham, either as a boy or as a player'. Nonetheless, it did not take him very long to decide that he liked West Ham, and the people around the club. 'It suited me. It wasn't slick, smart, it was honest and sincere. I felt a part of it ... It became my cup of tea, since I'd been brought up in the north ... and was a victim of good manners.'

Greenwood provoked strong feelings among supporters from the moment he arrived. Not only was he an outsider, but an Arsenal man to boot. There were warm personal relations between Pratt and the Gunners' board, and it was no surprise that he should look towards Highbury when choosing a new manager. Pratt and his colleagues saw Arsenal as a well-run club with a sense of tradition and an unwillingness to cut corners. But many West Ham supporters viewed it as a domineering, aloof club that had bought its way to success and enjoyed lording it over its London rivals, despite their lack of recent success. The attitude of those supporters to Greenwood might be summed up as, 'We didn't think very much of him, and since he came from Arsenal, he was off to a bad start already.'

Yet among the West Ham players was a feeling that Greenwood had been advocating the same things at Arsenal as they had developed on their own with the considerable assistance of Malcolm Allison. Noel Cantwell saw Greenwood as the hope for a new future at West Ham, and Ken Brown went even further, claiming that if 'Greenwood hadn't come, we would have been relegated'.

Greenwood introduced himself to his new team as they sat on the wall in front of the West Stand at Upton Park. He reportedly told them, 'Let's face it, you are a team that is just like your theme song. You're always promising – and then the bubble gets burst before you win anything. That's what my job is – to stop the bubbles being burst.' He went on to outline how he saw the game in general, what he was hoping for and what he intended to do.

The West Ham players were by no means all strangers to the new man. He had met some on coaching courses, others when they played for England at youth or under-23 level and still more when

Arsenal played West Ham. Within a matter of days, he began to realise what a goldmine he had inherited.

Yet he did so without a contract. On the one hand West Ham said they did not give one and anyway he did not want one. He felt the club directors could be trusted and such was his own self-confidence he felt he did not need to be handcuffed by a few lines of small print.

For the seven games since Fenton's sacking the team was selected by chairman Pratt and captain Cantwell. Greenwood was happy for that arrangement to continue for his first match in charge, a 1-1 draw at home to Manchester City.

However, for the remaining four fixtures of the 1960/61 season, pragmatism, rather than progressive coaching and entertaining football, was the order of the day. The priority for the new manager was to steady the ship and win enough points to stay in the First Division. Three successive draws proved sufficient to fend off the threat of relegation and, although they lost their final match of the campaign, West Ham finished in a relatively comfortable 16th position, but just four points above the relegation places.

His first management test came soon enough, and it involved veteran full-back John Bond. Before the game, away to Burnley, Greenwood was informed by physiotherapist Bill Jenkins that Bond would not be fit. However, the new manager had already picked up on the fact that Bond was in the habit of picking and choosing his matches, and he didn't fancy the trip to Turf Moor. So he was promptly dropped in favour of John Lyall, who kept his place at full-back for the following match at Cardiff City.

When Bond protested, he was told by his new manager, 'Let's be quite clear who is who in this club. I am the manager, and you are a player. I am in charge; I pick the team and that's something you'd better accept for your own good.' Eventually, Bond got the message.

As Greenwood gradually got to know the club and its players better, other problems became apparent. He identified that there were too many players on the staff, and, in one or two cases, the attitude was wrong. There were undercurrents, personal problems, personality clashes, and a few people outside the club whose influence with the players was too strong to be healthy – an early reference to Jack Warner. All these things had to be resolved before the club could move forward, and, to complicate matters, the maximum wage had just been removed and Greenwood had to work out new player contracts. He would probably not have thanked his friend Jimmy Hill for his efforts abolishing the maximum wage just then.

Greenwood would later describe chairman Pratt and his directors as 'intelligent, honest and caring men who did things for the right reasons'. Only twice in his 16 years at Upton Park did they say 'no' to him. In 1971 they refused to sack Moore, Greaves and other players after the tabloid newspapers splashed stories of their heavy drinking the night before an FA Cup tie at Blackpool, which was subsequently lost 4-0. The other occasion was a decade earlier in only his first month as manager.

When Greenwood joined West Ham the man in charge of their youth players was a part-timer, Tom Russell, who was headmaster of the school Moore had attended, the Tom Hood School in Leyton. He was doing a useful job and knew the area well, but the new manager felt that only a full-time coach would get the best out of the club's youngsters. As he wrote in his 1984 autobiography, 'There is no doubt in my mind that one of the best-paid men in any club – perhaps even the best – should be the youth coach. His job is investment. His responsibility is the future. It is not a position for a faithful Tom, Dick or Harry or for somebody who is cutting his own teeth.'

The man he wanted was Malcolm Allison, who was then playing non-league football for Romford after recovering from tuberculosis. Greenwood was well aware of his ability as a coach and that Allison was one of the men responsible for him inheriting such fertile ground. He felt Allison would make an ideal full-time youth coach but when he put the proposal to the board their reaction surprised him. They did not think Allison should come back to the club. They told him 'one or two things had happened which would not make it a good idea'. Greenwood could not make them change their minds and he had to accept their decision. He had not said anything to Allison, so it became a bright idea which never got off the ground.

Allison did not mention the possibility in his autobiography so the assumption must be he was unaware of it.

It does lead to the inevitable speculation about what might have been, and how Greenwood and Allison might have been able to work together. Allison's biographer, David Tossell, believed that at that stage in his life, he would probably have relished the chance to return to the game on a daily basis.

In Allison's autobiography *Colours of My Life* there is a chapter headed 'Those I respect'. He wrote, 'I have also felt respect for men with whom it would have been impossible for me to work. I couldn't get along with a Shankly for instance. I recognise his tremendous strength, his freakish enthusiasm, but I couldn't see any point at which our thoughts would meet.

'There is much about Ron Greenwood's work at West Ham which I admire deeply. When he arrived at Upton Park from Arsenal, he had a touch of excellence about his work. He knew that his basis would always be deep skill, and that is just about the most vital thing a football man can bring to the game. But there is a vast difference in our styles.'

In that 1975 book, Allison outlined some of the reasons the West Ham board would not have been keen to have him back, whatever his reputation as a coach: 'I had fought a series of battles with manager Fenton and chairman Reg Pratt. And it wasn't merely a question of rebellion for its own sake. I fought them only when I felt they had treated the players with a particular lack of respect.'

He had fought annual battles over his wages and had a deep mistrust of Fenton, who he once said, 'would cheat you out of anything'.

Once he had even threatened to lead the team out on strike – 15 minutes before the start of a league match with Nottingham Forest. The issue was a win bonus from a friendly against an England amateur team. The team got its bonus.

An earlier incident soured what had looked likely to be a promising relationship with chairman Pratt. Cliff Lloyd, secretary of the fledgling players' union, sent round a circular asking players to put down details of any under-the counter payments they might have received. It was part of his case that the maximum wage regulation was being abused by the clubs. Allison wrote, 'I was summoned to the presence of chairman Pratt who said, "I don't imagine that the players will be signing this union document." His tone and his manner were guaranteed to provoke me, and I told him we had all signed the document, which wasn't strictly true. He had been asked to argue on television that it was possible to run a football club without making some technically illegal payment.'

That Allison was not to continue to play an important role at West Ham was a surprise to some. John Cartwright recalls, 'We all thought that when Malcolm recovered from his TB [he had had to give up playing in 1958 due to the illness] he would come back into the club as a coach. He was the instigator in changing the club's footballing beliefs. But unfortunately, the directors were opposed to that and he never returned.'

Eddie Lewis adds, 'I don't think the directors liked Malcolm. His social life tended to come into that, and he was too over the top with his passion for the game. He upset too many people.'

With Greenwood in charge for the final four games of that transitional season, the Hammers drew three and lost one, scoring five goals and conceding six to collect three points.

1961-62

The arrival of Ron Greenwood did not create the immediate miracle that the more optimistic West Ham fans might have expected. He had to evaluate his existing playing resources and set them against the abundant youth talent available to the club. So, for a while, some of the old regulars were still to be seen trotting out of the tunnel. However, Greenwood promptly axed eight of them. The most senior of these was winger Mike Grice, who in six years at Upton Park had made 150 appearances, scoring 16 goals.

Professional football in 1961 underwent one of the most momentous and fundamental changes that it had ever experienced when the maximum wage was abolished. Like every other professional club in England, West Ham had to adjust to the players' new-found power which marked the dawn of a new era in the game.

The abolition of the maximum wage in 1961 made for extra strains between many clubs and their star players. Greenwood hated this new requirement to be haggling in his office when he could be outside with a ball. How was a manager supposed to squabble with his players over pay and then go out to the training pitch and demand they give blood? The new boss spent much of his first summer in E13 negotiating salaries and contracts. According to the club chairman Reg Pratt, the new rule brought two assessments of a player's value – his own view, and that of the management.

Greenwood did not want the confrontation. Indeed, he loathed it. What he certainly did not anticipate was that the most awkward, demanding player of all would be the diligent, dedicated Bobby Moore.

Now captain, Moore was offered £28 a week but held out for £30. After a stand-off Moore got his £30 – as did the rest of the players. This set a precedent for future wage battles, with Moore always the last to agree.

On the pitch, away to Spurs the team drew 2-2, and in an exciting return at the Boleyn Ground the Hammers won 2-1. The dismal away form of the previous campaign was forgotten with good wins at Aston Villa (4-2, which prompted Alan Williams of the *Daily Express* to declare that he would 'risk a modest bet that this poised and superbly schooled side will finish in a higher league position than any of their London rivals', and Sheffield United (4-1). After 12 games the 'old' regular left-wing pairing of Dick and Malcolm Musgrove had scored 15 goals between them.

Plymouth Argyle were narrowly beaten 3-2 in the League Cup at home, but the Hammers bowed out in the next round after losing 3-1 at home to Aston Villa.

Greenwood had hardly settled into the task of turning West Ham into a winning side when he was witness to a near riot at Upton Park. The date was 16 September 1961 and Chelsea the opponents. A tackle on Phil Woosnam by Tommy Docherty led to a flurry of flailing fists and flying bottles. Then in a separate incident goalkeeper Lawrie Leslie was knocked out in a collision with Bobby Tambling, from which Chelsea scored. This led to spectators encroaching on to the pitch. But even with ten men, in those pre-substitute days, and with Moore going in goal, West Ham held on to win 2-1.

Losing 3-1 at half-time away to Manchester City, the Hammers staged a remarkable comeback to win 5-3 despite Moore being sent off for the first and only time in his career with the club. Away form continued to improve as following a 2-2 draw at Arsenal there came a 2-1 win at Manchester United. At home against Wolves, Musgrove scored after 14 seconds and Moore added two more in a 4-2 victory. The Hammers moved into second place with that Wolves victory just before Christmas in 1961.

The FA Cup brought an all-too-familiar shock as the Hammers lost 3-0 away to Plymouth Argyle. February brought a 1-0 win at Chelsea followed by a 2-2 draw at home to champions-elect Ipswich Town. A disastrous March saw West Ham crash 6-0 at Burnley and 4-0 at home to Manchester City, where Johnny Byrne made his home debut.

During the Easter period the spotlight was on the goalkeepers. Against Arsenal, Leslie was injured and was replaced by John Lyall in the 3-3 home draw. At Cardiff City on 23 April, Brian Rhodes had to retire injured and midfielder Martin Peters replaced him. He made some good saves before being beaten for Cardiff's third goal. It was also notable as being the first match in which Moore, Peters and Geoff Hurst all played together.

The season ended with a 4-2 home win over Fulham, which left West Ham in a respectable eighth place. Greenwood felt his new team were heading in the right direction after his first full season. Spurs, 'a side of maturity, high quality and balance', and of course managed by his friend Bill Nicholson, were setting the standards to which Greenwood aspired. But he felt the West Ham way was going to pay a dividend in the not-too-distant future, by playing constructive, intelligent football at all times, even if this meant occasionally being turned over by a team that was direct and muscular in the traditional British way. He wrote, 'We seemed most at risk when the opposition played as if it was their last day on earth. Cup ties, particularly, are like this and in that first full season of mine we were soundly beaten at Plymouth in the third round. That hurt!'

Compromise, however, was out of the question. Greenwood's understanding of the complexities of what is often called a simple game was quick to influence players whose skills had been under-used for one reason or another. Greenwood enjoyed the practice sessions and spent hours discussing problems with the players; he put a special emphasis on the value of passing, and the basic skills such as when to hold the ball or move away into space as a decoy. The old power football made possible by tremendous fitness and featuring large centre-forwards fed by speedy wingers eventually made way for a more fluid, smoother style geared to a more sophisticated 4-2-4 formation.

Leslie, the Scottish international goalkeeper, had been signed from Airdrie for £15,000, but the most significant addition was Johnny Byrne, a club record £65,000 transfer from Crystal Palace. The purchase of Peter Brabrook, and Byrne in particular showed the great faith that Reg Pratt and the other directors placed in Greenwood's ability to judge talent. They were paying huge fees for a Third Division player, together with someone in Brabrook who they had not signed years earlier when they had had the chance. The importance of the purchases was summed up by the *Ilford Recorder*, 'Some knowledgeable people think West Ham has spent too much money to keep up with the Joneses … Just the opposite is true; the bank balance is positive … and the only reason for transfers will be by request. The days of the overnight transfer of star players to keep the finances straight are over at Upton Park. The club showed this when they spent £100,000 on Byrne and Brabrook, a change of policy which could not have announced Hammers' top-flight aims more patently.'

Byrne made his debut in a goalless draw against Sheffield Wednesday at Hillsborough and did not manage to score until six games later, a 4-1 win over Cardiff City at Upton Park on Good Friday, where Martin Peters made his debut.

Veteran Johnny Dick finished top scorer with 23 goals, while Moore was selected to go with the England team to the World Cup in Chile, and en route made his international debut against Peru in Lima.

Greenwood was keen that his players be exposed to coaching just as he had under the auspices of Walter Winterbottom. In the winter of 1961–62 he took most of his first team and reserve players away on a coaching course at Lilleshall. They took over the FA's coaching HQ – the first club to do so – for a whole week. At the end of it Ron Tindall gained his full badge while numerous others passed their FA preliminary exam.

To further broaden his players' understanding of the game and advance their coaching skills, the new broom sweeping through Upton Park also encouraged them to work in local schools in east London and Essex during weekday afternoons, teaching football to children.

Roger Cross said in an interview with *Ex Magazine* how, even having only just signed as a professional, he enjoyed the experience, even obtaining his preliminary coaching badge aged only 17. He was encouraged to think about the game from a very young age, and it could be no surprise that so many West Ham players of that era went into coaching and management.

As a reward for their season's efforts, the team were taken on a close-season tour of southern Rhodesia and Ghana in June 1962. Two notable stay-at-homes were Geoff Hurst and Ron Tindall. They were playing county cricket, which at that time was still a means for professional footballers to supplement their wages, only a year after the abolition of the maximum wage.

Logistically, everything went well until the Ghana leg of the trip. As Greenwood recalled in his autobiography, 'Nobody met us at the airport at Accra – the excuse given later was that they thought we were on another plane. By this time, though, we knew there was only one flight a day from Johannesburg to Accra. We then found ourselves being shown into a hotel that was nothing more than a dosshouse. The blankets almost crawled. Nobody slept, except Johnny Dick, who could sleep anywhere. The tour had a hidden bonus for us, however. Through all its adversity our team spirit grew stronger. The problems we shared welded us together. It also taught me a lot about the character of my players. I noted all those who had a good sense of humour, those I could count on, those who looked for problems and those who were idle. And on my first tour as manager, I discovered much about myself.'

When Greenwood took over as manager he had as little as possible to do with the press. Questions other than those dealing directly with performance were referred to club secretary Eddie Chapman. Greenwood was more cautious of the press than contemptuous; in his eyes the team would do the talking for him. But possible transfers always interest reporters, although the boss just would not talk about them.

Since the secretary would not comment on players, journalists had to depend on their own insights and imagination to describe what was happening. This may have made for more exciting if inaccurate copy, but it did not give the club the chance to shape its public image.

As a club, West Ham tried to ignore the growing tendency to concentrate on good public relations at a time when their First Division rivals, especially those in London, were courting publicity. The appointment of their first outside manager, especially one with an Arsenal and Oxford background, was a PR man's dream. But the Hammers did absolutely nothing to capitalise on it.

The early years of the Greenwood–Chapman relationship consisted of the manager doing things his own way and the secretary pointing out to him how the system had worked previously at West Ham. Chapman could 'say how we have been doing things around here', but no more than that. It was up to Greenwood to decide how he wanted to tailor his actions to fit the club and how much he wanted to alter the traditional approach.

During Greenwood's first two years, he did not handle transfer negotiations personally. After he had decided on a player he wanted, Chapman would negotiate the price and the final details of the transaction. When Greenwood took over control of transfer arrangements there was no opposition from Chapman. Greenwood was doing what the chairman wanted, and anyway, West Ham had never had a formalised division of responsibilities. The physical arrangement of the offices at Upton Park encouraged co-operation between manager and secretary. Only a few feet separated their offices, and each knew who was going in and out. Greenwood and Chapman had assumed their positions within a couple of years of one another, and that probably made co-operation easier.

1962-63

For Greenwood the biggest worry ahead of the new season was not fitness levels or injury problems, but contract wrangles. Four senior players – Moore, Woosnam, Ken Brown and Johnny Dick – had refused the club's offer of terms. By the start of the season the situation was still not resolved. Moore and Dick were placed on monthly contracts at £15 a week, while the other two players were left in the stands as West Ham lost their opening match 3-1 to Aston Villa.

Greenwood had insisted on being given carte blanche to run the playing side of the club as he wished, allied to responsibility for players' contracts and wages. Nevertheless, he was happy to retain the backroom staff that he inherited from Ted Fenton. Wally St Pier continued to serve the club as chief scout, the old guard of

Albert Walker, Ernie Gregory and youth coach Jimmy Barrett supported him at the training ground and on matchdays, while Eddie Chapman remained as club secretary.

Nevertheless, Greenwood was anxious to establish his own individual approach to doing things, be it tactics on the field or matters off it. He was a strong-willed man and could not be expected to put up with a 'business-as-usual' approach.

Early critics maintained that he did not understand or sympathise with the traditions of a club like West Ham. Among those critics was Jack Turner, the one person whose presence Greenwood did not welcome quite so warmly. Businessman Turner had forged a good relationship with Reg Pratt over many years and, as rumour had it, may even have been implicated in Fenton's sudden exit. Although not employed directly by the club, Turner held the title of property manager and he advised the players on all manner of financial matters, including savings, pensions and mortgages.

Turner, whose office was just along the corridor from Greenwood's in the old West Stand, was a father figure to some of the players and he also acted as an agent on behalf of club captain Phil Woosnam. However, when he offloaded the influential Welshman in late 1962, Greenwood explained his decision as one based purely on football, saying, 'He was an excellent skipper, motivator and full of ideas. But he smothered our younger players and robbed them of their individuality. He did everything with the best intentions but as a result the side lost much of its momentum'.

Some believed Greenwood's actions were not entirely unrelated to the fact that Woosnam had known ambitions to coach and even manage the club himself – and he was closely linked to

Turner, who Greenwood viewed with increasing unease. It was suggested that Turner's presence compromised the manager's own relationship with his players and the influence of such a financial advisor, especially after the maximum wage was abolished in 1961, became an unnecessary irritant to Greenwood. Turner was very unhappy when Pratt – who he had also represented on a business level – told him he was no longer welcome to work from the club. Difficult though the decision to oust Turner must have been for the chairman, he had again shown his support of the new manager.

Turner's view was, 'Greenwood didn't want me there ... I didn't blame him because he wanted to interfere with something he knew nothing about.' Yet it was hard to see a place for Turner at the new West Ham. The official explanation for his departure was that he no longer fitted in.

According to author Charles Korr, 'When Turner first came to West Ham, he was an extension of the board's traditional paternalism, but with an important difference. He dealt with the players as individuals and could not use the power of the club to push them. His success in establishing a personal relationship with many of the players vindicated what he and Pratt were trying to do but sowed the seed for his clash with Greenwood. By 1961, Turner's close ties with individual players existed regardless of his role at the club. The closer he got to players, the more he might find himself in the position of being between his club and his friends. When contracts became a negotiable item, how should Turner advise his friends, and in some cases clients, to react to offers made by their manager?'

Johnny Byrne had only joined West Ham in April 1962, but he could already appreciate Greenwood's influence, 'The way Ron wanted us to play did take a bit of getting used to … more for some than others though. And there were a few who expressed their doubts in no uncertain terms. And Ron's way was if you didn't want to play his way, you didn't have to, and you got dropped. He was a gentle, calm man, but he could be ruthless if pushed. He wasn't one to do his nut and as far as I was concerned you kind of knew what he was going to do as far as the team was concerned. But if you didn't understand his ways, he sometimes came across like a bit of an assassin.'

While preparing for his second season at Upton Park, it was clear to Byrne that Greenwood's emphasis on passing and holding the ball would suit him. Greenwood encouraged players to use space and move off the ball. Most of the West Ham players had been playing this way since their earliest days at the Boleyn Ground, under the influence of Malcolm Allison, but Greenwood had organised and developed the West Ham game and made it work in the 4-2-4 system.

Looking back, midfielder Ron 'Ticker' Boyce agreed that when Greenwood came in it was a complete change, 'He was a training ground manager, a teacher of the game, and once you took part in a training session under him it opened your eyes.

'He was very good at putting his ideas across and explaining the reasons behind them. People said that his man-management could be a bit suspect sometimes, but I never had any problems with him. I always thought he was good for making players feel confident by the way he spoke to you about the game.

'If you listened to what he said, you couldn't fail to agree with his views on football. He had such a great knowledge and I always found it very easy to understand what he was trying to get across.'

On the field, a poor start to the 1962/63 season saw heavy home defeats, 4-1 to Wolves and 6-1 to Spurs. After five games West Ham were bottom of the First Division. For game six, at home to Liverpool, Greenwood moved Geoff Hurst from wing-half to the forward line. He did not score in the 1-0 win, the Hammers' first of the season, but he looked the part and did find the net in the next game, a 6-1 victory at Manchester City. Blackburn Rovers were beaten 4-0 at Ewood Park, followed by a 5-0 demolition of Birmingham City, with Byrne scoring twice.

Byrne delivered a hat-trick in the League Cup as Plymouth Argyle were sent home 6-0 losers. But the trip to Rotherham United in round two brought a 3-1 defeat. West Ham had still to make an impact in this fledgling competition.

The year ended with goals as the Hammers drew 4-4 at Spurs and won 4-3 at Nottingham Forest, where winger Peter Brabrook scored twice. The 'Big Freeze' then hit the country, with many postponements through January and February. On a snow-covered pitch West Ham beat Fulham 2-1 in an FA Cup replay at Craven Cottage, after a 0-0 draw. There then followed two 1-0 FA Cup victories at home, against Swansea Town and Everton.

In the latter, play was held up by another bout of hooliganism. The threatened trouble finally erupted when referee Jim Finney awarded West Ham a debatable penalty. Against a background of total mayhem at the North Bank end, Byrne calmly slotted the ball past Gordon West. The incensed Everton fans threw dozens of bottles on to the pitch and a policeman was injured by a piece of flying concrete. It was the worst display of football hooliganism seen post-war in England to date and a catalyst for the growing cancer of violence within the game.

The Londoners' FA Cup campaign finished in the quarter-finals, where a late Roger Hunt goal saw them downed 1-0 at Liverpool, and from a mid-table position Nottingham Forest were dispatched 4-1. The scorers were Hurst, Moore and Peters. West Ham finished their season with another 6-1 demolition of soon-to-be relegated Manchester City and a 12th-place finish. Hurst fully justified his manager's faith in him by finishing as top scorer with 13 goals.

West Ham's youngsters reached the FA Youth Cup Final but trailed 3-1 to Liverpool after the first leg on Merseyside. When the Reds took an early lead in the return, it looked like the Hammers were on the verge of losing their third final. However, before a crowd of 13,200 the youngsters staged a remarkable comeback to win 6-5 on aggregate. In the home tie, Martin Britt scored four, all with his head. Nine of that side would go on to play for West Ham's first team.

Greenwood was allegedly 'over the moon'. He wrote in his autobiography, 'We won the FA Youth Cup in 1963 and I find it impossible to describe how much pleasure this gave me. Jimmy Barrett was our youth coach and I spent so much time working with him that Bobby Moore said to me jokingly, "You're more interested in the youngsters than you are in the first team."'

Harry Redknapp was a member of that cup-winning side in 1963, a feat Greenwood said brought him 'indescribable pleasure'. Redknapp recalled, 'He came and saw us play on a Saturday in the semi-final of the FA Youth Cup rather than watch the first team that day and loved it. If the first team was playing at home on a Saturday, he'd be at Chadwell Heath in the morning to watch our South-East Counties League match. He took a big interest in us kids. In 1963 I remember Ron bundling six of us into his car and driving us to Wembley to watch the European Cup Final between Benfica and AC Milan.'

Redknapp wrote that he had signed for West Ham because, 'I noticed that whenever I went to watch the youth team play, Ron Greenwood, the manager was present. He really cared about the kids. He didn't just put in the odd appearance to impress you into signing. He knew you, how you were progressing, how far you had to go.

'Ernie Gregory, the first team coach, saw us [the apprentices] as more of a nuisance. He came out one day and moved us on from the forecourt. When Ron found out, he gave Ernie the most frightful bollocking. "As long as they want to stay out there, as long as they are doing something useful, as long as they are playing football, we'll stay here with them as long as they want," he said. He loved the fact that all his apprentices just wanted to play.

'Ron was another old-school, like Bill Nicholson. The manager's door was always open in those days. But even senior players wishing to see Ron had to make an appointment. And you had to be in the first team a good few years before you were on first-name terms. Until that point, he was always Mr Greenwood.'

Some of the old Ted Fenton favourites were moved on. In early September 1962 Johnny Dick, who had found his new manager less forgiving than his predecessor, left for Brentford (his goals helped Greenwood's old club win the Fourth Division championship), after nine seasons as a Hammer. When Lawrie Leslie broke his leg against Bolton in November, Greenwood turned to Jim Standen from Luton, a keeper he had known from his Highbury days. Phil Woosnam departed for Aston Villa, which opened the door for Ron Boyce to claim a place in midfield. Malcolm Musgrove, despite, like Dick, still being one of West Ham's leading goalscorers, moved across east London to Leyton Orient just before Christmas.

These comings and goings, allied to the promotion of the younger players such as Hurst, Peters, Boyce and Jack Burkett, marked a watershed in Greenwood's tenure at West Ham. By early 1963, after two years in charge, he was assembling the core of the squad which would bring trophies to the Boleyn Ground.

But with so many changes in personnel it was hardly surprising that West Ham struggled to find any consistent form throughout the 1962/63 season. Twelfth place in the league was far better than could have been hoped for after the disastrous start to the season.

During the summer of 1963 West Ham were invited to play in the American Soccer League tournament. Fourteen teams took part, split into two groups. The Hammers did not start very well, drawing 3-3 with Kilmarnock and losing 4-2 to the Italian side Mantova. Fortunes changed when Moore and Byrne, who had been playing for England, joined the squad. Oro of Mexico, Valenciennes of France and Preussen Munster of West Germany were all beaten, with Hurst scoring six times. The final group game against Recife of Brazil was drawn 1-1, sufficient for them to win the group.

The championship play-off was over two legs against Górnik Zabrze. In the first game Johnny Byrne gave the English side the lead, but the Poles equalised for a 1-1 draw. In the second leg, Hurst scored and Górnik had two goals disallowed which upset their fans, who invaded the pitch and attacked the Scottish referee. After a half-hour delay play was resumed and West Ham held on for a 2-1 aggregate win.

This qualified them to meet Dukla Prague in the Challenge Cup Final. The first leg was played in Chicago and was an even contest before the Czechs won 1-0. In front of a 15,000 crowd in New York, Tony Scott put the Hammers in front before a Josef Masopust goal levelled the scores. West Ham may not have won the trophy, but the experience was invaluable.

Czech international Masopust predicted that 'West Ham would win a major European tournament within two years' and manager Greenwood claimed, 'We learned more that summer than we would have done in five European campaigns about how the game was evolving around the world.

'It could have taken two or three years at home to gain the experience we achieved on our American adventure. We faced the skill of Brazilians, the quick minds of Italians, the controlled strength of Germans and Poles and the all-round quality of the Czechs. Every one of our ten games was a lesson in itself and our reward came in the form of increased confidence, understanding and team spirit. I was convinced even bigger things lay just ahead of us.'

Greenwood had only been in the job for two seasons but already he was admitting to a niggling feeling, 'Perhaps we were better suited to cup football than league, that we were sprinters rather than marathon men. A year before the opposite had seemed true; now I was not so sure. The blame was partly mine of course. I began to wonder – not for the first time – if I had put enough concrete into the mixture. Was the team hard enough? Was I being too idealistic? Questions like this are easier to ask than to answer but one thing never wavered: my faith in good intelligent football.'

1963-64

Bobby Moore once claimed that he had enjoyed those early days with Ron Greenwood 'because we were mostly local lads down at

Upton Park who had grown up with the youth team together and knew each other like class-mates'.

Now came the pay-off. At the start of his third full season at Upton Park, Greenwood had put together a team which bore little resemblance to that which he had inherited from Ted Fenton. The line-up which took the field for the opening fixture of the campaign away at Chelsea included just three players – Moore, Joe Kirkup and Ken Brown – who had survived from Fenton's final match in charge.

Greenwood had benefited greatly from the youth programme instigated by his predecessor, and five of the other players on display at Stamford Bridge had been nurtured through the club's junior ranks during the late 1950s.

The promise West Ham had shown in that summer tournament in the United States began to bear early fruit in the 1963/64 season. Johnny Byrne, especially, stood out in his deep-lying centre-forward role, while Moore, who had been switched to sweeper in Greenwood's revised 4-2-4 system, emerged as the master defender and great unflappable at the rear.

The Hammers won two and drew two of their first four league games to top the early-season table. This being West Ham, two home defeats were to follow, before a 2-1 victory at Liverpool – their last Anfield triumph until 2015.

The League Cup saw neighbours Leyton Orient eliminated, then Aston Villa were beaten away, to progress to the fourth round for the first time. After a further six league games without a win the Hammers beat champions Everton 4-2 and followed up with a 1-0 victory at Manchester United. Swindon Town were the next League Cup opponents; a 3-3 draw at the County Ground was followed by a 4-1 win in the replay. Fourth Division Workington provided the next challenge and Byrne scored a hat-trick in a 6-0 win.

On Boxing Day, the home crowd were shocked as visitors Blackburn Rovers crushed the hosts 8-2. Two days later, with just one personnel change – Eddie Bovington for Martin Peters – the Hammers travelled to Blackburn and won 3-1. Bovington was told to 'put Bryan Douglas out of the game'. A 3-0 home win in the FA cup against Charlton Athletic was followed by a 3-0 victory against neighbours Leyton Orient.

The Hammers were still in the League Cup, and in the first leg of the semi-final at Leicester City they lost 4-3. The second leg was six weeks later, but West Ham could not rescue the tie and a Gordon Banks-inspired 2-0 home defeat meant a 6-3 aggregate loss.

Meanwhile, West Ham had knocked Swindon out of the FA Cup in round five thanks to a 3-1 win at the County Ground. February also saw home wins against Tottenham (4-0), and Sheffield Wednesday (4-3), Johnny Byrne notching another hat-trick. Burnley were eventually beaten 3-2 at Upton Park in the FA Cup quarter-final to set up a semi-final against Manchester United. A week earlier the Mancunians had beaten West Ham 2-0 at Upton Park, and were clear favourites in the rain and mud of Hillsborough, but Moore inspired his side to a 3-1 victory.

John Helliar had been watching West Ham since 1958, and in his book *West Ham United – The Elite Era: 1958–2009,* he wrote, 'With hindsight, the quarter-final tie at home to Burnley could be taken to mark the moment when the Hammers finally came of age, exhibiting a ruthless determination that had often been lacking in their make-up.

'But if the epic game with Burnley had shown West Ham to possess previously unseen grit, then the semi-final with Manchester United exhibited further steely qualities, belying the reputation of a team that many considered could only play football on the firm, flat pitches of autumn and spring.

'At the final whistle West Ham had done what few believed they were equipped to do. The tactical battles were all won by Moore and co. – and the ultimate architect of the triumph, Ron Greenwood.'

In the hysteria after the semi-final, it was Greenwood who made perhaps the most telling comment when he proclaimed, 'Look at them – this is the greatest day of their lives. I have been proud to be associated with this bunch of youngsters. Now the world and his friend will claim them. I accept that this must happen, but I will not let the leeches, hangers-on, glad-hangers destroy what they have built for themselves. I will do everything I can to protect them from the wrong sort of reaction to this success.'

The players celebrated wildly on the way back from Sheffield and the drink was flowing. Family, friends and fans joined them, and there were so many people crammed into the team carriage that Greenwood became visibly upset. 'It was like the January sales, Wembley Way and the London rush hour all rolled into one,' he complained.

When Moore and Byrne asked the manager why he looked so downcast, he said the day was being ruined by hangers-on. 'I wanted the journey home to be memorable,' he told them. 'But this is a disgrace. We don't need all these people. Is this success?' The baffled players returned to their boozing.

The Wembley final was against Preston North End. The Hammers struggled against their Second Division opponents and were twice behind before finding themselves level at 2-2 with a minute remaining. Johnny Sissons and Geoff Hurst scored the two equalisers. Then Ron Boyce headed a last-minute winner, and the east London club were FA Cup winners for the first time.

At half-time Greenwood had endeavoured to shake his side out of their first-half inertia, telling his players, 'All right, Preston have been in front twice and they've played well enough to deserve their lead. We just have to play better. We can do it and we're going right out there to win the cup if it kills us.' In truth, Greenwood had averted a major disaster with a half-time talk as inspired as it was timely. Preston, with Alan Spavin, Tommy Lawton and Howard Kendall running the midfield, had dominated the first half and looked anything but Second Division underdogs. Ken Brown was struggling to combat the twin aerial threat of Alex Dawson and Alec Ashworth, so Greenwood made some tactical adjustments.

Greenwood wrote later, 'It is at moments like this that managers earn their keep. I felt we were giving Preston too much time and room in midfield and that our setup wasn't right for the dual threat of Dawson and Ashworth. They were making good use of the big pitch and Moore was being bypassed. He was doing nothing. My answer was to play squarer at the back than I'd have liked, with Moore shifting up alongside Brown to mark Preston's two strikers, and to push Bovington forward to make earlier impact. In short, we reversed our tactics and it worked.'

Moore would later label the final an anti-climax, 'A lot of finals are like that anyway because you pour so much into striving to be there that winning a semi-final and setting up a trip to Wembley seems like a major achievement in itself. But it was more than that. We were playing against Preston North End, a Second Division side. We'd been magic in the semi-final against Manchester United, Wembley should have belonged to West Ham. We won and it was good to win the first major honour. Apart from that it was a wash-out. We played badly. We spluttered. We didn't fulfil anything we had promised ourselves. Most of us felt let down. We were lucky to beat Preston. Who could explain it? That was West Ham.'

Two years earlier, Greenwood went to watch Spurs play Burnley in the 1962 final. He had stood just behind the players' tunnel, and as Bill Nicholson and Harry Potts led their sides out, he felt tears in his eyes. They were managers he knew personally so he identified with them and shared their pride. He also wondered what he would feel like if the chance came his way. But when he led West Ham out in 1964, he claimed he felt no emotion at all; he was just doing his job. Only once had he shown real excitement at a match – when West Ham scored their winner against Liverpool in the final of the FA Youth Cup at Upton Park a year earlier. He had jumped to his feet and later reflected, 'I was, you might say, over the moon.' His chairman Reg Pratt had turned to him and asked what the matter was.

There is a narrow margin between victory and defeat and Greenwood knew the result could have gone either way. He knew his side had underperformed on the day, but still managed to achieve a famous triumph. Nevertheless, confessing that he felt no emotion strikes one as an odd thing for a manager to say as he looked back on one of the highlights of his career. It was this perceived emotional frigidity that would eventually bring him into conflict with some of his players, not least Moore.

The cup winners had a celebratory do at the Hilton, where the manager slept with the FA Cup under his bed, the same trophy he had first seen as a boy growing up in Cornholme. Then on Sunday came the journey back to Upton Park, which started quietly and ended with a real East End knees-up.

On the eve of the final, Moore collected his Footballer of the Year award, a trophy for which Greenwood could claim considerable credit.

And on the Monday before Wembley, West Ham staged a testimonial for John Lyall when an All Star XI were beaten 5-0 by the club's first team.

'As a human being he was absolutely kind and honourable,' said his successor. 'The best example I could give you was when I badly injured my knee. He told me to take a year off to see if it got better, but it didn't, and I had to stop playing early in 1964. But he told me not to worry and said, "We'll look after you." And that was the great thing about Ron Greenwood – it was always "we" not "I", because he involved everybody.

'He played his first-choice team in my testimonial game on the Monday before the FA Cup Final to ensure a big crowd. People told him he must have been crazy to do it, no matter how much he liked or respected me or wanted to help me. But he just simply said that if a player got injured, he was injured. Luckily, no one did get injured that night, but it wasn't a problem for him anyway.'

Greenwood could go away for his summer break content that West Ham had won the elusive FA Cup at long last. But their performances in the league still disturbed the manager. Here again it had been the same old inconsistency, the same old habit of losing to the cannon fodder, while beating hell out of major talent. If his wry smile was occasionally replaced by a frown, it was understandable.

A paragraph in the FA's yearbook for 1964/65 was another niggling reminder of the fickle achievements of his team in the league where they had finished only 14th, 'West Ham were inconsistency itself, with a double win against the champions, Liverpool, wins against Manchester United, Everton and Spurs, and losing three points to Ipswich Town and Bolton Wanderers and two points to Birmingham City.'

1964-65

The FA Charity Shield match against First Division champions Liverpool at Anfield kicked off the 1964/65 season. A crowd of 38,858 were treated to a wonderful game which finished 2-2, with Hurst and Byrne scoring for the visitors. Each team then held the trophy for six months.

Journalist Brian Glanville wrote, 'West Ham are a consistently interesting side to watch because they are consistently trying to do something interesting. They are, in the approved contemporary fashion, a counter-attacking team, playing the ball out of a massed defence to an inventive forward line.'

For Greenwood, the obligations about European football now lay ahead, but he remained passionately dedicated to making his team worthy of the greatest prize in English football – the Football League championship. He felt he now had the players to achieve a major breakthrough and could approach the coming season with high hopes.

His team had responded with alacrity to his persuasive coaching methods but, alas, the old goblin which had haunted the side began to grin again as it had done during decades of Hammers history. Once again, the team proved consistently inconsistent, although in their defence they had to do so without their great anchor man, Moore, when he suffered a long-term 'groin injury'.

After winning 2-1 at Fulham on the opening day, the first home game was a sell-out against Manchester United, the Hammers winning 3-1. Wolves were beaten 5-0, and in a 3-2 win against Tottenham Byrne scored a hat-trick. He went on to net 11 in the first 12 league games.

The first tie in the European Cup Winners' Cup was in Ghent against the Belgian side La Gantoise. It was a nervous start for the Hammers, but they won 1-0 when Boyce headed in a corner from Alan Sealey. The second leg saw the Hammers give another below-par performance. Peters scored an own goal to give La Gantoise the lead, but Byrne managed an equaliser to earn a narrow 2-1 aggregate victory.

The second round of the League Cup took the Londoners to Sunderland, where they found themselves 4-0 down after only 38 minutes. Peter Brabrook pulled a goal back, but Sunderland finished worthy 4-1 winners.

The 'groin injury', which we now know to be his first brush with the cancer that would kill him 30 years later, forced Moore to miss the next three months of the season. Nevertheless, November was a good month with away victories over Arsenal and Chelsea, both 3-0, and an excellent 3-1 home win against Leeds United.

The Hammers' next opponents in Europe were the Czech side Spartak Sokolovo, now known as Sparta Prague. It was goalless at half-time in the first leg at Upton Park but ten minutes into the second half John Bond opened the scoring with a 30-yard piledriver, and eight minutes from time Sealey added a second goal. The return leg in Prague was far tougher. Johnny Sissons put West Ham ahead after only 14 minutes, but then Bond conceded a penalty which Standen saved. The Czechs scored two second-half goals, but West Ham held on for a 3-2 aggregate victory.

In their defence of the FA Cup, West Ham started at home to Birmingham City. The away side even went into a 2-0 lead but two more goals from Hurst helped give the Hammers a 4-2 victory. The fourth round brought Chelsea to Upton Park where a sell-out 37,000 crowd saw Tambling give the visitors a 1-0 win.

League form was also declining, and in January and February there were only two victories.

Lausanne-Sport of Switzerland were the next opponents in Europe. Brian Dear scored first in Lausanne and Byrne added a second after half-time with the Swiss scoring late on. In the return leg both sides made defensive errors, but the home side got a 4-3 win.

Helped by successive home wins over Arsenal and Aston Villa, West Ham were comfortably in mid-table in the First Division. In the Good Friday match at home to West Bromwich Albion, Brian Dear scored five goals in a 21-minute spell and Martin Peters got the other in a 6-1 win.

The opponents in the semi-final of the Cup Winners' Cup were Real Zaragoza of Spain, who had a forward line nicknamed 'Los Cinquos Magnificos', or 'The Magnificent Five'. A packed house at Upton Park saw Dear and Byrne produce a 2-0 lead inside 25 minutes, but the Spaniards came back and the Hammers finished hanging on to a slender 2-1 lead. Greenwood's team flew to Spain for the return leg without Byrne, who had been injured on England duty. Zaragoza went ahead but just before half-time Sissons drove in the equaliser. The visitors held off a second-half onslaught to send themselves to a date in the final at Wembley.

The league season finished with West Ham in a respectable ninth place, with Byrne and Hurst scoring 42 league goals between them.

And on 19 May 1965 a crowd of 100,000 witnessed West Ham's 2-0 victory over the West German side 1860 Munich, who at the time were among the leading sides in their nation. There were chances at both ends in the first half. Sissons and Dear had shots well saved by goalkeeper Petar Radenković, while West Ham were troubled by the pace of the German centre-forward and captain Rudolf Brunnenmeier. In the second half Sissons hit an upright before West Ham took the lead on 69 minutes as Boyce passed to Sealey, who crashed home a shot from an acute angle. Two minutes later Moore's free kick found Sealey, who stabbed it into the back of the Germans' net.

Moore collected his second Wembley trophy in 12 months, while Greenwood would say, 'It was the way we won, for me it was fulfilment.'

Their manager had drummed in the message to his men before the start, 'Getting to Wembley means nothing in this competition or any other. Nobody is interested in losers. You are here to show millions of people what West Ham can do.'

The 2-0 victory, which made the Hammers only the second British club to win a European trophy, produced in the words of captain Moore 'probably one of the greatest nights for a celebration the East End had known since VE night'.

Everybody seemed to think it had been one of the finest games of football they had ever seen. Greenwood's happy bunch of Hammers were on their way to scale fresh heights. Or were they?

A post-match tribute came from the former Wolves and England captain Billy Wright. He said, 'West Ham have the potential to dominate the English game for years to come. They are a young team and there are no limits to the heights that they can attain.'

Unfortunately, it is an eternal paradox of sport that the most expert practitioners tend to be the least reliable pundits. This is especially true of football, and, sadly, Wright's words ultimately proved to be way off the mark. Incredibly, West Ham were about to drift into years of decline and mediocrity. It would be exactly ten years before they won another trophy, by which time all of the successful team from the mid-60s had departed.

It added fuel to the argument that their style of football was only suitable for success over a shorter span of games, like a cup run, and it could not be sustained throughout the marathon-like league programme with its interminable onslaught of fixtures. In later years, Greenwood acknowledged the problem but by then it was too late.

The bubbles were going flat even before the night was over. After a buffet at Wembley for players, officials and directors – but not wives, who were forced to loiter outside – the players were taken back on a coach to Upton Park.

The dispersal of the conquering heroes was not how Moore believed the club should enjoy what remains the greatest night in its history. Spotting Greenwood heading to his car to go home, the captain told his manager, 'You know the trouble with this club, boss? We don't know how to celebrate and enjoy the good times.'

After the Hammers' victory, the whole of Europe applauded their performance and messages of congratulation poured into Upton Park. One even came from their great London rivals Chelsea, which read, 'Well done, you East End lot. A real West End show.' Another came from Liverpool's manager, Bill Shankly, whose injury-hit team had been beaten by Inter Milan in the semi-final of the European Cup the previous week. Shankly's typically aggressive message said, 'Well done. I feel that British teams are more than ready for these European people.'

Even the prime minister, Harold Wilson – a big football fan – who had watched the game on television in Downing Street, sent a telegram of congratulations saying, 'Splendid match and a wonderful victory.'

The praise for the Hammers' performance in the following day's newspapers was almost overwhelming. The sports pages across Europe were magnanimous as they heralded the triumph. The leading French sporting newspaper *L'Equipe* ran a headline stating 'West Ham have discovered a new football formula'. Similarly, the Fleet Street press boys went into raptures. The *Daily Express* carried a banner headline on the front page of its paper saying 'Forever Blowing Bubbles – Night of Glory'. One of the match reports announced, 'There could have been no greater match to place before the greatest night audience in English football history.'

The highly respected reporter, Bryon Butler, graphically wrote, 'Moore and company used Wembley's green carpet as an artist uses his canvas. Their movements were precise, their designs bold and imaginative. They were a credit to themselves and English football.' The esteemed J.L. Manning described it as 'the best football match I have seen at Wembley since the stadium opened 42 years ago'.

Geoffrey Green of *The Times* also gave his blessing, pointing out, 'This was the night when Wembley for the first time was available to the genuine supporter of the club, the man who lives on the terraces through the winter. No longer did the majority of seats go to "outsiders". The true-blue fan at last took his rightful place in the national theatre of the game to cheer his own side. That was one agreeable sidelight. Another was the memorable way Wembley cheered the losers from the field; the way the Munich banners also saluted West Ham in their lap of honour; and how Olympic Way itself was lined by cheering thousands waving farewell to the German supporters in their coaches going home. The East End that night was aglow with bonfires and singing and dancing in the streets until dawn's early light.'

Another scribe said, 'West Ham's display was so majestic that, at times, it seemed they were touched by the gods. They are going to be greater than Bill Nicholson's double-winning Spurs and greater than the pre-Munich Manchester United.'

It was praise indeed and given the exultation rightly being accorded to West Ham, it was difficult to disagree with such a proud sentiment. After all, never before had the club experienced such euphoria and success. It was not unreasonable to assume that winning the FA Cup and European Cup Winners' Cup in successive seasons would be the beginning of a long period of unbroken success.

Geoff Hurst wrote in his 1970 autobiography, *The World Game*, 'It wasn't so much HOW West Ham played that night that thrilled me but WHY.' He also described the unusual role he played in those European matches, 'Although I had knocked in a few goals over the previous seasons, Mr Greenwood decided that my strength was better employed in midfield as a first line of defence. This kept down my shooting chances considerably, but I didn't mind, as this was another stage in my development as an all-round player.'

Twenty-year-old winger Johnny Sissons was the youngest player on the pitch that day, but already a veteran of five Wembley finals. He did everything but score at Wembley, hitting both crossbar and post amid the Hammers' second-half onslaught, after missing an easy chance from close range early on.

In an interview with *Ex Magazine* in 2005 he talked about his time at West Ham, and in particular his relationship with Ron Greenwood, 'Who always referred to me as "Young John" even years later when I was one of the senior players. He did more for me as a player than anyone else. If things weren't going as well as they should, Ron would pinpoint the problem at half-time, make the adjustments needed and we'd go out and do what was needed. He never blamed anyone for first-half errors at half-time or even at the end of games. Nothing was usually said until the following Monday.'

Sissons says that Greenwood put a lot of trust in his players on and off the field, some of whom abused it, 'Ron believed in treating his players like men and expected them to behave like men, but it's fair to say that one or two abused the faith he put in them and we could have done with more discipline. We should have gone on to become a great side; it just needed a small bit of fine tuning.'

Brian Dear had had his most successful season in a claret and blue shirt. Although he had his ups and downs with Greenwood, Dear paid tribute to the manager's influence, 'He was a brilliant tactician, as everybody knows. Ron changed it tactically in the final too. He played me alone up front, with Sealey and Sissons on the wings and Geoff a bit behind the line. We normally played 4-2-4 but Ron gave the three of us up front carte blanche to go wherever we felt we should be.'

West Ham might not be the only all-English team to triumph in Europe – Manchester City repeated the achievement in 1970 – but they were certainly the most local. Nine were Londoners (the exceptions were the Geordie Joe Kirkup and Geoff Hurst, from Ashton-under-Lyne) and six were even born within a mile or two of Upton Park.

Leslie Page wrote in the magazine *Soccer Star* a few weeks after the final, 'West Ham were something of an enigma in league and cup, always promising so much and yet somehow finding themselves beaten by teams who were not truly their equals.

'Maybe they saved something for this European competition and if they did then Ron Greenwood and the West Ham board deserve all the praise we can give them for not only was the match a magnificent game of football resulting in a brilliant win for West Ham, but was also the biggest, best and brightest boost that the game has had for many a year.'

For that display, West Ham became the first football team to win the World Fair Play Trophy, awarded by Fair Play International having been inaugurated by UNESCO and several international sports governing bodies.

The final word must go to Greenwood, who had masterminded the whole European campaign, 'I was just a player when I saw the 1953 Hungarians, and I never imagined for a moment that one day I would see a side of my own applying so many of the same principles. But when West Ham beat Munich 1860 in that Cup Winners' Cup Final, they played in a way very different from the standard English game. They moved on and off the ball in a way similar to the Hungarians – not exactly of course, because our overall methods were adapted to the players we had – but the basics were the same. That West Ham side proved a point for me.

'The match exceeded my wildest hopes. We won with two second-half goals by Sealey, but it was the manner of the victory that counted most of all. I said to my players before the start, "Here's our chance to show the world what we can do." And that is precisely what we did. Three years of hard work and faith went into our win. Our principles were justified: we proved that football at its best is a game of beauty and intelligence. Players and ball were in happy harmony, while skill and men had flourished together. Ideas and passes flowed. For me it was fulfilment.'

Greenwood had left nothing to chance in his quest to conquer Europe. His meticulous planning included compiling a dossier for his players, detailing each of their opponents in simple terms they would understand, by comparing them to English players they were more familiar with.

He continued, 'Clearly our preparations had to be first-class. I remembered the Spanish dossier I had found in a hotel drawer in Porthcawl in my early days as West Ham's manager, and I decided to give my players a similar service, with an original extra. I watched each opposing club as soon as I could after every draw, so that I could give each player of mine a vivid word-picture of his likely immediate opponent. To do this I related every opposition player to a British player my men would know.'

When Munich met Torino of Italy in a replay of their semi-final in neutral Zürich, Greenwood despatched his whole team to Switzerland to watch their potential final opponents first-hand. The only person missing from the Hammers' party that night was the man himself, who was being confirmed at Loughton, the Essex town where his family lived after moving from Twickenham.

Only three weeks later the new holders of the European Cup Winners' Cup defeated Munich once again, 2-1 in the International Soccer League in New York, with Sealey again netting the winner. But the Hammers flopped badly in the rest of the tournament to finish bottom of their group.

'The Munich team were great to us,' said centre-half Ken Brown. 'Afterwards, their players invited us to a German beer garden, and it spoke volumes for the good time we had together that night that neither team won another game in that tournament!'

The first home programme of the 1965/66 season, against Sunderland, heaped suitable praise on the European Cup Winners' Cup winners. The standard 16-page issue devoted four pages to the events at Wembley and noted that two of their opponents – Spartak Sokolovo and Lausanne – had won their respective leagues, testimony to the strength of the opposition West Ham had had to face.

You could also buy an 8mm film of the final, though the 90-minute sound version would set you back £52 – an awful lot more than a ticket to the match itself.

All that had happened in the past 12 months, or perhaps since Greenwood had taken over at Upton Park four years previously, was of little consequence compared to what was achieved on that balmy May evening at Wembley. Many would say that nothing the three former West Ham managers had accomplished in seven decades could compete with Greenwood's achievement in bringing to a small, homely and friendly East End club one of the greatest prizes in European football.

Such a point of view would, in fairness, be disrespectful not only to the aforementioned trio, but to Greenwood himself. He was a different type and breed of manager to the likes of Syd King, Charlie Paynter and Ted Fenton, who in their eras were as far-seeing as Greenwood was in his. The difference in his outlook was his ability to focus on the tactics that were necessary in the modern era during each individual game, and to appreciate that the various strengths and weaknesses of each opposing side had to be overcome in contrasting ways. He was the master tactician.

Yet little did all those associated with West Ham United realise that night, and in the ensuing weeks – cocooned in the euphoria of the victory while dreaming of greater glories to come – that this would stand as the pinnacle of the club's achievements for a decade. Once again, those immortal words within the Hammers' theme tune would ring true, 'Just like my dreams they fade and die.'

10

1966–1974: Decline

1965-66

In June 1965, West Ham returned to New York to compete once again in the American Soccer League. But this time they lost all bar one of their games, once again beating 1860 Munich. Ron Greenwood admitted that his team's performances had been 'disgraceful', but added, hopefully, 'Still, the beatings we have taken over here should have cut us down to size. After this we will not start the new season with any preconceived notions of our own greatness, and that is a good thing.'

But just 90 seconds into the new league campaign the Hammers were trailing at West Bromwich Albion, who added two further goals without reply as Greenwood's team seemed to find it difficult to adjust to league form after the euphoria of the Wembley win. The new season commenced with Alan Sealey, Johnny Byrne and Brian Dear all out with long-term injuries. That defeat at The Hawthorns paved the way for some dismal early performances.

By the end of September, the Hammers had won only twice in the First Division and had conceded five goals in successive games against Sheffield United, Liverpool and Leicester City, the last two at home. They even managed to lose to Northampton Town, giving the Cobblers their first win at the 14th attempt.

In the League Cup, Bristol Rovers were beaten 3-2 in a replay at Upton Park after a 2-2 draw at Eastville, and although they continued to struggle in the First Division, the Hammers progressed steadily in this competition with victories over Mansfield Town (4-0), Rotherham United (2-1) and Grimsby Town (1-0) heralding a path to the semi-final.

In the European Cup Winners' Cup, for which they had qualified as holders and been given a first-round bye, West Ham had a comfortable second-round home win over Olympiakos of Greece. In the return in Athens two Martin Peters goals produced a 2-2 draw for a 6 2 aggregate win. The referee in that second leg was Tofiq Bahramov. The following summer the moustachioed official would become famous – or infamous if you were German – when he was the linesman at the World Cup Final at Wembley who allowed Geoff Hurst's controversial second goal, England's third of their 4-2 win.

In the League Cup semi-final first leg at Upton Park in December, Cardiff City were well beaten 5-2. The second leg didn't take place until early February, but a 5-1 victory at Ninian Park took West Ham to their third final in as many years. Hurst scored two goals to maintain his record of having scored in every round.

In the third round of the FA Cup, Oldham Athletic of the Third Division were beaten 2-1 in an Upton Park replay after a 2-2 draw at Boundary Park. The fourth round brought Blackburn Rovers to Upton Park and a 3-3 draw meant yet another replay, but the Londoners were beaten 4-1 at Ewood Park.

It was odd to see Johnny Byrne's name in the programme for the game against Northampton on 15 January 1966 alongside the number 12. West Ham put in a miserable performance against this to-be relegated team to draw 1-1. Even the goal was a penalty by Hurst, and one reporter wrote, 'At all times West Ham struggled to capture the urgency and grace which have made them such a power in European football. But they were always failing.'

Thankfully, league form did improve and three four-goal victories were gained in succession, against Aston Villa, Blackburn and Sheffield United.

Next up in the Cup Winners' Cup were Magdeburg. It was only 1-0 to West Ham at Upton Park, but a solid performance in East Germany saw a 1-1 draw and progress to another semi-final.

The League Cup Final against West Bromwich Albion was the last in that competition to be played over two legs. A year later it would have been a one-off at Wembley. In the home leg, goals from Moore and Byrne gave West Ham a slender 2-1 lead to take to The Hawthorns. Unfortunately, an excellent first-half display there by the Midlanders gave them a 4-0 lead by half-time. Peters pulled a goal back, but the Albion were convincing 5-3 aggregate winners.

Hurst wrote how, after the game, Greenwood 'acted right out of character by insisting no one left the hotel for a drink after our defeat, perhaps the worst display we had ever put on since he took over. For the first time, despite a plea by Bobby Moore on our behalf, he refused to budge, "No one goes out tonight."

'Even then, this wasn't a reprisal against the players, or any form of punishment. "You are staying in." He told us right out, "Not to pay you back for losing, but to make you think about why you lost. You would like to go out and have a drink or two and forget. I want you to sit here and remember. This defeat should not have happened, and certainly not the way it did. Think where you went wrong, think what this means to each of you and your reputations as top-class players. And make up your minds not to ever feel this way again.'"

The significance of the League Cup loss at West Brom was that it was the first of three cup defeats, halting the sequence of cup successes which had taken the club from being also-rans to winners. Moreover, they had been winners with style, allied to a steely core, and that had pushed the name of West Ham United to the forefront, not only on the domestic scene but also internationally. In less than 12 months they had slipped back to being just another First Division side who promised much but failed to deliver.

But that defeat to West Brom was swiftly edged aside with the news that Bobby Moore wanted to quit West Ham and wouldn't be renewing his contract. The timing of the announcement – on the eve of the club's Cup Winners' Cup semi-final with West German side Borussia Dortmund at Upton Park – was particularly unfortunate and Greenwood promptly stripped his former right-hand man of the captaincy in favour of Johnny Byrne, but still played Moore against the Germans. Greenwood was even quoted as saying, 'Let's face it, we shall probably be murdered,' a public utterance that was completely out of character.

In that Upton Park first leg, Peters gave the home side a lead they held until the closing minutes when Lothar Emmerich scored twice for the Germans. In the return leg Emmerich scored twice in the first half. Johnny Byrne pulled a goal back before half-time to give hope, but Gerhard Cyliax added a third for the Germans near the end. Dortmund would go on to win the trophy, beating Liverpool 2-1 at Hampden Park.

In the programme for the following game against Arsenal, on 16 April 1966, the following lament appeared, 'After two years of campaigning on the continent we regretfully said farewell to European competitive football in Dortmund. It would be better to use the German expression of "auf wiedersehen" rather than "farewell", this being in keeping with the language of the country where we made our exit and of a less definite nature than its English counterpart, as we must hope that this reverse is temporary rather than final.'

The Hammers travelled home no longer holders of the European Cup Winners' Cup. It would be nine long years before they were able to participate in the competition again.

The second leg had been their 20th cup match of the season, virtually the equivalent of half a league campaign.

But First Division victories over Arsenal, Spurs and Manchester United helped the team to finish in 12th place as Hurst was named Hammer of the Year for a season in which he had contributed 40 goals.

In his 1984 autobiography, Greenwood admitted, 'Now was the time I should have begun to make changes because little cracks were appearing in the fabric of the side, but one of the reasons for keeping the team together was more success in the Cup Winners' Cup in 1965/66.'

One day in early April 1966, just a couple of months before the World Cup finals, Greenwood had called Moore into his office, told his stalwart defender to sit down, and then sacked him as captain. There was no row – just cold, silent acceptance.

Greenwood not only stripped Moore of the armband but went to a newspaper with a remarkable public attack on the deposed skipper. The outburst was untypical of a measured man and very oddly timed coming just a week before the first leg of the Cup Winners' Cup semi-final against Borussia Dortmund, the biggest match of West Ham's season. But Greenwood evidently felt a need to pour out his frustration.

Brian Scovell of the *Daily Sketch* was the reporter handed the exclusive. The article, on Monday, 4 April was headlined 'West Ham sack Moore'. If that was eye-catching, the quotes from Greenwood were even more extraordinary. From the high of Wembley, West Ham had spent much of the winter in distress in the relegation zone. Was Moore one of the reasons for the decline? 'I am absolutely sure of it,' Greenwood told Scovell. 'Moore has not been really playing for us for eight months. We got into the big time with that cup final win at Wembley and some of the players think they are still playing at Wembley. They have been playing in the past.'

Greenwood had convinced himself that Moore was distracted. He had been stripped of the captaincy because 'we can't have a man leading the side who doesn't want to play for us'. The understanding was that Moore wanted to join his friend Jimmy Greaves at Tottenham.

The manager never publicly blamed referees or linesmen for any injustice against his team, but he was not afraid to stand up to his best player, even if he was the Golden Boy of club and country, if he thought West Ham United was being undermined by what he perceived to be the self-interests of one player. When Greenwood believed that Moore no longer had the heart to give his best for the club, he dropped him and stripped him of the captaincy for a brief period.

After the glories of the previous two seasons, West Ham had not lived up to their reputation as England's coming force. They had done well enough in the cups, reaching the League Cup Final as well as a European semi. But the First Division campaign had been disastrous with long months spent perilously close to the relegation zone.

On Good Friday 1966, the Hammers had travelled to White Hart Lane and thrashed Spurs 4-1, with Moore watching from the stand. The following day they went to Chelsea with Moore reinstated and lost 6-2.

Moore was quoted in the *London Evening News* as saying, 'Only two people, Mr Greenwood and myself, knew I was not going to renew my contract at the end of the season. We agreed that it would be kept secret until the end of the heavy Easter programme. I kept my end of the bargain.'

And Greenwood countered, 'If the picture has been presented wrongly, I am to blame. After a talk with the board, I decided it was time the public knew what was happening – they have a right to know.'

Greenwood felt that his captain was too preoccupied with Alf Ramsey's plans for his international team for the World Cup finals in England that summer. The England captain's listlessness while wearing his West Ham shirt worried his club manager, but if Moore sometimes performed without his usual authority, his leadership was still strong enough to see the team out of several embarrassing scrapes.

In a twist to the tale of Moore failing to sign a contract, Greenwood answered Alf Ramsey's summons to the England team's Hendon Hall Hotel to get the captain's signature on a month's contract that would enable him to play in the World Cup tournament. By FIFA regulations, an unattached player – which, technically, Moore was – could not play in the World Cup. This was a temporary end to an impasse that Moore and his club manager had reached shortly before the end of the season.

After the tournament concluded, and Moore was lauded as the new icon of world football, he could virtually write his own contract at West Ham, who doubled his wage to keep him from going to Spurs. Moore got his way. But Greenwood could claim he had made his point.

In the build-up to that summer's World Cup, Ramsey had included Hurst and Peters in his England team, as well as the already well-established Moore.

Brian Glanville of the *Sunday Times* provided a prescient preview of why Hurst and Peters would ultimately serve their international team so well, 'Geoff Hurst had been something of a marginal choice for the party. Like Bobby Moore, he owed much to the coaching and percipience of Ron Greenwood. He was superbly built, tall, with immense muscular thighs, a fine jumper, shot and header, but he had originally been no more than a moderate wing-half. He was marvellously philosophical about the harsh treatment he often got from opponents, superbly unselfish and intelligent in his movement off the ball.

'Martin Peters was the third West Ham player in the party, a quiet, almost withdrawn Londoner, technically exceptional, a right-half by preference and position who had just made the England team in time the previous May, when Ramsey had chosen him against Yugoslavia at Wembley. Now he would blossom in a new role as a midfield player exploiting his flair for the unexpected.'

England won the World Cup and West Ham had the unique honour of contributing three players to the team. Moore's captaincy earned him the title of Player of the Tournament, Hurst's hat-trick earned him a special reward as England's top scorer, and the goal that put England into a 2-1 lead in the final was scored by Peters.

The headline in the *Stratford Express* said it all: 'West Ham 4 West Germany 2'.

But West Ham's – and Greenwood's – contribution to England's success wasn't just three players. The use of a near-post cross, rather than to the far post, an innovation that Greenwood took from the 1953 Hungarians to West Ham, was a distinctive ploy.

According to Matt Dickinson's 2014 biography of Moore, *Bobby Moore: The Man in Full*, 'The equaliser comes just six minutes later. Moore is instrumental, Ron Greenwood too. When Moore is fouled by Wolfgang Overath as he turns to shield possession midway into the German half, the captain quickly gathers the ball to take the free kick. He is looking up, alert to the possibilities, just as he had been taught on West Ham's training ground.

'Geoff Hurst knows exactly what is coming next. Timing his run to attack space in the heart of the penalty area, the striker can rely on Moore's chipped free kick arriving precisely when and where he needs it. "It was like Ron always coached us," Hurst says. "If something is on quick, take it." It is a move straight out of the Greenwood manual as Moore flights the ball into the German penalty area and Hurst's header draws England level at 1-1.'

In his biography of Moore, *The Life and Times of a Sporting Hero*, Jeff Powell described the mid-1960s West Ham thus, 'Like a delicate cobweb glistening in the sunlight, West Ham were beautiful to behold but inspired no feeling of permanence. On so many days they spun a silken web of delightful football, only to be blown into tatters by a storm of old-fashioned British sporting aggression.

'It was well known,' said Moore in that same book, 'that everyone enjoyed playing against West Ham as much as they enjoyed watching them. We had endless discussions about what went wrong but nobody seemed able to put their finger on it.

'Maybe it was a question of emphasis in the minds of the management. Ron Greenwood and John Lyall shied away when you mentioned putting some stick about. The emphasis was on skill.'

What bothered Moore most was that when he looked through the West Ham team he, like the fans, could find no glaring weakness, no excuse for repeated failure. 'You looked at a few of the individuals and felt there might have been room for improvement. But the 11 pieces of the jigsaw fitted when we won the cups. They'd put the ingredients in the cocktail shaker and the team had come out right. It's like a drink. Sometimes a cocktail is fabulous, sometimes it's diabolical. But when you get it right it's a crime to let it go.'

Another West Ham hero, Billy Bonds, perhaps put his finger on the Greenwood enigma in his own biography *Bonzo*, published in 1988, 'England manager was his proper level. With players of international ability, Ron did not need to waste his energies upon the motivation that is necessary in the bread-and-butter stuff of club competition. Motivation was definitely one of his strengths as a manager. When he took over with England, he worked with a squad of the best players who needed no gee-up. He could concentrate upon tactics – collective and individual – and at that he is the best.

'The Hammers learned this playing in Europe. Ron's assessment of the opposition was always spot on. When the action started you felt as if you'd been playing them for years instead of for the first time.

'So why, with such an excellent manager and three of England's 1966 World Cup-winning side, did West Ham not achieve more? Perhaps part of the answer is that Ron was, at times, too much of an intellectual.'

Charles Korr, in his *West Ham United: The Making of a Football Club*, suggested, 'The first [1964 FA Cup] win seemed to open up an almost unlimited horizon to the club. When the Cup Winners' Cup and the World Cup victories followed in quick succession, only the most sceptical supporter did not predict a glowing future for West Ham. Even the national press, which tended to treat the club and its supporters with a certain amount of condescension, became interested in what was happening at West Ham.

'Greenwood and his players were expected to restore a flair to English football and acquire trophies that would blot out the memory of years of frustration, but in fact during the 11 years between cup finals the club was unable to sustain a victorious pattern. Many journalists hoped that West Ham represented the way football would develop in the future. When success did not follow, they had to come up with something about West Ham that would redeem it: that West Ham did not have enough hard men; that the club was more interested in playing good football than in winning; and that it lacked a hungry ambition to win. These ideas could have been applied to other football clubs, but they stuck to West Ham and became its public personality.

'The story was that West Ham did not win as much as it should, but at least it lost with dignity. It was supposed to be a club that would not stoop to unethical backroom procedures and would not allow its players to become thugs on the pitch just to win a match. Entertainment and ethics became code words to describe West Ham United. This led journalists to look at West Ham's history to find out why it was different from other clubs. That meant looking at the club's unwillingness to sack managers, its attitude towards money, its antipathy to hangers-on, and it's supposed dependence on local players. These characteristics are exactly what West Ham wanted to believe about itself.'

West Ham's past had been so mediocre that winning anything was still a novelty when Greenwood arrived. By the end of his second season in 1963 many supporters had come to believe that there was something special about the team and began to expect, even demand, winning matches as well as good performances. The FA Cup victory in 1964 cast a new light on what supporters expected and what Greenwood thought about them. Success was not impossible for West Ham; why should the supporters be expected to settle for mediocrity?

The events of 1966 were a triumph and a test for West Ham. The club's contribution was a source of personal, patriotic and professional pleasure to Greenwood. The aftermath, however, reinforced his ideas about the shallow nature of many supporters and the dangerous trends that were taking place in football. His reaction to the exuberance that greeted his team was to draw even further back from the public and give the impression of total immersion in the world of training and tactics. His conduct violated the expectations that East Enders had of their manager. He was the leader of a club, their club, and they wanted him to show in public that they were together in something that was important to both of them.

Greenwood's approach both to the game and to the club changed little over his years with West Ham. This was no surprise to the men who employed him. Greenwood was what Reg Pratt and his fellow directors wanted, and they stayed with him because he was consistent. Pratt wanted somebody who would teach good football, bring victories and set standards. The manager had to be able to work within the structure at West Ham, to realise that money did not grow on trees, and that the directors would not stand for being embarrassed.

Another reason for West Ham's post-1965 decline was that Greenwood could not control his players' behaviour off the pitch. They needed someone a lot stronger who could keep them in check. Johnny Byrne would claim, 'He could do nothing to stop us, and we went completely berserk, living it up, day in and day out.'

But chasing players was just not Greenwood's way. He wanted them to act like adults and thought the only way that would happen was if they were treated and trusted like adults. He believed that they had to take responsibility for themselves and deal with the consequences.

1966-67

Despite the feelgood factor generated by 'West Ham winning the World Cup', the Hammers still lost their first three matches of the 1966/67 season – 2-1 at home to Chelsea, away to Arsenal by the same score, and 5-4 at Leicester – even though Moore, Hurst and Peters were in the side. The first win of the season was not until the sixth game, 4-1 at Manchester City.

But then the team embarked on another extended run in the League Cup that would take them past Spurs 1-0 at home, Arsenal 3-1 at Highbury, and a full-strength Leeds United 7-0 at Upton Park. Allegedly the latter score caused such disbelief in the offices of the *Yorkshire Post* that they asked for confirmation three times! At that time Don Revie's men were at the pinnacle of English football.

Byrne was described in one of the match reports as 'the nearest thing we have in English football to [Alfredo] Di Stéfano'. It summed up Greenwood's West Ham, who on any given day could produce a performance like that. But in the league they lost twice to Leeds that season, and did not beat the Yorkshire side once in the next 14 meetings.

Blackpool were beaten 3-1 at Bloomfield Road in round five but eventually the bubble burst with a 4-0 semi-final first leg thrashing at West Bromwich Albion. A 2-2 draw in the second leg at home meant West Ham missed out on a third visit to Wembley in four years.

A purple patch over nine league games in November and December, which witnessed 32 goals, included a 6-1 home win over Fulham with four goals for Hurst, a 4-3 victory at Spurs – 'the best soccer show seen in London in years' according to the *Evening News* – and an incredible 5-5 draw at Chelsea on 17 December after leading 5-3. Then, as was their wont, the Hammers added fuel to the countless jibes about 'coming down with the Christmas decorations' as a 3-3 home draw to Third Division Swindon Town in the third round of the FA Cup was followed by a 3-1 defeat in the replay.

Come the spring, West Ham embarked on an appalling run of seven successive First Division defeats, including a 6-1 loss to Manchester United which allowed the visitors to clinch the title at Upton Park.

At least there had been an interesting April trip to the Houston Astrodome in the States for a friendly against Real Madrid. In front of a 33,000 crowd the English side lost that game as well, 3-2. A final-day 1-1 draw at home to Manchester City meant the Hammers finished 16th, hardly a sign of progress.

Eighty league goals scored in 42 games was an impressive total but 84 conceded showed where the Hammers' weakness lay. Only two clubs had let in more.

Hurst finished with 41 goals in all competitions, with 29 of them coming in the league, and was again named Hammer of the Year, while Moore was given an OBE in the New Year's Honours List.

Hammers fans were clearly unhappy. Some of them damaged Moore's sports shop in Green Street – only months after that afternoon at Wembley.

After 455 Hammers appearances, Ken Brown left to join Torquay United. In February, Johnny Byrne returned to former club Crystal Palace. Across 205 appearances he had delivered 107 goals and had won ten England caps while with the Hammers.

Peters was one who thought that a First Division club with three World Cup winners and West Ham's resources should have been good enough to challenge regularly for the major prizes in the English game, but they weren't.

Yet he stressed that as a teaching academy West Ham were one of the finest in the land. The calibre of player developed by the club in the 1960s was outstandingly high. Everything he learned from ages 15 to 25 he owed to West Ham in general and Greenwood in particular. Peters said, 'They taught me good habits that served me well throughout my career, both on and off the field. I shall be eternally grateful to Ron and all the coaches at West Ham who helped shape me both as a player and a person.'

Yet in the seasons after that European triumph at Wembley the club failed to progress in the way many expected and Moore and Peters, in their different ways, both criticised their manager's lack of ambition and poor man-management. It was a criticism that was to haunt Greenwood for the remainder of his time at the club.

Yet it was Brown, one of the 1960s stalwarts, who felt unappreciated by his boss, saying, 'I don't remember receiving any praise from him, and I don't think he was particularly happy with me.'

The evidence against Greenwood began to mount in the years following the Wembley triumphs. Greenwood's ideas on man-management were built on the concept of mutual respect. He simply assumed that players would always do the right thing. He wrote, 'I was always "Ron" to my players, rather than the "Boss", because that was the kind of relationship I wanted. I did not want to force anything on them. Respect is not something a manager can demand or expect.'

But what Greenwood saw as a mature and democratic philosophy of leadership, others saw as weakness. Byrne admitted players took advantage of their manager's refusal to crack the whip, either in training or after a match. Others like Brown wanted a more physical approach to training, with more fitness work. Brown admitted he often went for a long run after training because Greenwood's sessions focused on technique rather than building up fitness.

The drinking culture was certainly a factor in the relative demise of the Hammers after 1965, but another aspect of their success was also probably part of the reason why the side was unable to sustain its achievement: consistency of selection. In the FA Cup-winning season Greenwood had called on 22 players, but five of them played no more than half a dozen matches. Another three turned out fewer than 15 times. For most of the games, Greenwood would rely on the 11 players who would go on to win the FA Cup.

After one of the most demanding – and financially rewarding – seasons the club had ever known, not a single new player was brought to Upton Park for 1964/65. This time a squad of 21 was used to defend the FA Cup, as well as contest the League Cup, the Cup Winners' Cup and cover the First Division programme, but again in the main, it was the FA Cup Final side plus Martin Peters that bore the majority of the burden. It seems likely that the board and maybe the manager were not ready to invest in their success or were willing to see players burn themselves out and hope that the youth policy on which the team of the 1960s had been built would produce ready-made replacements. Unfortunately, the plan failed, although sufficient talent did come through to maintain mediocre cup and First Division performances for the better part of a decade.

Such parsimony could affect the best managers. In the summer of 1962 Ipswich Town were league champions, yet manager Alf Ramsey bought in just one new player, keeping all 28 of the previous season's squad. It was 'an act of reckless loyalty' according to his biographer, Leo McKinstry.

After the high of the World Cup, there was frustration ahead with West Ham whose early promise under Greenwood was compromised by maddening inconsistency.

Popular folklore would have it that they were southern softies, but there had always been a hard streak in the Hammers, even under Greenwood.

Look no further than Eddie Bovington, who replaced Peters in the 1963/64 side after the 8-2 mauling from Blackburn Rovers. Bovington, for one, was insistent that it would have been better for everyone if Moore had been allowed to go to Spurs, 'Bobby should never have stayed at West Ham. He should have gone to Tottenham, a bigger club, bigger crowds, trophies. West Ham weren't big enough for him. You've got three of them [Moore, Hurst and Peters], and if you can't form your side around three World Cup winners there's something wrong ... It might have been better for Greenwood. Really, there should have been a rapport with the coach and manager to make it work and they never had that.'

Bovington added, 'My relationship with Greenwood was never good, we just failed to click from the time he arrived ... I don't think he liked a young whippersnapper standing up to him.' He pointed to the 1965/66 League Cup to underline his perceived low rating in Greenwood's eyes. He said, 'I played in every game of each round up to the final, but he dropped me for the first leg of the final, at home to West Brom. I don't think our personality clash was the reason he decided not to pick me. I wished Ron had been more straightforward and not pussyfooted around.'

By 1967 West Ham were committed to replacing their goalkeeper. The situation seemed perfect for England's Gordon Banks to join up with his international skipper as Peter Shilton was set to replace him at Leicester. The *Ilford Recorder* made the case for the deal under the headline 'Why the Hammers must switch to Banks'. He would be ideal for West Ham, according to the newspaper, and it was reported on 13 April 1967 that he could be available for £50,000. Banks was 28; Bobby Ferguson, the goalkeeper from Kilmarnock under consideration by the Hammers, was 20. Banks had experience, skill and drawing power; Ferguson had only youth and potential. The paper continued, 'Too often in the past, West Ham have damaged themselves by their less than ruthless attitudes in a world where the quality of mercy is very much strained. Whatever agreements have been reached with Kilmarnock must be put aside. Banks of England is the man.'

Leicester boss Matt Gillies actually phoned Greenwood after the World Cup to inform him that Banks was for sale. 'We could certainly have afforded him, and I was told that Banks was keen on joining us,' Greenwood confirmed.

Banks might have been the man for the *Recorder*, but not for Reg Pratt and Greenwood. The argument against Banks was simple – Greenwood and Pratt had made a commitment to Kilmarnock and that was too important to set aside. Personal honour was involved; West Ham's word had to be good if the club were to be trusted in future negotiations.

In the past, West Ham officials had been contemptuous of other clubs that went back on their word. In the future, Greenwood would be furious when West Ham lost a player he felt was committed to signing while his own club touted him around for a slightly higher price. The Hammers refused to participate in a football version of 'gazumping' and turned down the opportunity to bring in the best goalkeeper in the world.

Phil Woosnam, Johnny Byrne and now Ferguson had ended the legend that West Ham would not spend, but another set of standards remained firmly in place and Banks became a Hammer who never was.

It was his signing of Ferguson instead of Banks that would ultimately cause Greenwood most regret. To almost every football manager in the land the decision to sign either England's number one or Scotland's number two was what they now call a no-brainer. But for a man of Greenwood's integrity, it was simply a question of honour. Explaining how one of his most admirable strengths could also be a weakness, he said, 'To sign Banks I would have had to have broken my word to an old friend and I just could not do that. There was a mountain of an obstacle: my conscience. I had just made a huge and firm offer for Bobby Ferguson of Kilmarnock.'

The Ferguson fee was £65,000, a record for a British goalkeeper. Kilmarnock's manager was Malcolm MacDonald, a good pal from his playing days at Brentford, and they had shaken hands on the sale.

Greenwood said, 'I told the West Ham directors about my dilemma, admitting that I would prefer Banks, but I insisted we went through with the Ferguson deal. The story that Banks was for sale and that we were interested came out in the papers, and Malcolm MacDonald phoned me to ask if I still intended to stick to our agreement. "I've given my word – the deal is still on," I told him. Roland Brandon, one of our directors, told me it was the biggest mistake West Ham ever made. He said we should have pulled out of our deal with Kilmarnock and gone for the best man. I know he was right in one sense. Professional football is a hard, little, world. Promises are broken daily. Expediency rules. Nice guys are supposed to finish last. But I did what I thought was right, and honesty should matter. Only if that is wrong was I wrong.'

Greenwood admitted too, 'Hindsight tells me that was one of the biggest mistakes of my life – but the reason for the decision was at least honourable. I can only wonder what we might have achieved if Banks had joined us.'

Harry Redknapp, by the time of his 2014 autobiography *A Man Walks on to a Pitch* a manager of some considerable experience, wrote of his view. To him it was 'a strange decision', but one which could have hinged on Greenwood not being willing to match Banks's wages, which were £50 higher than Ferguson's.

But Greenwood had form with failing to sign goalkeepers around that time. He had reached agreement with Millwall to sign their promising goalkeeper Alex Stepney for £40,000 in 1966, but when Greenwood refused to pay a signing-on fee, Stepney signed for Tommy Docherty's Chelsea instead.

Chelsea already had a very good keeper in Peter Bonetti, so Stepney soon moved on to Manchester United. Greenwood was convinced Docherty had only signed Stepney to spite West Ham. Indeed, in 1966 'The Doc' had already turned down Greenwood's bid to sign Bonetti. West Ham's, and Greenwood's, policy of refusing to pay signing-on fees also cost them Terry Venables's signature.

1967-68

Bobby Moore had ended his first autobiography, 1966's *My Soccer Story*, by posing an interesting question, 'What effect, I wonder, will England's triumph have on ordinary football in this country? Will new standards be accepted, new levels of skill demanded by crowds used now to seeing the world's best?'

Moore's optimism was at the time justified after the euphoria of victory, but he could not have seen the almost catastrophic decline of English football, which came sooner than imagined. The game, shackled to 4-4-2 formations, became increasingly negative, and certain clubs who should have known better resorted to thuggery and bullying to gain them success. Increasing violence on and off the field did nothing to raise the morale of young fans inspired by Alf Ramsey's triumph. Gates began to decline, playing standards fell and British football seemed to be on the skids.

West Ham did clinch one title in 1967. According to the Football League they had enjoyed the best disciplinary record of any First Division team over the past five years. And according to many pundits, therein lay the root of the Hammers' problems. Greenwood's team was too nice and was too tame in defence. For the Hammers, Brown and Moore were the men at the heart of the defence, and while both men were strong players and were in no way shrinking violets, when it came to tackling neither had that extra, nasty edge which could terrify forwards.

West Ham entered the new season feeling eternally optimistic about their First Division chances, but again this proved misplaced and the team had to settle for a mid-table 12th place.

Greenwood was rightly worried about his defence, signing the man with the heavy metal legs from Celtic, John Cushley, to add a 'bit of stick' at the back. Another arrival – in March, effectively to replace Cushley, who failed to take his opportunity at Upton Park – was centre-back Alan Stephenson from Crystal Palace, signed for a then club record fee of £80,000. Greenwood had also spent that £65,000 on Kilmarnock goalkeeper Bobby Ferguson, who would never make the impact of Ernie Gregory before him or Phil Parkes after him.

But one new arrival did make an immediate mark in the first team. Trevor Brooking, a local lad from Ilford, made his debut at Turf Moor against Burnley in a 3-3 draw in August 1967. Another West Ham favourite-to-be began to make a name for himself at right-back after his £47,500 transfer from Charlton on 13 May 1967: Billy Bonds, in Brooking's estimation, 'The club's most successful venture into the transfer market.'

The new defenders did not settle in quickly and 18 goals were conceded in the first six matches with only one win, 4-2 at home to Burnley. The Hammers' league form improved when Geoff Hurst scored twice in the 5-1 win at Sunderland, and four days later Martin Peters scored twice in another 5-1 win in a League Cup tie at Walsall.

The next league game was at home to bottom club Wolves, on 16 September 1968, and marked my first trip to watch West Ham. Naturally they lost, 2-1.

The League Cup fourth-round tie at home to Bolton was a personal triumph for Geoff Hurst, who scored all the goals in a 4-1 win. Then in the next round the Hammers lost 2-0 at Second Division Huddersfield Town. There was a small piece of history made when Harry Redknapp replaced Ronnie Boyce to become the club's first League Cup substitute.

West Ham's defensive frailties were never more apparent than against Stoke City at home when, leading 3-0 at the interval, they contrived to lose 4-3.

Brian Dear came back into the side during December and responded with a hat-trick in the Boxing Day home win over Leicester City. Four days later he scored two more in another 4-2 win against the same side.

In the FA Cup, two goals from Martin Peters helped the Hammers to a well-deserved 3-1 triumph at Burnley, and a week later Fulham were crushed 7-2 at Upton Park. The good form continued with a 3-0 triumph at Stoke City in the fourth round of the FA Cup. It was expected that the Hammers would beat bottom side Sheffield United in round five at Upton Park, but the Yorkshiremen triumphed 2-1. I had again travelled from Hereford for that match, my second trip to Upton Park. There was a pattern emerging.

Greenwood admitted that his team did not deserve a replay, saying, 'We played badly as a team and never got on top of them.'

A few days later, England under-23 centre-half Alan Stephenson was signed from Crystal Palace in an attempt to fill the problem position at the heart of the defence.

In April, Newcastle were beaten 5-0 at home, with Brooking scoring his first hat-trick, but during a 2-1 win at Sheffield United, Frank Lampard broke his leg and would be sidelined for a year.

The season dribbled to a conclusion with a 1-1 draw with Everton which left the Londoners in 12th place. This was also the day when West Ham bade farewell to the East Terrace, popularly known as the 'Chicken Run'.

Even the best club managers have made bad signings. But Greenwood's failure to adequately replace centre-half Ken Brown and keeper Jim Standen proved an ongoing problem he never really resolved. In May 1967 he had made three defensive signings that he hoped would add much-needed steel to the rearguard, while ignoring Moore's recommendation to bring in Manchester United hardman Maurice Setters alongside him at the back. The manager went instead for Celtic's 23-year-old John Cushley for a fee of £20,000. Cushley had been the understudy to the legendary Billy McNeill and was on the fringe of the side that lifted the European Cup in May 1967, when he swapped east Glasgow for east London. Moore would blame Greenwood for ruining Cushley by instructing him to temper his naturally aggressive style in favour of a more controlled and measured approach.

Peters later wrote, 'At one point Ron decided that we needed a tougher presence alongside Bobby Moore in the heart of the defence. He signed an uncompromising centre-half, John Cushley from Celtic. He was as tough as old boots and a formidable tackler, but he wasn't really Ron's type of player. "We don't do that sort of thing here," Ron told him at the end of one match. After a couple of reprimands, and a total of 46 games, he was sent back to Scotland.'

Cushley was an educated man who was also a qualified teacher but according to Moore, Greenwood was 'buying a compromise that satisfied his conscience', adding that the Scotsman was 'a nice lad who could get stuck in'. At times, though, even Cushley was too forceful for the Corinthian ethics of the Hammers manager, and he would fail to make a significant impression during his time in east London.

Greenwood would later admit, 'Our basic trouble [in the summer of 1967] was in two positions: centre-half and goalkeeper. We had good goalkeepers and good centre-halves, but not at the same time.

'Cushley was not much taller than Setters, but he was a defender who was positive and strong, he had done well in Europe, and he was a man of character. He had his moments, but he sometimes struggled in the air. Perhaps Setters would have been a better bet after all.'

While Cushley and Ferguson are generally regarded as two of Greenwood's most lamentable signings, the manager did mark the 1967 'Summer of Love' with a third signing that all Hammers fans would take to their hearts over the next two decades.

A fee of £47,500 bought William 'Billy' Bonds to Upton Park from Charlton Athletic as a right-back. Arguably, he didn't reach his peak as a player until John Lyall's time in charge but said of Greenwood, 'I could talk all day about Ron and the influence he had on me as a player. He signed me as a big, strong 20-year-old right back in 1967 and turned me into a central midfielder – the position in which I believe I enjoyed the best years of my career. He was a great coach who was years ahead of his time, and I think anyone that worked under him would say that he helped to make them a better player. Everybody respected his knowledge and vision of the game.

'To Ron, football was entertainment. He never once compromised his beliefs or changed the style of his team. I suppose you might say that, after the success of the mid-60s, West Ham slightly underachieved in the years that followed, but Ron wouldn't have changed his methods or approach.

'He always called me William. To everyone else I was Bill or Bonzo, but Ron was a stickler for formality and called everyone by their full Christian name.'

After Cushley, Greenwood turned to Alan Stephenson in the hope of finding the right central defensive partner for Moore, later admitting, 'He didn't do a bad job but, once again, technically, he wasn't quite up to the mark.'

Stephenson was interested to read Moore's comments that Greenwood's footballing principles had ruined both him and Cushley as defenders who were afraid to tackle. He said, 'I was surprised to read that in Bobby's book, because Ron certainly never said anything to me about him not wanting me to be aggressive or to adapt my style for West Ham in any way. I played for them the way I had always done. Maybe Ron might have said something about me to Bobby, but he never said anything to me in that respect.

'To be honest, when he first signed me, he didn't go into detail about what he expected from me. But having watched me a number of times for Palace, he knew what he was buying, and, at 23 or 24 years of age, it would have been silly of me to try and change my game. Ron never criticised me at all. Although, having said that, he hardly said anything to me. Ron went about his business quietly.'

Stephenson did agree with Moore's view that Greenwood, brilliant and inventive coach though he undoubtedly was, might have coaxed a better response – and therefore results – from his players if he had got tougher with them whenever standards or attitudes fell unacceptably short. After the team had been hammered on the field, Moore said he wanted the manager to show his disgust in the dressing room there and then, rather than delay his response until expressing a more considered analysis on the following Monday morning.

'I thought there was something lacking discipline-wise at the club,' said Stephenson. 'Players were taking training too light-heartedly, whereas the emphasis I'd been used to at Palace had been a disciplined approach and hard work. I don't think the West Ham players hurt enough after a defeat – there was never any shouting in the dressing room. I was a little bit surprised to find when I came to West Ham that there were a lot of players who were disillusioned with the club, which may have influenced the behaviour of certain people. We weren't going to challenge for the league title because the discipline wasn't there among the players. The general attitude wasn't right, there were a few cliques, and the club wasn't bonded. Given the amount of talent around we under-achieved. If anything, as a club, West Ham were too friendly.'

1968-69

There were no additions to Greenwood's squad, though Peter Brabrook left for Orient and Jack Burkett for Charlton. The Hammers at last got off to a good start in the First Division, losing just one of their opening 12 matches. By the end of September they were comfortably placed at fourth in the table. That heady period also witnessed a 7-2 League Cup win over Bolton Wanderers, but in the next round a 0-0 home draw was followed by a 3-2 defeat to Coventry City – managed by ex-Hammer Noel Cantwell – in a replay.

Harry Redknapp became the first West Ham player to be sent off in seven years after a bust-up with Leeds United's Billy Bremner at Elland Road. Bremner's run-in with Redknapp, when compared with an incident later in the match, illustrated a major problem with English football at the time. Stephenson fouled Johnny Giles and the latter retaliated but received no punishment. One newspaper commented, 'In the case of Giles there was sympathetic silence from spectators who have been educated at Elland Road that treachery is a part of soccer success.'

But a week later, on 19 October 1968, Geoff Hurst got his name into the record books when he scored six against Sunderland at Upton Park in an 8-0 win. He thus equalled Vic Watson's feat against Leeds in 1929. As one match report put it, 'West Ham played no better than when I saw them draw with Tottenham and Sheffield Wednesday. There is genius in their play, but they are balanced on such a knife edge that they can as easily fall one way or the other. Yesterday they fell the right way.'

After Christmas, West Ham made it through to the fifth round of the FA Cup, but then fell victim to yet another giant-killing act as Mansfield Town dispatched them 3-0 at Field Mill, in a tie which had suffered five postponements. When they beat Wolves at home 3-1 on 24 March, they were sixth, and with a real chance of Inter-Cities Fairs Cup qualification. But then they failed to win any of their last nine matches, with only four goals being scored. The total of 66 league goals was the lowest of Greenwood's tenure, but 50 conceded was the best defensive performance of his reign and the club's lowest since the war.

They finished a respectable eighth, but with thoughts of what might have been, given their sparkling form earlier in the season. Hurst was again top scorer with 31 goals and bagged another Hammer of the Year award.

Leeds skipper Bremner, perhaps safe in the knowledge that his team had just clinched the championship for the first time, acknowledged West Ham's skill in a television interview. 'They let you play,' he said. Such was the reputation of the Hammers – they let other teams play good football. What Bremner really meant was that the majority of their title rivals had favoured a more defensive outlook in a bid to stop his team.

Outside the East End, Greenwood's reputation was still high. There was a story that a First Division club were prepared to offer him a £10,000 signing on fee to join them, with a generous salary, and a seven-year contract. He turned the approach down.

1969-70

West Ham won their first two league matches, 1-0 at home to Newcastle United, and 2-0 at home to Chelsea, which put them top of the First Division, but then they decided to give up on the rest of the season as five defeats and two draws in the next seven games left them down in 20th.

The team finished 17th, the lowest since Greenwood's appointment. Away form was poor from the outset with the first victory not arriving until December, a 2-0 win at Tottenham.

One high note came on 17 January 1970 when 41,643 spectators entered Upton Park to witness a 0-0 draw with Manchester United, a new ground record.

Cup competitions offered no respite. The Hammers went out of the League Cup in the third round with a 1-0 defeat away to Nottingham Forest, and fared even worse in the FA Cup, where Second Division Middlesbrough beat them 2-1 in the third round at Ayresome Park.

It had been a depressing season, which for the first time in living memory saw supporters protesting. The only consistent thing about West Ham – yet again – was their inconsistency. The Upton Park faithful would see victories against Chelsea, Derby, Liverpool and Newcastle – all top-seven teams. Contrast that with dropped home points against struggling sides like Southampton, Ipswich, Sunderland and West Bromwich Albion.

Alan Stephenson just didn't seem to fit the bill as the hoped-for long-term replacement for Ken Brown at centre-half, despite making 118 league and cup appearances before going on loan to Fulham in 1971/72. And neither did Peter Eustace, a £90,000 acquisition from Sheffield Wednesday in January 1970, look to be in the same class as Martin Peters. Even if it's generally agreed that Peters was virtually irreplaceable when he chose to leave for Spurs in March 1970, Eustace didn't even come close to filling the World Cup winner's boots. A northerner who preferred game shooting to a few lagers, the unpopular Eustace didn't fit in at Upton Park and was on his way back to Hillsborough within 16 months, after only 49 appearances in a West Ham shirt and seven goals. Allegedly calling the East End a dump compared to his native Sheffield didn't help endear him to the natives.

Peters was sold to Spurs in a £200,000 transfer, with Jimmy Greaves moving to Upton Park, in a record-breaking deal completed five hours before the transfer deadline in March 1970. Greaves scored twice on his debut at Manchester City, thereby maintaining his record of scoring on all of his first outings for club and country, sparking a late-season revival of fortunes with just one defeat in the remaining five games. Peters would also score on his Spurs debut but his new team lost 2-1 at home to Coventry.

Peters was the first of West Ham's most famous trio to leave. He cited what he believed was the club's lack of ambition for wanting to better himself at Tottenham – not, as Greenwood later claimed, because he wanted to quit the Boleyn as he felt in any way overshadowed by the two other World Cup heroes. Greenwood's opinion was that Moore and Hurst were getting most of the credit and rewards after 1966, and that Peters saw himself as a sort of

RON GREENWOOD

quiz question, 'Who scored England's other goal in the World Cup Final – with most people getting the answer wrong.'

Peters would trace the first real sign of a breakdown in his relationship with Greenwood to a match at Nottingham Forest in April 1968. He was left out of the team and the manager embarrassed him in front of team-mates by accusing him of saving his best performances for England. It was an accusation Greenwood had levelled at Moore two years earlier.

He wrote, 'The beginning of the end of my career at West Ham came on the day Ron Greenwood accused me of saving my best performances for England. It was an affront to my professionalism and something I never forgot. Occasionally, he'd have a quiet word, but I'd never known him set upon one of his players in this way. Perhaps he felt under a bit of pressure himself. I think in his heart of hearts Ron knew, much as Geoff, Bobby and I knew, that the way West Ham played wasn't conducive to winning the big prize in English football. Why? Because other clubs played a different kind of football.

'Our one-touch, passing game was based on flair and freedom of expression. Ron encouraged his players to attack. The crowd at Upton Park loved us for it because the football we played was entertaining and exciting. On our good days, we were brilliant, there was no better team, but we couldn't sustain that style of play throughout a 42-match programme.

'Our game was not designed to close space and grind out 1-0 victories. We could put together a run of good performances that would win one of the cup competitions, but over the nine months of the league programme we were consistently inconsistent. It was one of our endearing qualities!'

152

In October 1969, Peters was dropped again for a game at home to Burnley. He had only scored one league goal all season but he professed to being shocked at the demotion.

Explaining the background to his move to Spurs, Peters said, 'I wasn't playing very well, for whatever reason, and Ron dropped me. Fine, anyone can be dropped, but it caused mayhem in the football world. I had a private meeting with Ron. I said that the team wasn't winning anything – we were already out of the League Cup and not doing well in the league – and I was 25, coming up for 26, I felt that I needed a fresh start somewhere. We made a verbal agreement that if we didn't do well in the FA Cup, he would let me go. We shook hands on that.'

West Ham duly lost in the third round at Middlesbrough in January. Greenwood did not renege on the promise he had made to Peters at the training ground that day. For his part, Peters claimed that he didn't push his manager into letting him go and that the move to Spurs came out of the blue.

Greenwood wrote, 'Martin was a very likeable person, but he became fed up and eventually sure in his own mind that things would be different elsewhere. He began to ask for a move regularly, but I did not agree immediately because once again I felt it important that he should go to the right type of club. He needed a manager who understood what his game was all about.'

Regarding Peters, Greenwood added that he 'is a player that perhaps only West Ham could have produced. I believe he would have done well with half a dozen other clubs, but it was our style and philosophy which enabled him to flower properly. He did not need to adjust with us because he found the understanding he needed at Upton Park. He had players around him who were on the same wavelength. We were right for him. He was right for us. The result was a player who did full justice to his talents.'

In fact, the papers were already speculating that West Ham could eventually be a destination for Greaves, either in March or perhaps during the summer. But there was no suggestion that his former England team-mate Peters might be heading in the other direction.

Having arranged a secret meeting with his Spurs counterpart Bill Nicholson in the car park at Chingford greyhound stadium, Greenwood then suggested the audacious trade.

'Bill was getting the better of the bargain because Jimmy wasn't doing much at Spurs,' conceded Greenwood. 'But I knew a change could sometimes work wonders. I fancied a go. Jimmy was a Dagenham boy and now he was coming home.'

Greenwood recalled Greaves telling him, 'Give me a blank contract and I will sign it.' But while he took such a response as genuine enthusiasm, it might equally have been a reflection of a 'couldn't care less' attitude.

'I wish to God I had told Bill [Nicholson] that I was not interested,' Greaves would later say, but he was swayed by the prospect of playing alongside his great friend Moore and also only having to travel 15 minutes to the Chadwell Heath training ground.

In the pre-electronic, fax-less world of 1970, Greenwood then drove to the Football League headquarters in Lytham St Annes in Lancashire to personally deliver the transfer papers that showed Greaves was valued at £54,000 in the £200,000 exchange. It is hard to envisage a modern-day manager making a frantic midnight dash to the Lancashire coast to register their latest signing, but it was all in a day's work for him.

One wonders if Greenwood already knew, or Nicholson just omitted to tell him, about Greaves's drinking habits. Presumably Moore, his great buddy at the bar, was all too aware but did not let on to his manager.

Quite how much Greaves was allowing his game to erode with his off-field activities is difficult to gauge, but he did admit that his social drinking in the late 1960s was already considerable and was moving towards more dangerous territory by this time. 'Knocking back the booze became more than just a habit,' is how he recalled this period. 'It started to become a necessity, like water to a plant.'

According to Hammers physio Rob Jenkins, before Greaves made his debut at Manchester City he had to tell the striker to stay away from Greenwood because he stank of drink.

Yet it took no time at all for Harry Redknapp to become aware of his new team-mate's lifestyle. 'His first day at the club we all went over to the Slater's Arms with Jimmy because we all wanted to be with him. We were still in there at seven or eight at night after getting in there at half past one. It was too much to keep that pace up, but Jimmy kept going.'

During the summer of 1970, Moore, Hurst and Peters were in Mexico with England to defend the World Cup.

Greenwood also spent the summer at the tournament as a member of the FIFA Technical Committee, which prepared reports on the tactics and preparations of the 16 competing teams.

Greaves was also there, though not as a player. He competed 16,000 miles as a co-driver in the World Cup Car Rally, which finished in Mexico City. His car was placed a very creditable sixth out of 26.

1970-71

On a personal note, I moved from Hereford to college near London in the autumn of 1970. This meant I could watch the Hammers regularly. Well, I certainly picked the right season.

Jimmy Greaves opened his season's account in an opening day 2-2 draw at his old club Tottenham, who had Martin Peters in the side, but he had to wait a further two months before notching his 350th career goal in a 2-1 defeat at Stoke City.

In September came the announcement that John Lyall – then in charge of the Hammers' youth team – was to be promoted to Greenwood's assistant. The Ilford-born full-back had made 36 first-team appearances for the club in the early 1960s before having to retire due to injury. Greenwood, who prided himself on his close relationship with his players, was becoming increasingly out of touch, partly because of the ever-widening age gap between him and the players and having the 30-year-old Lyall on board could help to bridge it.

A Geoff Hurst hat-trick at home to Burnley on 3 October brought the team's first league victory – at the 11th attempt. The next home match against Spurs was another 2-2 draw, but was also notable for Hurst displacing Jimmy Ruffell as the club's second-highest scorer; a record Upton Park attendance of 42,322; and Tommy Taylor making his debut after an £80,000 switch from Orient, in yet another attempt by Greenwood to solidify the centre-half berth.

West Ham's only cup victory that season came with a narrow 1-0 win over Hull City in the League Cup, but even that came with an extra cost. Billy Bonds was sent off, and with a 21-day suspended sentence already hanging over his head the right-back incurred a further two-week ban and a £120 fine.

His absence allowed John McDowell to make his league debut in a 2-1 win over Blackpool at the end of October. This took the Irons to 16th in the table, their highest league position of the season since the brief hope of August. But the team from the Lancashire coast were to have the biggest impact on West Ham's imploding season.

On Saturday, 2 January 1971, West Ham lost 4-0 away to Blackpool in the third round of the FA Cup. Blackpool would subsequently finish bottom of the First Division. On the same day 66 people lost their lives, and 200 were injured at an Old Firm game at Ibrox Stadium in Glasgow. Yet it was the Blackpool episode that would dominate the headlines for days, if not weeks.

As Hammers fans travelled back to London a petition was circulated demanding Greenwood's dismissal, albeit signed by only 370 names, alongside talk of a mass boycott at the next home match. But chairman Reg Pratt would come out in his manager's defence, declaring, 'We have hit a bad patch, but we have every confidence in the manager.' He also told reporters, 'I gather they [the players] were not drinking heavily, just a beer or two. But even if they had only had a lemon squash it would have been the same. In view of all the problems we have been facing, and the position we are in, we can imagine no more irresponsible behaviour.'

Post-Blackpool, four players, including Bobby Moore, were fined a week's wages and, with the exception of Clyde Best, were dropped from a team desperately trying to dig itself out of a big hole that was getting bigger by the game. A 2-0 defeat at Arsenal followed, then Leeds left Upton Park with a 3-2 victory, but it was the subsequent 4-1 home loss to Derby County on 6 February – with Moore a substitute – when angry fans showed their growing discontent by unfurling banners, the first of their kind seen at Upton Park, including 'Greenwood Out' and 'Moore substitute – the Final Sick Joke'. A section of fans standing in the new East Terrace further showed their disapproval with anti-Greenwood chants.

Moore had many friends in the media and fans. After two games out the England captain was given a place on the bench against Derby and with the visitors leading 3-0 at half-time he was brought on. An improved performance in the second half prompted one reporter to ask Greenwood if he was pleased with the impact his substitution had made. It was a question which brought a somewhat unexpected and uncharacteristic answer from the normally reserved manager, 'Moore coming on was immaterial to the side's improvement. We played well for ten minutes before he even touched the ball.'

A run of five league defeats was halted three days later with a vital 1-0 win at Coventry City. A reinstated Greaves scored the all-important goal, with Moore back in the side.

The next point came at home to Manchester City, with John Lyall taking control of the team for the first time. Greenwood was in Newcastle on a scouting trip, and by the time his side faced Nottingham Forest at Upton Park three days later it included Bryan 'Pop' Robson, signed for £120,000 from Newcastle United. He duly scored in a much-needed 2-0 win.

On 30 March 1971, West Ham were away to Everton. It coincided with Greenwood's daughter Carole's wedding in Loughton, Essex. He gave his offspring away then was off to Stansted Airport to catch a flight to Liverpool. West Ham's 1-0 success even delivered their first win at Goodison Park in 11 years.

A sequence of three successive victories amid a run of 15 games, of which four were lost, helped ensure the team's survival, albeit in 20th place, seven points clear of relegated Burnley.

The 31-year-old Greaves then announced his retirement, complaining, 'The game had gone a bit sick.' The Greaves era at West Ham was of limited success. The goal magician of Chelsea, Spurs and England rarely showed his old form, though 13 goals from 38 league appearances was a reasonable return in a struggling side. But he was unhappy in the East End.

He wrote in *Don't Shoot the Manager: The Revealing Story of England's Soccer Bosses*, 'I made the mistake of signing for Greenwood when he was having an uncomfortable time as manager of West Ham after a long run of comparative success. I had always promised myself that the moment I stopped enjoying my football I would quickly hang up my boots, and from the start of my only full season with West Ham in 1970/71 I was thoroughly miserable about West Ham's game and my contribution to it. There was a lack of confidence and cohesion in the side, and Greenwood was in danger of losing the rapport that a manager needs with his players. I will hold up my hands and admit that I did little for West Ham's cause in a season when the threat of relegation was hanging over the club. I needed a manager who could relight the fuse for me, but Greenwood was not that man.'

The club had decided to disband its Metropolitan League team, thus necessitating a pruning of the playing staff. Seven players were given free transfers, including Brian Dear and John Charles. Transfer-listed players included Jimmy Lindsay, Peter Eustace and Trevor Brooking. He had been dropped after the Derby disaster and had made just one further appearance as a substitute. Now

22 years old, Brooking had become frustrated with his prospects at West Ham. Years later he would admit that he 'had to think seriously about whether I should continue in football'. Fortunately, he stayed put, and was able to reclaim his midfield place when Tommy Taylor was moved back into defence at the expense of Alan Stephenson.

In September the Hammers played an exhibition match in New York against Santos of Brazil. The game ended in a 2-2 draw, with Pelé scoring both Santos goals and Clyde Best getting a brace for the English side.

It took place after a 2-0 loss at Newcastle, the Hammers' ninth consecutive game without a league victory, but it marked the only occasion Greenwood had considered resigning. He and his players were aboard a jumbo jet taking them to America when Greenwood confided his feelings of despair to Moore and Greaves over drinks at the bar on the upper flight deck and resignation was broached. On that occasion Moore talked him out of throwing in the towel while at the same time lacing Greenwood's glass of coke with Bacardi – though Ron's version of events is that he knew his drink was being doctored and was happy to go along with the prank.

According to Moore, 'He blurted it out, "I'm going to resign."' Moore sensed that he might have crushed Greenwood there and then. One savage sentence would have applied the final push. The respect of his most famous player would have been publicly torn away. Moore, instead, said, 'No, Ron. Be bigger than resigning.'

Two months later West Ham staged a testimonial for Moore, against Celtic. There were 24,448 present, and they witnessed an exciting 3-3 draw. The England captain supposedly made £15,000 from the game.

Blackpool

The Imperial Hotel looks out on to Blackpool's seafront. On the first day of 1971 the hotel was still filled mostly by those who'd taken advantage of the establishment's new year packages. It was also a temporary home to an additional party who had checked in during the late afternoon, the footballers of West Ham United, there to face Blackpool in an FA Cup third round tie the following afternoon.

Icy weather threatened a postponement, and with the game likely to be called off, Greenwood had placed no restrictions on his players' activities. There wasn't much on television to grab the attention of young, red-blooded males, the centrepiece of BBC One's programming being a gala performance of ballet and opera from the London Coliseum, while ITV was pinning its late-evening hopes on a two-decades-old movie. The one scheduled sports programme of the evening, BBC Two's highlights of the second day of the third Ashes Test in Melbourne, had been washed out.

The tie was played, though arguably the Londoners did not bother to turn up. After West Ham had been thrashed 4-0 on an icy Blackpool pitch it emerged that four players – Bobby Moore, Jimmy Greaves, Brian Dear and Clyde Best – had spent the early hours of Saturday refreshing themselves in a local nightclub.

All four, who admitted breaching club rules, were fined a week's wages, and with the exception of Best – who hadn't drunk alcohol – were excluded from a team desperate for points. It was the first time that Moore had been dropped in over a decade.

It's a matter of debate whether more damage was done to the England captain's public image, having just featured on the ITV programme *This Is Your Life*, or to his relationship with Greenwood, who described what became known as the 'Blackpool Affair' as the lowest point during his 16 years at West Ham.

Within 24 hours of the match on the Lancashire coast, word had reached Greenwood back in London that a fan had phoned the national press, claiming that he saw four players, along with physio Rob Jenkins, drinking in ex-boxer Brian London's 007 nightclub until the early hours of matchday.

They had failed to keep their late-night visit a secret and a devastated Greenwood was all for sacking the guilty parties there and then. That included Jenkins, who he 'really had a go at' and said should have known better. Moore was the captain, but the manager felt so badly let down that he was prepared to sacrifice his leader on the altar of integrity and discipline. 'There is a right time for a drink – and a wrong time. A nightclub in Blackpool a few hours before an important cup tie is the wrong time,' he said.

Greaves would describe it as 'the day Fleet Street went mad'. A *Sun* headline was 'Lights Out for Bobby Moore' and even *The Times* considered the incident worthy of its front page.

After Blackpool, the manager was in no mood to indulge his big-name players. He felt his trust had been abused beyond repair and wanted to take drastic action. But for only the second time in their 16 years working together, chairman Reg Pratt would not sanction Greenwood's call for heads to roll. The board said they would agree to sacking Dear, who had blown the second chance Greenwood had given him, but not the other four. The manager countered by saying it would be unfair to single out one person and let the others escape. He might have kept the matter in-house but the fact that the antics came to light via the press meant there was no possibility of it not becoming an embarrassment to the club.

In the end West Ham settled for fining Moore, Greaves and Dear one week's wages (about £200 in the case of Moore) and they were dropped for the next match – a 2-0 First Division defeat to Arsenal at Highbury. The club also suspended all three players for two weeks. Best, the least culpable of the four, was treated more leniently and kept his place. As Greenwood confirmed that Moore, Greaves and Dear were being dropped from the team to play at Arsenal, Matt Busby was excluding George Best from his Manchester United line-up to play at Chelsea after he had once again been absent from training – and then missed the train to London.

And with Arsenal on their way to a First Division and FA Cup double, manager Bertie Mee used the example of Greaves and his pals to remind his players of their responsibilities. 'He told us that fines would not be the Arsenal way,' said goalkeeper Bob Wilson. 'If any player was caught letting down the club in this way, I don't think he would expect to play for Arsenal again.'

Even years later, Moore still couldn't believe what all the fuss was about and was still sickened by Greenwood's handling of the affair, 'I suppose we all realised at the time that we were leaving ourselves vulnerable. But it was hardly a diabolical liberty. Whether people like it or not, whether they care to admit it, footballers are always doing what we did in Blackpool. The problem was not the drinking, it was the result.' It seems incredible that he was unable, or unwilling, to connect the two.

But his manager, facing what he called the lowest point of his career, felt that the four players, plus an important member of his staff, had 'let me down badly'.

Greenwood said, 'Moore even said he thought I'd let him down by not denying the story to the press. "It was you who went to that club before a big match. Not me. Not the fans who came banging at the front door. And you tell me I've let you down!"

'Moore and the other four let everyone down. I felt this, so did the fans, and so, in a way did the newspapers. If there was no harm in a spot of nightlife before a big match, they would not have given the story the treatment they did. But the issue went deeper than this. There was a heavy social scene available to many of the players.

'Moore's world was particularly big. I had no objection to any of the players enjoying themselves. A good social life is one of the rewards of success. But here are built-in dangers, and self-discipline is required. Collective responsibility does matter because a player never lets just himself down. He lets the whole team down. I trusted the players and they owed me that. I believed in their ability to make the right decision off the field as well as on it.'

Greaves has never forgiven Greenwood either. He claimed he had consumed about a dozen lagers in the club but wasn't drunk. Moore and Dear drank about five each.

'The story screamed from the front page of every newspaper. It was as if we had perpetrated a heinous crime. I still feel anger and resentment at the way the West Ham board, in particular Ron Greenwood, handled the situation. We were out of order, me more than anyone. Disciplinary action had to be taken but I felt the matter could have been dealt with in private,' Greaves wrote.

Greenwood even claimed that 'Greaves came in and cried his eyes out', although the striker recalled merely being angry that what he saw as a minor indiscretion was being painted as 'the crime of the century'. 'It gave me first-hand – and painful – experience of how Greenwood the manager handles (I would say mis-handled) an incident that was blown out of all proportion by the media,' he said.

'This was when Greenwood, in my opinion, showed that he was not the manager he was cracked up to be. He should have handled it as an internal matter, but I got the feeling we were being thrown to the wolves. The story was plastered all over the front pages as if we had been guilty of the crime of the century.

'I was particularly nauseated by the treatment handed out to Bobby Moore after all that he had done for the club. The only favour they did him was withholding the announcement of our suspensions until the following Thursday. Like me, Ron Greenwood was in on the secret that Bobby was to be booked by Eamonn Andrews on *This Is Your life* on the Wednesday evening.'

Though he never played for the club again, Brian Dear was actually the most contrite over the episode, 'I knew I'd let Ron down, more than myself, which over the years has hurt me quite a bit. He had nothing to do with me after that. I knew I'd never play for him again.'

Another West Ham player was said to have told the *Daily Express* that team-mates were aware of the late-night session as early as the next morning but thought nothing of it until after their heavy defeat. 'This was the most crucial match we had played at the club for years and the feeling was we had been badly let down by a group of players,' read the quote, which comes across like something Greenwood might have said. There were, however, some in the dressing room who shared that opinion. Trevor Brooking, at the time a relative newcomer to the team, would look back at the incident as 'probably the most spectacular betrayal of the boss'.

Harry Redknapp and Billy Bonds had been watching television at the hotel before going to bed, and, according to Bonds, 'We imagined everyone else was too.' They only heard what had transpired when they saw the news stories, although Bonds's observation on the game was, 'It was pretty clear from the start that one or two of us didn't fancy it.'

Bonds also remembered the players opting to keep heads down and mouths firmly shut rather than speaking to the press, but he recognised the extent of the hurt Greenwood felt, 'He trusted players to behave responsibly and was not the sort of manager to go around knocking on doors.' Bonds, a future West Ham manager himself, added, 'The whole 11 of us let down Ron and our supporters.'

Greenwood's weaknesses as a boss stemmed from his naivety about professional footballers. He expected them to be self-motivated, as passionate about the game as he was, and have pride in their profession. The Blackpool incident shattered his belief in professional footballers and wounded this deeply sensitive man.

So the final straw for this proud manager must have been the sight of 'Greenwood Out' banners on the North Bank, following Moore's suspension after Blackpool.

Blackpool was a scandal which had a certain inevitability given West Ham's relish for boozing and sinking morale at the club. The mood was low and form wretched.

However irresponsible the players had been, to sack three of them for one drinking session would have been draconian. But this was not Greenwood responding to one lapse. It was an outpouring of accumulated frustration; a belated realisation that he had been too indulgent and a sign that his relationship with Moore was broken.

'He was very close to tears when I spoke to him about it a week or so after the whole affair,' Brian James of the *Daily Mail* said. 'I think he felt terribly let down by Bobby. He thought, "I built my team around this young man and he knows I'll do anything to assist his career." But the relationship was purely professional, nothing personal, certainly by then.'

It was a dire period at Upton Park, and not just because of one late night. There was another piece by James in the *Daily Mail* on the Monday after Blackpool, which is particularly noteworthy because it was written even before the boozing scandal had erupted and was not coloured by the subsequent media storm. James highlighted the roles of Moore and Greenwood in the club's malaise, and his strident and prophetic piece provided a revealing snapshot of a dysfunctional club. He talked of Greenwood's idealism coming apart on and off the pitch, and how the trust and honour system at West Ham was crumbling. He wrote about how the manager's theory of trusting players like adults and expecting them to respond was scornfully regarded as a weakness by a significant number of players and how irresponsible behaviour had destroyed West Ham.

There were numerous reasons for West Ham's troubles, from Greenwood's failings in the transfer market to his refusal to compromise his tactical principles, and Moore could hardly be scapegoated given that he remained the outstanding world-class talent. But the captain was part of the problem. There was a slackness about West Ham which had been eroding team discipline for some time, and Greenwood had confirmed that neither he nor his skipper were addressing the issue.

When Jimmy Greaves arrived in March 1970, he found training and the general running of team affairs to be lax, at times disorganised and occasionally shambolic. At the same time, fans could read in the newspapers of the boozing at their club. Greaves told writer David Miller, 'The booze didn't develop out of the World Cup; it came more out of my move to West Ham. West Ham were a bad side when I got there. Hurst had lost a bit of his enthusiasm. There was some question of Moore going, and the atmosphere was bad. I wasn't on my way to be an alcoholic at Spurs.'

At West Ham, alcohol had become something Greaves could no longer function without. 'I don't know how come he began drinking,' said former Spurs colleague Phil Beal, 'but we know it was at West Ham he really started.'

Hammers defender John Charles said of the drinking culture that Moore and Greaves inhabited at Upton Park, 'We'd go to and from away matches to places like Newcastle by first-class train. By the end of the journey home the bottles of miniatures were piled up in a big heap and we'd thrown half out of the window. We were always on the piss. We went from club to pub. Mooro was as good as gold on the field and off the field, but he was a pisshead. God could he drink.'

In Greaves's sole season with the club, he and Moore were the leaders of the drinking gang. Greenwood gave them several lectures but they just dismissed him as an old killjoy.

In his 2013 book *Harry: My Autobiography*, Harry Redknapp wrote, 'I don't think Ron approved of Bobby's lifestyle really, the drinking culture that existed in football in those days … I imagine it drove him mad to see the boys get well beat somewhere like Newcastle and then pile on the train and drink all the way home.'

Redknapp also recalled being so angry at being substituted in the Newcastle game that he finished a post-match row with Greenwood by throwing a bottle at the dressing room door as the manager departed.

'You're a nice one Harry,' said Greaves, who had been watching the conflict with a beer in his hand. 'Oh, don't you start,' Redknapp snapped back. 'You could have picked an empty one,' Greaves elaborated. 'That was our last lager, wasn't it Mooro?'

Alf Ramsey had never experienced any trouble with discipline when he was manager at Ipswich. But with England it was very different, because in the side in the mid-1960s were three of the heaviest drinkers ever to wear the white shirt – Jimmy Greaves, Bobby Moore and Johnny Byrne. It was no coincidence two of them played for West Ham and the other one would.

1971-72

When the Hammers kicked off the 1971/72 season with no sign of a goal or point after three games, another nine months of struggle looked to be in the offing.

In match five Clyde Best scored a goal, and the team secured a 1-0 victory over Everton – five days after the first point had been secured with a 0-0 draw at home to Ipswich. This first win of the season prompted a recovery, as during September Best scored two against Coventry in a 4-0 win, followed by another brace in the 2-1 defeat of Chelsea. There were 53,334 inside Old Trafford to see Brooking and Best score for West Ham but it was United's other, more famous Best who scored a hat-trick to secure a 4-2 win.

However, between August and October, over 12 league and cup outings, this was the only defeat, which hoisted the team up to ninth place. Then as surely as a West Ham night would follow a West Ham day, so four successive league defeats came in November.

In January, Everton chairman George Watt described West Ham as 'the best side I have seen in years' despite watching his own side beat them 2-1 at Goodison Park. At least it was better than Jack Charlton's description of the Irons the previous season as 'the worst West Ham team I've ever seen'.

In December a three-goal lead had been surrendered in a 3-3 draw at Southampton. But Manchester United were well beaten 3-0 on New Year's Day and a Brooking goal in the 2-0 home win over Tottenham in April helped the team to a league double over their London rivals on their way to a final position of 14th. An improvement over the previous season, but only by two points.

In the League Cup, the Hammers made hard work of getting past Second Division strugglers Cardiff City in round two, winning 2-1 in the replay after a 1-1 draw at Upton Park. They then had to face title-chasing Leeds United at Upton Park. After a 0-0 draw, when the home side had two seemingly good goals ruled out, a Best header in extra time decided the replay at Elland Road and earned a first victory of any sort over Leeds since the 7-0 demolition in 1966. This set up another home clash, with Liverpool, who were also chasing the First Division crown, and a goal from 'Pop' Robson sealed a 2-1 victory. This brought Sheffield United to east London in round five, where a Robson hat-trick propelled the Hammers to a 5-0 win, and a semi-final with Stoke City.

When Hurst and Best struck to claim a 2-1 win in the first leg at the Victoria Ground on 8 December, Wembley was in the

Hammers' sights. But a solitary goal by Paul Ritchie for Stoke in the second leg at Upton Park, where the home side played abysmally, took the tie into extra time. With just three minutes remaining Harry Redknapp was hauled down by keeper Banks, and Hurst's penalty was strong and accurate but somehow the England keeper saved it.

A third match at Hillsborough was goalless after two hours. In the second replay, at Old Trafford on 26 January, Moore replaced Bobby Ferguson in goal for 20 minutes after the latter had been concussed in a collision. The captain even managed to block Mike Bernard's 33rd-minute spot-kick, but the Stoke man scored from the rebound. Despite temporarily playing with ten men the Hammers scored twice through Bonds and Brooking, but with a dazed Ferguson back in goal the men from the Potteries scored twice to take them to a Wembley victory over Chelsea, while Hammers fans were left to rue what might have been.

The FA Cup third round saw Luton Town beaten 2-1, with Hurst missing another penalty and Moore being stretchered off after eight minutes. The next round saw a trip to non-league Hereford United following their famous victory over Newcastle United in the third round. A crowd of 15,000 crammed into Edgar Street, including your author, watching his hometown club, to see a tense 0-0 draw. Hurst scored a hat-trick in a 3-1 win in the replay, which was also notable for being played on a Monday afternoon due to power shortages during the miners' strike. The crowd of 42,271 was a post-war record in the FA Cup. However, hopes of success were to be dashed in round five at Huddersfield Town as the Yorkshire side triumphed 4-2, although a week later the Hammers gained a modicum of revenge with a 3-0 league victory. For the second season running West Ham had exited the competition away to a side destined to be relegated. At least this time, there weren't the same repercussions.

Hurst scored his final goal for the Hammers at Manchester City on 8 April 1972 in a 3-1 defeat. His final appearance came a week later in a 2-0 home loss to Liverpool. Over 499 appearances he had amassed an impressive 248 goals – one every other game. Not a bad record for someone who had started their career as 'a bit of a cart-horse at wing-half'.

Hurst joined Stoke and would still score 30 goals for the Potters over 100 appearances in three years. Greenwood's problem now was how to replace such striking power.

Football and Racism

Racism was rife among football crowds in the 60s and 70s, but Greenwood was always his own man when it came to picking his team. He had given John Charles, West Ham's first black player, his senior debut at left-back in 1963, just after he had captained the youth side to the FA Youth Cup Final win over Liverpool.

And Charles has another claim to footballing fame – as the first black footballer to play and score for an England representative team. Charles made footballing history when he started for England under-18s in a 3-1 defeat of Israel in 1962, scoring on his international debut, and he also helped England to win the UEFA Under-18 Championship.

Greenwood made history again nine years later when, on 1 April 1972, he selected three black players for the first time in an English top-flight team. Nigerian Ade Coker, who scored,

Bermudan Clyde Best and Clive Charles – John's younger brother – all played their part in a 2-0 win over Tottenham.

Forward Best entitled his autobiography *The Acid Test*, for in 1970 he had received a threatening note: 'The letter stated that, as I ran through the tunnel, they were going to throw acid in my face. I was petrified and I probably never moved so much and so fast on a soccer field in my life.

'The only person who knew was Ron Greenwood, my manager. Ron had become a father figure to me at West Ham. He had always tried to keep the press away from me to stop me getting exposed at too young an age. When I handed the acid letter to him, he remained utterly calm, hiding it away in a drawer and telling me not to worry. I don't know to this day what happened to it.

'I was, and remain, so grateful to Ron Greenwood for having faith in me. Ron was simply one fantastic human being. He understood the mentality of his players and instilled in us the way he wanted to play. We always remembered what he drilled into us: that when we went on the football field, we had to entertain the crowd. I knew I wanted to play for him from the day I signed for the club.

'Ron was ahead of his time in my opinion, just like Martin Peters. I think he'd have done brilliantly if he'd managed on the continent because he wanted his teams to play with control and technique. He always said, "Think of the fans, they're the ones who pay your wages."

'All I can say from my time at West Ham is that Ron Greenwood didn't treat me any differently. In fact, he was the first coach to give us black players an opportunity to showcase our talent. Under Ron Greenwood's leadership skin colour had no relationship to skill or ability. Ron used to say, "When you hear all those remarks, first of all ignore them. Second, stick the ball in the net. That will shut them up!"

'For all the recognition of Greenwood as a great coach and motivator, he struck an equally telling blow to those who thought the colour of a man's skin was an impediment to his ability to play.'

No acid was thrown at Best that day, but he would play for six years under a hail of abuse, yet still he went on to demonstrate that the stereotypes of black players – foreigners who were unable to cope with the weather, the banter or the physicality of the English game, gifted athletes but ill-disciplined, hopeless thinkers – were all wrong.

Best was eventually idolised at Upton Park, and in the early 1970s Greenwood's West Ham side became the most diverse in the land.

In his 2006 book *The Black Hammers,* Brian Belton interviewed most of the black players who turned out for West Ham. Best, Coker and the two Charles brothers embraced the Greenwood era.

The late 1960s and 1970s were periods of pronounced hostility to black players, with West Ham considered to have some of the most racist fans. In their autobiographies, Les Ferdinand – eventually to become a Hammer after a successful career primarily with Queens Park Rangers and Newcastle United in the 1990s – and John Barnes singled out Irons supporters as among the most racist in the country. According to Barnes, who lined up against West Ham for Watford, Liverpool, Newcastle and Charlton Athletic in the 1980s and '90s, 'Of the away grounds Upton Park was the worst. If I tried to make a joke about the bananas, the West Ham fans intensified their abuse.'

Brendon Batson spent his career with Cambridge United and then West Bromwich Albion in the 1970s and early '80s, before becoming deputy chief executive of the Professional Footballers' Association. He said, 'The noise and volume of abuse at some grounds was deafening – Upton Park was among the most hostile and vicious places to be a black footballer.'

The much-travelled former England international Carlton Palmer claimed that while warming up as a substitute at Upton Park, 'The crowd, relishing their role as tormentors in chief, rained down their racist abuse at me.'

Yet John Charles would claim he could 'never remember any real racism, certainly not from other players at West Ham, or our crowd'.

Barnes found upon visiting Upton Park with Watford, 'West Ham fans cheered their black player, Bobby Barnes, while tossing bananas at me.'

When Bobby was an apprentice at West Ham, he received free tickets for home games, yet he was so concerned about the possibility of being racially attacked as he left the ground, he used to leave early and sprint all the way along Green Street, not stopping until he got a mile away.

Barnes was even nicknamed 'Superwog' by the West Ham fans, a strange term of acceptance by a group of fans well known for their racist following. Black players who played for opposition fans were mere 'wogs', Bobby was the claret and blue version.

At the time of the 1972 appearance of Coker, Best and Clive Charles, there were probably fewer than ten black footballers playing professional football in England or Scotland at that time, so for these three to be included on one side was quite a milestone.

Two years earlier, on 2 April 1970, the Irons hosted a First Division game against Leeds United. That day, forward Best took the field with his great friend, the defender John Charles. It was the full-back's final game for the club and the first time that the Hammers had included two black players in their line-up.

Years later, Coker recalled that he had only subsequently understood the importance of that spring day in 1972 and how it would have impacted on young black players in Britain. He believed it motivated a feeling that there might be opportunities for young men of colour to break into major football. However, it is also telling that he saw West Ham as the one club where an occasion of such consequence could have taken place at that time. For Coker, Upton Park, under the sway of Greenwood, was a place that looked to and shaped the future, seeing skin pigmentation as having no bearing on the endeavour to unearth skill and promise.

There had been a black presence in English professional football since its inception. West African Arthur Wharton played in goal for Preston North End in 1887 and later pioneers included Walter Tull at Tottenham on the 1920s and Jack Leslie at Plymouth Argyle in the 1930s. After the war came Roy Brown, Charlie Williams and Lindy Delapenha.

Perceiving them as a form of imperial exotica, the press rendered these players in the bright tones of an unreflective stereotypical racism. Delapenha was described in the papers as 'lithe as a snake ... the coffee-coloured king of the wing', who played with 'the spirit of calypso'.

Leslie was good enough to be picked for England, but his invitation to play for the national team was mysteriously withdrawn in 1925. He retired from professional football in 1935. Many years later, he would join the backroom staff at his local club – West Ham – at the behest of Greenwood, who recognised his stature in English football. During his time in the boot room at Upton Park he cleaned the footwear of the World Cup trio and Harry Redknapp.

Interviewed on the podcast *Coming in from the Cold*, Redknapp and Best admitted that they were unaware of Leslie's playing career as he never talked about it. 'Maybe we should have been doing his boots,' Redknapp said.

In a 2020 interview, Best said, '[I] remember playing at Goodison and the Everton crowd were on me, and I thought, "I've had enough of this." I picked up the ball from the halfway line and as the goalkeeper approached, I sold him a dummy and he sat down on his backside and I dinked the ball over the top of his head and the crowd were mesmerised. Joe Royle and Howard Kendall came up to me after the game and said, "Clyde, that is the best game we have ever seen." That was a way to silence them. People of colour play football too.'

Arguably, the tipping point for black players came in the mid-1970s when Ron Atkinson's West Bromwich Albion fielded three, six years after the Hammers trio had faced Tottenham. There was a blaze of publicity with Atkinson labelling his trio of Cyrille Regis, Brendon Batson and Laurie Cunningham the 'Three Degrees' after the female singing trio popular at the time.

In April 1978, Viv Anderson became the first black player to be picked for England when he appeared against Czechoslovakia. National team manager Greenwood told the press that Anderson, and the West Brom trio, were as English as any of their team-mates.

On *Coming in from the Cold*, the next generation of black players such as Anderson and Chris Hughton acknowledged that Best and the Charles brothers had been trailblazers for them.

Best not only won hearts and minds in a stronghold of Powellism, but he also inspired the generation of Afro-Caribbean players who were about to break through. 'It was important for me to see Clyde Best, a black man,' said one interviewee in an oral history project. 'I was proud to be black. I couldn't wait for Clyde Best to come down here to see this big, black man, as a centre-forward, playing. The guy was a legend, a hero. Seeing a black man out there was tremendous. It was a good feeling to see one of you and be able to say "if he can do it, I can do it".' And from the early 1970s that is precisely what the new generation of black British players did.

Negative attitudes towards black players were not restricted to club boardrooms or the terraces. In his 2015 book, *Pitch Black*, author Emy Onuora, cites an interesting reflection on racist attitudes at the FA.

During the 1999/2000 season Richie Moran was invited to be a guest speaker at an event at Watford. It was also attended by the former England manager Graham Taylor, who provided Moran with an insight into the attitudes of senior FA officials towards black players.

The book quoted Moran as saying, 'Graham Taylor come up to me and said, "Look, I'm going to tell you something … I'm never going to admit it, I will be sued for libel. When I was manager of England, I was called in by two members of the FA, who I won't name … I was told in no uncertain terms not to pick too many black players for the national side."'

Taylor was England manager a decade after Greenwood, and it begs the question if similar pressure was put on him. But, if true, it puts Greenwood's insistence on playing black players, at West Ham and for England, in an even more positive light.

1972-73

Ron Greenwood may have bemoaned the lack of goals in 1972/73 – the 47 scored was the second lowest in the club's top-flight history – but Geoff Hurst, having requested a transfer, was allowed to join Stoke City. Other departures included Harry Redknapp who moved to Bournemouth for £31,000, while Alan Stephenson switched to Portsmouth for a similar fee. Redknapp's replacement was Dudley Tyler, who had impressed for Hereford United in the two cup games.

A 5-2 home win against Leicester City gave Tyler his first – and only – goal for the club, and Robson was also off the mark with a brace. He scored two more in a 3-2 defeat at Anfield, and a further two in the 2-2 draw with Manchester United. In September there was a good 3-1 win at Stamford Bridge, with First Division newcomers Norwich City being dispatched 4-0. 'Pop' Robson continued his good season with two more goals in a 3-2 win over Stoke, and another brace in a 2-2 draw with Spurs. Old boys Hurst and Peters both scored against the Hammers.

It was a pleasant surprise that West Ham should enjoy a relatively successful season given the lack of replacements up front. So credit should really go to Hammer of the Year Robson, whose tally of 28 league goals was only one short of Hurst's post-war record. Robson scored two goals in a game eight times and finally got a hat-trick against Southampton on Good Friday. Only one defeat in the last ten matches pushed West Ham into sixth place.

Nevertheless, the search for a partner for Robson had continued until Ted MacDougall joined in February 1973 after an unhappy five months at Manchester United. His first goal was in a 2-1 win over Manchester City. The fee was a club record £170,000, and he contributed four goals in ten games that season.

There was a corresponding improvement at the other end of the pitch, with full-back Frank Lampard winning his first England cap against Yugoslavia.

The Hammers missed out on UEFA Cup qualification by one point to fifth-placed Wolves, and the domestic cups were an all too familiar story. The League Cup saw the Hammers fall 2-1 at Stockport County – the club's first defeat to a Fourth Division side. The FA Cup exit came at Second Division Hull City in the fourth round, 1-0.

1973-74

The new season was a return to 'normal', with one win in 20 games. An awful start did not witness a victory until the 12th attempt, 1-0 at Coventry City. Goalkeeper Bobby Ferguson was dropped after remarking, 'There are too many gutless, spineless men in the team.' That was surely hardly a controversial comment given the results. Teenager Mervyn Day came into the side and, despite the poor results, played well and kept his place for the remainder of the season.

Bobby Moore was omitted from the team at Manchester United in September because of, according to Greenwood, 'unexpected adverse publicity that was bad for morale'.

Three weeks later the Hammers lost 1-0 at home to Burnley, with MacDougall being sent off. The knives were really out for the manager – even on *Match of the Day* – but Greenwood still claimed, 'I'm certainly not quitting, and I have no intentions of resigning.'

He still had his chairman's public backing, but the press gossip was that he would be moved to the role of general manager.

Scoring goals was now a problem. McDougall netted only twice in 15 appearances and was allowed to move to Norwich City in part-exchange for midfielder Graham Paddon. Bobby Gould was recruited from Bristol City in November, but Robson was lost for four months due to injury. West Ham reached Christmas bottom of the First Division.

Yet on Boxing Day the team won 4-2 at Chelsea after being 2-0 down, and on New Year's Day Norwich were beaten 4-2. A ten-match unbeaten run between January and March saw the Hammers manage to claw their way out of the relegation zone, which had just been expanded to three teams.

But this form wasn't carried over to the FA Cup. Hereford United were now in the Third Division and held West Ham to a 1-1 draw in the third-round tie at Upton Park. The home side had only been spared greater embarrassment by an 88th-minute equaliser from Pat Holland. But in the replay, Hereford – now with Dudley Tyler back in their team – dispatched the First Division outfit 2-1.

There was worse news. In the first tie Bobby Moore had sustained twisted knee ligaments, and it would prove to be the great man's 642nd and last appearance in a West Ham shirt.

The captaincy passed to Billy Bonds, now operating permanently in midfield. His 13 goals, including a hat-trick against Chelsea, earned a well-deserved Hammer of the Year award and helped drag the team to safety. A final-day 2-2 draw with Liverpool saw the team finish 18th, just one point above the relegation zone.

One shaft of light in a dismal season came in April when Trevor Brooking won his first England cap, in a 0-0 draw away to Portugal, Alf Ramsey's last game in charge.

Despite his injury, Moore was in another of his restless moods. But Greenwood could be stubborn too, especially when rival managers tried to lure away his best players. He gave Brian Clough the cold shoulder when the outspoken Derby County boss sauntered into his office one day at the start of the 1973/74 season and arrogantly told him he wanted to sign both Moore and Brooking for a combined fee of around £400,000. Greenwood simply recommended to his board that they reject this audacious offer, which they did.

Clearly frustrated at not being allowed to join Derby, Moore said he wanted to move on, and Greenwood promised him a free transfer at the end of the season.

On transfer deadline day, 14 March, Moore signed for Second Division Fulham for £25,000. Even that left a bad taste and Moore was dismayed to find a fee had been demanded. 'West Ham had years of service from me and now they were using me to balance the books,' he said, feeling that Greenwood's earlier pledge had been broken.

But Moore had left on Greenwood's terms – the manager revealed he had previously endured threatening phone calls and letters, even threats to bomb his home, from irate fans insistent that their blue-eyed boy should never be sacked or sold.

One of Greenwood's reasons for becoming disillusioned with football in the mid-70s was his family becoming the subject of abuse – for a decent and proud man this was the final straw. Greenwood had not forgotten being booed and vilified by the fickle

North Bank crowd following the Blackpool incident in 1971. But he could take that in the knowledge he had done the right thing by his terms. What he could not take was the abuse his children received at school.

And by 1974 he was losing enthusiasm with the game itself. He was sickened by the 'professionalism' of people like Don Revie and their cohorts, calling them 'cheats'. His old mentor Walter Winterbottom said, 'Ron was always angry when he saw ruthless and brutal aggression getting the better of skill. He deplored the spread of negative football and was disenchanted by the modern obsession with money.'

In his own autobiography, Greenwood's long-term friend Bill Nicholson recalled, 'It was around this time that football plummeted to a level never before experienced in this country. There was a meanness about the way the game was played. I had to admit I didn't enjoy watching it. There were fewer goals and more arguments, more dissension, more professional fouls.'

These words could easily have been written by Greenwood himself.

11

1974–1977: Football and Society Changing

Greenwood moves Upstairs

By the mid-1970s, the old post-war consensus was breaking down, with the trade unions asserting their own power in an unprecedented, often bullying manner. Politicians of all parties seemed impotent and bewildered. The country was in a state of near permanent crisis, reaching the nadir under Edward Heath of the three-day week in 1973, designed to cope with the shortage of power supplies.

Things were little better on the football field. The glory of 1966 was quickly forgotten as manager Alf Ramsey came in for a barrage of criticism over his approach. He was seen as too defensive, too unimaginative and too dour, encouraging brutality rather than flair. Far from being a moment that invigorated English football, the World Cup win was followed by a prolonged spell of introspection in which Alf was blamed for undermining the sport as a spectacle.

Goals were drying up – thanks to Alf, it was said – while defences and midfields were packed. In 1961, when Spurs won the title, they scored 115 goals. In 1969, Leeds won the championship after scoring 62 goals.

Denis Law, however, claimed, 'You can't blame Alf for the decline of English football, you must blame the people who followed his example.'

Perhaps more than any other sporting moment of the decade, it was the swaggering German 3-1 victory on the sacred Wembley turf in April 1972 in a European Championship quarter-final that heralded another Hungary-style moment of introspection. The English players had been outclassed, said *The Observer,* with their 'cautious, joyless football' years behind the times.

In the 1948/49 season the league clubs had sold more than 41 million tickets, but by 1975 numbers had fallen to just 25 million.

This was part of the general decline of collective entertainment, comparable to the decline of the holiday camp and even the pub. With money in their pockets, working-class men and women preferred to devote their time to their families and their homes; there were simply more kinds of leisure and entertainment to choose from.

Between 1964 and 1974, as managers adopted increasingly defensive tactics, the average number of goals scored in the First Division fell by 30 per cent. 'In England,' the former Manchester City striker Rodney Marsh told an American audience in 1979, 'soccer is a grey game played by grey people on grey days.'

Marsh and George Best were typical examples of a new breed of football stars in the early 1970s; self-styled entertainers who seemed more interested in making money and modelling clothes than in knuckling down, playing for their country and winning trophies. To young men brought up in a world of increasing affluence, irreverence and individualism, the cautious deferential values of Ramsey and Ron Greenwood seemed laughably old-fashioned.

'Has football a future?' Brian Glanville asked in the *1974 Charles Buchan's Soccer Gift Book*. 'The public have been voting with their feet. Attendances in Britain have dropped alarmingly … Great changes of some sorts are coming, but no-one knows quite what they will be.'

Hooliganism

The sporadic outbreaks of football-related violence that had been peppering the newspapers in the early 1960s had, by the mid-70s, turned into the defining feature of British football culture.

The train-wrecking exploits of Liverpool and Everton fans in the early 1960s earned them the title 'Merseyside Maniacs' in the popular press at the time. Their antics probably constitute the first emergence of hooliganism as a regular phenomenon in one of its recognisably modern forms.

However, hooliganism was not restricted to supporters from Merseyside. As early as 10 November 1963, the *Sunday Times* was able to comment on an 'undeniable increase in irresponsible crowd behaviour' and to describe a situation in which 'scarcely a week goes by without a report of incidents'.

That same month, Everton became the first English club to erect fences to segregate fans. They were not responding to an invented phenomenon, although the press reacted with a measure of surprise and shock.

Eric Dunning, Patrick Murphy and John Williams, in their *The Roots of Football Hooliganism: An Historical and Sociological Study*, point to the start of the 1966/67 season as witnessing the first references in the national press to the activities of hooligan gangs inside and outside stadia.

There were stories describing Saturday afternoons 'somewhere between the storming of the Bastille and a civil rights march in Alabama', and accounts of court cases in which skinny youths from Liverpool or Manchester pleaded guilty to possession of flick knives or kicking policemen. Violence was particularly common at games in London, partly because the capital had 11 league clubs but also because its transport links made it easy for visiting fans to attend games – and hard for the authorities to police them. By the end of the 1960s many of the familiar ingredients of football hooliganism were already present.

By 1974, when two general elections were required to produce a knife-edge Labour majority, both British polity and British football stadia were beginning to look ungovernable.

The headlines belonged to the football hooligans, who had marked the 1975/76 campaign with an orgy of violence surpassing anything that had gone before. On its very first day, hundreds of Manchester United fans ran amok in Wolverhampton, stabbing 14 people and causing damage worth thousands of pounds. But worse was to follow. When Chelsea visited Luton on the last Saturday in August, enraged away fans invaded the pitch, attacking players and officials, punching the Luton goalkeeper to the ground, and leaving one steward nursing a broken nose and another with stab wounds.

On the same day, 50 Manchester United supporters were arrested after fighting broke out at Stoke, 60 Rangers fans were arrested outside Ibrox, and dozens of Liverpool followers set fire to the train carrying them home from Leicester.

The return leg of the final of the UEFA Cup in Feyenoord in May 1974 had incited some of the worst hooliganism for years. The shock of seeing his own supporters create havoc had such a profound effect on Spurs manager Bill Nicholson that it contributed to his resignation months later.

Author Duncan Hamilton described football at this time 'as faintly repellent, like a sour smell, a crude primitive pastime played by long-haired yobs and watched by the dregs of society, a game whose supporters were more likely to end up with a knife between the ribs than to see a genuinely exciting sporting occasion'.

West Ham supporters would not be excluded from the disease of hooliganism. It has already been noted how Greenwood had hardly settled into his new job when he witnessed a near riot when Chelsea visited Upton Park in September 1961. The origins of West Ham's links with organised football-related violence started in the 1960s with the establishment of the 'Mile End Mob'. West Ham fans would go on to achieve further notoriety for the levels of hooliganism and antagonistic behaviour towards both their own and opposition supporters. The 'Inter-City Firm' was another infamous Irons-aligned gang, content to cause trouble at any game, home or away.

Increased media coverage of hooliganism could have contributed directly to its escalation. Trouble in and around London grounds, for example, gathered momentum towards the end of 1967 and, as this happened, so the role of the press in helping to trigger incidents became more pronounced. *The Times* reported in October 1967 how a Chelsea fan convicted of carrying a razor said in court in his defence that he had 'read in a newspaper that the West Ham lot were going to cause trouble'.

It was also in the 1966/67 season that northern fans 'arrived' in London, an event which played a part in stirring the embryonic capital ends into developing greater levels of cohesion. In May 1967 Manchester United went to Upton Park, taking with them a large travelling contingent. Young United supporters, fast gaining notoriety at the expense of their Merseyside neighbours, arrived in London seemingly intent on claiming the north's first terrace success in the capital. At the match damage was widespread as fighting spread inside and outside the ground, and 20 people were hospitalised.

It was the day, according to the press, when British fans finally succeeded in outstripping their continental and Latin American rivals. Under the headline 'Soccer's Day of Shame', the *News of the World* edition of Sunday, 7 May proclaimed, 'For years we have despised the Latins for their hysterical and violent behaviour. In 1967, British fans are themselves held in disgrace by the rest of the world.'

By the mid-1970s, popular newspapers had even begun to publish league tables of fan violence. Manchester United's Stretford End, for example, was placed at the top of the 'League of Violence' published in the *Daily Mirror* in May 1974.

On 12 September the same year the *Daily Mail* joined the bandwagon by publishing a 'Thugs League' of clubs in the London area, writing, 'Chelsea, London's soccer violence champions for two years running, are in line to land a hat-trick. They share the lead with West Ham in Scotland Yard's league of violence – 97 fans having been thrown out of each ground up to August 24.'

At Manchester United's match at Upton Park in October 1975 they found the East End in a state of readiness for a siege. Staff on the underground had decided to strike rather than ferry United supporters to the ground. Hundreds of police and stewards were employed in what was described as a massive security operation. Despite these precautions, serious disturbances occurred in and around the ground, 100 fans were reported to have been injured, and the match was halted for several minutes as fighting fans and those seeking to protect themselves poured on to the field of play. Nevertheless, newspaper reports carried little hint of condemnation. Instead, the West Ham fighting crews were cast, alongside the police, in the role of 'avenging angels'. *The Sun*'s report of 27 October was jubilant and headlined 'The Day the Terrace Terrors were Hunted like Animals and Hammered'.

General Manager

The Tottenham v West Ham fixture is among the highlights of the season but at White Hart Lane in September 1974 it was unusual. For years, the two managers in the opposing dugouts had been Bill Nicholson and Ron Greenwood. Now, though, times were changing.

A few weeks earlier, Greenwood had stood down as manager of West Ham after 13 years. Nicholson had also decided to resign after a poor start to the 1974/75 season which included losing 4-0 to Middlesbrough in the League Cup. Nicholson later said of his departure, 'The simple truth was that I was burned out, I had no more to offer.' He added, 'Players have become impossible. They talk all the time about security but are not prepared to work for it.'

Nicholson wrote a revealing passage in his autobiography, *Glory Glory*, about the player Alfie Conn. Only towards the end did he really cut to the chase, 'There was another reason I was unhappy with Alfie Conn. He wore his hair extremely long in an unbecoming manner for a professional footballer. Around that period a lot of players wore their hair long and it sickened me.'

Oddly, Nicholson was also convinced of the essential decadence of 'abroad'. In his autobiography he warned sternly against English teams 'making the mistake of adapting to the continental way'. Nevertheless, Nicholson did pretty well out of abroad, where, in fact, he was one of the progressives. His Spurs team won the Cup Winners' Cup in 1963 and performed in Europe with some distinction.

Trevor Brooking, in *My Life in Football*, wrote, 'This upheaval [in 1974] involving some of the nation's most distinguished coaches, suddenly threw the spotlight on to the mounting pressures that managers faced as they sought to satisfy the increasing demands of players and fans.'

When Nicholson left Tottenham after 33 years on the payroll he even had to go on the dole for a while. He still had the urge to get back into the game and started visiting the training grounds of the other London clubs. One day he was at West Ham's Chadwell Heath when Greenwood asked him what he was doing. 'Not a lot,' Nicholson admitted. Greenwood offered him a job as a consultant and Nicholson was delighted to accept. He spent a happy year at West Ham until the call came from Keith Burkinshaw to take up a similar consultancy at his old stomping ground, White Hart Lane.

While Greenwood had coached Oxford University at the outset of his coaching career, Nicholson had coached Cambridge University to gain experience and earn some extra money.

Something else the two men had in common was the coaching inspiration of Walter Winterbottom. According to Nicholson,

'Walter was an exceptional man. He had more influence over the game in England than anyone and he worked prodigiously hard. He travelled the country on his own, lecturing non-stop. He persuaded dozens and dozens of players to take up coaching and he was like a Messiah, spreading the word.'

Winterbottom, Greenwood and Nicholson loved football with a passion and wanted to improve it, to make it more entertaining. These coaches weren't in it for the money or material goods; they never besmirched the game, and they upheld the old, Corinthian creed of fair play.

With fans having called for Greenwood's head at various times over the past decade there would presumably have been mixed feelings when it was announced that John Lyall would assume responsibility for first-team affairs, including training and selecting the team. Greenwood, now aged 52, would become general manager and oversee scouting and financial matters.

Chairman Reg Pratt insisted that there was no question of Greenwood being demoted, 'He is still my manager.' But Lyall took a different slant, 'It is now my team and I'm going to stamp my personality on the side. Ron and I have disagreed on a couple of matters, but now the team will reflect my ideas.' It was not long before Lyall was officially confirmed as 'team manager'.

West Ham would win the FA Cup in Lyall's first season, but Greenwood would say, 'By the time we won the FA Cup in 1975 … there was a different team – and it was John Lyall's team.'

Greenwood and Lyall each gave credit for the FA Cup triumph to the other. They, it appeared, were as much a team themselves, in the continental tradition of general overlord (Greenwood) and tracksuited manager (Lyall).

Brentford team group 1952/53. Ron Greenwood is back row, third left

Ron Greenwood playing for Chelsea against Manchester City: 16 April 1954

Greenwood taking Arsenal training — note use of technology!

The new man at Upton Park: April 1961

Probably Greenwood's best signing: Budgie Byrne moves to Upton Park in 1962

The manager with his 1964 FA Cup winning side

Another season, another cup: The 1965 European Cup-Winners' Cup side

Greenwood's contribution to English football: West Ham's 1966 World Cup winning trio

Greenwood presents Clyde Best with the Footballer of the Month award, September 1971

Greenwood leads out his England side for the first time, against Switzerland at Wembley in September 1977

Ron Greenwood is back in a tracksuit, taking England training in September 1977

A proud manager with his 1982 World Cup squad

Ron Greenwood shows off his OBE after his investiture at Buckingham Palace

A minute's silence is held for Ron Greenwood (and Peter Osgood): England v Uruguay, 1 March 2006

Greenwood had overseen five games in the new season. Only one was a victory, with three defeats.

Typically, the decision to replace Greenwood with Lyall was glossed over by the club, with a statement reading, 'Ron Greenwood has not been demoted. John Lyall will be in charge of the first team but Greenwood, as club manager, will search for new players.'

There were early results from Greenwood's new position. Two new strikers arrived in September 1974: Billy Jennings from Watford for £110,000 and Keith Robson from Newcastle for £45,000. Alan Taylor joined in November from Fourth Division Rochdale for £40,000 – on condition the player would not be cup-tied. An important proviso, given his impact on the 1974/75 FA Cup run.

Greenwood secured first option on the signing of Plymouth Argyle's prolific striker Paul Mariner in 1976. A fee of £200,000 was agreed, only for the Second Division club to enter into discussions with Ipswich Town. 'It's not possible to do business with people like that,' stormed Greenwood.

When West Ham were relegated in 1978, Lyall had been manager for four years. Yet local reporter Trevor Smith still blamed Lyall's predecessor for their demotion: 'I accuse Ron Greenwood. The downward spiral path began the day the team won the 1975 cup final. His failure since 1975 to sign the right players at the right time must surely be regarded as the single biggest factor in the circumstances which combined to result in relegation.'

Nevertheless, Greenwood was reported to have turned down the chance of a new career in the North American Soccer League. The offer, which he described as 'the best I've ever had', was reportedly worth £35,000, but Greenwood added, 'There are some things more important than money.'

In early November 1976, on the eve of a game against Spurs, chairman Reg Pratt had made a surprise statement, denying press gossip of a rift between Lyall and Greenwood. Shortly afterwards, Pratt had to quash rumours that Bobby Moore was being offered the managership. The situation was exacerbated by comments Moore had made about his former manager in his recently published biography.

A few days before the 1977/78 season kicked off, it was announced that Greenwood had been released to become acting England team manager for the next three internationals, and thereby end a 16-year association with the club.

John Lyall

Recalling his decision to promote John Lyall from assistant manager to first team manager soon after the start of the 1974/75 season – it was officially announced in the programme for the home game against Sheffield United on 17 September 1974 – Greenwood wrote, 'We sent him on courses and as a man with the right qualifications and attitude, he began to grow with the job. By 1971, his youngsters were coming through into the first team and to provide continuity I decided to make him my assistant manager. Ernie Gregory was a bit disappointed, and I could understand why, but I felt we needed a younger man.'

Over time the senior players would recognise the difference in approaches between the two men. For Billy Bonds, 'Ron was more, "This is how we are going to win today," while John tended to take a more balanced overview of situations – maybe pointing out that we were losing too many goals at set pieces and putting that right before exploring our own attacking options.'

By 1974, Bonds and Trevor Brooking were the established central midfield partnership, a perfect blend of craft and graft. They were probably Greenwood's greatest legacy on the playing side when he decided he wanted to take more of a back seat that year. But surely his greatest gift to the club was the man he had groomed to succeed him.

Greenwood had said, 'Nothing lasts forever in football. A manager can stay in a job too long. He can begin to take things for granted. He can stop being hungry and start being cosy. Things had not reached that point when I decided John Lyall should take over in 1974. I simply felt it was better early than late, and the decision was made easier by the fact that in John the club had the perfect man to take over from me.'

Greenwood admitted he was becoming 'increasingly angry at the way the game was developing'. More and more teams set out simply to stop their opponents from playing, rather than to attack themselves. Defences were beginning to dominate and there was a growing cynicism within the game. 'I wince when I watch some games,' Greenwood said. 'Control and touch are often poor, passes are stabs in the dark, movement off the ball is statuesque and sometimes the only rhythm is provided by the music at half-time. Yet the whole is wrapped up with so much pace and soaked with so much sweat that there is general approval.'

Greenwood had no fears that the standards he had set at Upton Park would be in any way compromised by his successor, 'Our relationship was a very good one. John is a strong character with a Scottish background, stable, straight and single-minded. He has a nice, easy manner and I discovered very quickly that he was a person after my own heart. He wanted to know everything about the job but, more than that, he cared passionately about the club and the game. He was also a family man and he cared about people for their own sake.

'The time came when I knew he was ready to take over. "You be team manager and concentrate on that," I told him, "and I'll become general manager and deal with financial matters, look at opponents, size up players we might want to buy and handle everything else." I told John tactics and selection were now his job and I wouldn't even go near the training ground. We'll have two voices hammering away and two opinions. I remember what happened to me at Arsenal and I don't want it to happen here.

'Inside it hurt me. I hated the idea of divorcing myself from the players, but I felt I had to be absolutely fair to John.'

It said a lot about the autonomy with which Greenwood ran West Ham that he suggested the change to Lyall without first going through the formality of getting approval from the board. Before he had a chance to inform them, the news was revealed in the *London Evening Standard* and it was a somewhat embarrassed Greenwood who attended the board meeting the next day. He explained how the story had leaked out and not only did they fully understand what had happened, they backed his decision to promote Lyall all the way.

Lyall had once asked Greenwood what it was really like to be a manager. The reply was, 'You'll never know until you're on your own.'

Greenwood's last words on his departure from West Ham were, 'When I left West Ham to take the England job, I knew

I was leaving the old club in very good hands. John Lyall is a harder man than me and I know that over the years he not only noted the things I did which worked but he also benefited from my mistakes.'

Even though he had formally cut all ties with West Ham three years earlier to take the England job, it was Greenwood who ensured that Billy Bonds was available to play at Wembley in the 1980 FA Cup Final. He had been sent off for fighting with Birmingham's Colin Todd and was hauled before the FA. He seemed certain to be banned for one game until Greenwood intervened. According to Bonds, 'I don't know what Ron said to his colleagues at the FA before the disciplinary commission met, but they let me off and allowed me to play in the final against Arsenal. If it hadn't been for him, I wouldn't have played at Wembley.'

A much worse fate would have befallen Keith Robson two years earlier when another timely intervention by Greenwood saved the wayward Hammer from a likely jail sentence. Robson had been arrested for drink-driving among other charges but his old manager rode to the rescue. The articulate, smooth-talking Greenwood appeared at Stratford Magistrates' Court on behalf of the wayward Geordie, who was let off with a £600 fine and three-year driving ban. 'Ron performed like Perry Mason in the witness box,' said a grateful and repentant Robson years later.

Greenwood and Lyall, between them, spent three decades in the manager's seat at Upton Park. Lyall did not agree with the view that West Ham sides under-achieved after 1965, even with a World Cup-winning trio.

He told *Ex Magazine*, 'You pick the best West Ham side of the '60s and then select a best XI from all the other sides in the First

Division in them – and you'll find that those clubs have as many good players and more than West Ham so, proportionately, West Ham performed a miracle.'

Lyall used the development of defenders John Bond and Ken Brown as good examples of the Greenwood effect, 'They were good players before Ron arrived, but as soon as he came, they moved into another dimension. They were senior players who could have easily not listened, but they were so enamoured with what Ron was teaching them that they took it on board.'

The two men did disagree. But their relationship was one of trust and debate, and each would listen to the other's opinions. If Greenwood tried something and it didn't work, he would hold his hands up and admit his mistake. Above all, Lyall would benefit from what he had learned from Greenwood, believing he could not have learned as much from anyone else.

John Lyall would label the years learning about coaching from Ron Greenwood as 'Probably the most exciting and stimulating period of my career.' Lyall would even claim that he did not aim to be a coach after seeing his playing career ended by injury at the age of 24.

He would enter coaching with no practical experience but once under Greenwood's wing he would discover that he couldn't learn enough. Lyall would enter coaching with a completely open mind. He devoured all his mentor's ideas, and said that he could 'listen to him talking about the game for hours'.

Greenwood would create pictures of situations for his players. He told Lyall that every time he took a training session he should do likewise. He should aim to create the picture that helped the players understand what was required.

While Greenwood preferred players with good habits, this didn't mean that they held a teacup with the correct degree of finesse (though he did admire good behaviour and good manners in his players). What he meant was that players who consistently did the right things on the playing field would develop good habits and become good players. He argued that players with bad habits would also become inconsistent players. One of the most important arts of the game was the ability to improvise, alongside the ability to surprise the opposition with the unpredictable. 'The complete footballer was the one who could combine good habits with improvisation.'

The longer Lyall worked with Greenwood the more he realised that his greatest strength was his ability to spot the key problems every time. His method was to sit the players in the dressing room and say, in straightforward terms, where his men were at fault and what could be done to rectify the problem.

Greenwood could be a dogmatic man, but then a coach had to be like that. He would always put his ideas across in a creative and intelligent manner, and if you had a football brain, his ideas were easy to understand.

'You have only to look at the number of his players who went on to become internationals, and often coaches and managers themselves, to realise that the vast majority of them learned a great deal from Ron Greenwood.'

Lyall once went on a coaching course at Lilleshall but only got average marks. Greenwood asked how it went and upon being told by Lyall that he 'enjoyed' it, the former boss replied, 'I assume you got a distinction.' 'No,' said Lyall. 'I got marked down for over-coaching.'

Greenwood then wrote a letter of complaint. Lyall's tutors told him that he stopped play too frequently and gave too much advice. But this was how Lyall had been coached at West Ham, where attention to detail and a resolve to improve an individual's technical ability were fundamental principles of coaching. Perhaps the incident was indicative of the gulf between the conservatism of the FA and Greenwood's pioneering methods.

Trevor Brooking believes, 'John Lyall took on the West Ham reputation for playing attractive, attacking football, but what he also added was that little bit of drive and edge. He didn't stand any nonsense. If he didn't feel you were putting in the effort that he thought you should – irrespective of who you were – he would let you know in no uncertain terms.'

Greenwood and Supporters

In his history of West Ham, Charles Korr quotes a long-standing West Ham supporter, 'West Ham United's existence matters to thousands of men, women and children, many of whom have never seen a professional football match ... West Ham was rooted in the various communities and subcultures that made up the East End ... The club has touched the lives of tens of thousands of people in ways that have nothing to do with what happens on the field. The Hammers have been part of something much larger than the club, the League, or even the game of football ... it has been a way of life.'

Yet, for the first few years of Greenwood's reign, it was noted how most team members never acknowledged the supporters. There were some exceptions to this, most notably Geoff Hurst, but in the main, players became remote, self-absorbed figures. The likes of Bobby Moore and Martin Peters always gave the impression that they were doing the fans a favour by playing.

Signed from Sheffield Wednesday to replace Peters, Peter Eustace got the cold shoulder off to a fine art. Foolishly, he admitted he missed the dressing rooms at Hillsborough. One writer even labelled him, 'Every inch a Greenwood player. Totally cold, remote and passionless.'

Moore was very concentrated and studious on the pitch. But off it he was accused of making the detached coldness of Greenwood and Ramsey his role model.

A reporter even went so far as to accuse the West Ham 'establishment' of treating their supporters with more than a hint of contempt, with the Greenwood era representing an almost total cut-off from contact with the fans and seemingly the rest of the world.

Brian Belton, in *The First and Last Englishmen: West Ham United in the 1960s*, wrote, 'Greenwood's attitude to the great unwashed of the East End had everything of the Victorian butler about it. He saw it "an area of swaggers ... they would love somebody like [Malcolm] Allison". This shows how out of touch he was with the fans. Allison was never much liked by the crowds at West Ham. Arrogance has never gone down well, hence the general low-level disdain for Ron.'

Greenwood continued to be something of an enigma for West Ham supporters. For some reason he was not as loveable as the likes of Bill Shankly or Matt Busby; he lacked the panache of Allison or the no-nonsense appeal of Tommy Docherty. He didn't carry himself like Joe Mercer or Jock Stein; he lacked the slight mystique of Alf Ramsey.

A supporter named Paul, who was 15 at the time of the Cup Winners' Cup triumph, reflected on the man at the helm of Upton Park, 'Bill Shankly, Joe Mercer, Jock Stein and Matt Busby seemed to have a different attitude to the game than Greenwood, who didn't seem to have any sense of humour or fun. Maybe his very serious attitude to football had something to do with the fact that, unlike Shankly, Stein and Busby for example, he had never really done anything else. I mean, when you've had to work at a coal face down a pit you probably have some idea of proportion. You might get upset about results, but maybe not fall into a deep depression, or, as it sometimes seemed from a distance in Greenwood's case, a sulk.'

12

Greenwood, Ramsey and Moore

Greenwood and Moore

Sir Alf Ramsey was born on 22 January 1920, but the 100th anniversary of the birth of the only man to guide England to World Cup glory passed virtually unnoticed. He had died aged 79 on 28 April 1999, 22 months before Ron Greenwood passed away.

And Greenwood is not the only former England manager to be buried in a Suffolk municipal cemetery. Twenty miles away in the Old Cemetery at Ipswich lies Sir Alf Ramsey. Between them, the two men can be said to have been the architects of English football's finest moment. Crucial to England and West Ham's success in the mid-1960s was the captain of both sides, Robert Frederick Moore. This section seeks to look at the relationship between the player and his managers for club and country.

Trevor Brooking, in *My Life in Football,* wrote that Ramsey 'reminded me very much of my club manager Ron Greenwood. They were contemporaries as players. Another thoughtful, defensive player like Alf, Ron treated his players with respect and, again like Alf, expected his players to return the courtesy.'

It seems incredible now but, in the spring of 1972 Greenwood left Geoff Hurst and Bobby Moore out of his team specifically so that they'd be fresh for England's European Championship tie against West Germany. West Ham were 15th in the table, with relegation a growing threat, when Greenwood decided to rest the two players for a game at Highbury to help Ramsey. It's almost impossible to imagine any club making such a sacrifice for the England team today. They would be more likely to withdraw their player with an 'injury'.

Johnny Byrne was one player who did not fall under Ramsey's spell. One night, long after he had retired, he told Moore, 'I can hear his talk now. The same old talk. Let's face it, Bob. He didn't hold a candle to Ron Greenwood in his knowledge of the game. Not in the same street.'

Ultimately, Ramsey's debt to Greenwood would be a tangible one.

In the 77th minute of the 1966 World Cup quarter-final against an obdurate Argentina, Peters picked up the ball, went down the left wing, and then hit a curling cross towards the near post. Hurst, who had timed his 15-yard run to perfection, met the ball with a glancing header, sending it across the keeper and just inside the far post. It was a beautifully worked move, simple yet devastating, one that Peters and Hurst had practised thousands of times on the West Ham training ground. 'We'd worked on near-post goals until it became an automatic action,' said Peters. 'I wouldn't even have to look. I knew Geoff would be there.'

It was much the same in the final against West Germany, when England's equalising goal – which arrived just six minutes after the Germans had gone in front – came via Moore quickly setting up Hurst in a move straight off the West Ham training ground.

Greenwood was in charge of the England youth side and scouting for new talent when he first came across Moore as a sturdy 16-year-old, an early sighting that said more about his discerning eye than Moore's obvious abilities. Greenwood would hand Moore a record 17 appearances for England's youth team in 1957/58, while championing him around the FA. Greenwood saw a ball-playing centre-half and a boy with the temperament to go a long way. At least in those early days, Moore seemed a manager's dream; just the type for a thoughtful coach like Greenwood.

After the England youth days, Greenwood was promoted to take charge of the under-23s and he was soon bringing Moore along with him.

The pair's careers were about to become entwined even more closely when West Ham looked for a new manager in April 1961. When the news emerged that Greenwood had got the job, the players rushed to ask Moore what the new boss was like. 'If you want to learn, there's no better teacher,' he told them.

Virtually the first knock on the door when Greenwood installed himself in his new office was a fretful Moore, wanting to know if he had prospects. Greenwood made a bold promise that would stick in both men's minds, 'I know you; I like you and I am going to build this club around you.' The chance to build a team around Moore was one of the reasons he had been attracted to the job at Upton Park.

Hurst is in no doubt about the deep and lasting significance of the tactical switch that turned the young Moore into a masterful defender. 'Perhaps Ron's masterstroke,' he maintains, which is quite an accolade considering that Hurst himself was transformed, in a brilliant piece of coaching alchemy, from a middling midfielder to a powerhouse centre-forward who would make an historic impact.

Ken Jones of the *Daily Mirror* believes that it is hard to overstate how the new tactics shaped Moore's career, 'I'm convinced that the change in the way the game was played helped to make Bobby Moore a truly great player. Without Greenwood Moore might not have been a world-class defender; he might not have been much of a defender at all.'

Malcolm Allison had always encouraged Greenwood to play from deep, and in his own coaching career he preached from the same gospel. When Moore's ambition proved costly in one game, with possession lost and a goal conceded as he tried to carry the ball out of defence, Greenwood told the press that he would much prefer to see a well-intentioned mistake of over-elaboration than a clearance hoofed into the stands.

Greenwood and Moore would lead their club to an FA Cup win, a European triumph and a League Cup Final in three successive seasons.

Yet one day in early April 1966, Greenwood called Moore into his office and sacked him as captain. He not only stripped Moore of the armband but also went to a newspaper with a remarkable public attack on his now ex-skipper.

One headline on 4 April 1966 read 'WEST HAM SACK MOORE'. According to Greenwood, Moore had been coasting all season. From the high of Wembley, West Ham had not lived up to their reputation as England's coming force. 'We got into the big time with that win at Wembley and some of the players think they are still playing at Wembley. They have been playing in the past,' said Greenwood.

Greenwood convinced himself that Moore was distracted by captaining England in the forthcoming World Cup on home soil. Moore had been stripped of the captaincy because 'we can't have a man leading the side who doesn't want to play for us', according to the boss. Moore compounded the offence in the eyes of his manager by refusing to sign a new contract.

West Ham drew plaudits for their cultured approach, but they were not competing for honours. There was a sense of unfulfilled ambitions after the high standards set with the cup triumphs of 1964 and 1965. They had been talked about then as a growing force in English football and the World Cup had only heightened expectations. Greenwood's footballing principles were widely admired, but they began to grate with Moore who believed it was all well and good for the manager to believe that the growing obsession with results would be the ruination of English soccer but there was a balance to be struck – and Greenwood did not get it right.

Moore wanted Greenwood to sign big players to lift the place, but his principles were also costing the club in the transfer market, most famously when he declined to sign Gordon Banks because he had given his word to the Kilmarnock manager to buy Bobby Ferguson.

As Moore became increasingly disillusioned, feeling a growing detachment from his manager, so Greenwood was becoming frustrated with his captain.

Trevor Brooking agreed that his boss was a great coach, but he could not get his players to run through walls for him like Bill Shankly or Brian Clough. He also claimed that Greenwood would take the easy way out, dropping younger players if changes were needed: 'He didn't like confrontation with the senior ones. In the circumstances it was probably inevitable that indiscipline would creep into the club, and a booze culture too.'

There was therefore a certain inevitability about the Blackpool scandal in January 1971, given West Ham's relish for boozing and sinking morale at the club. With it, finally, came the realisation by Greenwood that he had been too indulgent and a sign that his relationship with Moore was broken.

According to West Ham's physiotherapist Rob Jenkins, who had also been one of the Blackpool drinkers, 'He was a funny guy, Greenwood. Although he was a wonderful manager with his football, he didn't impose himself with certain players and that's where the problems came in. Some players became slight enemies. That's what Bobby did.'

Moore would tell journalist and friend Jeff Powell for his biography, *Bobby Moore: The Life and Times of a Sporting Hero*, 'I know very little of Ron as a man. We are different. I have a lot of enjoyment outside the game, but I don't know if Ron has much of a life outside football.' This was the essence of the contrast. Moore's character and lifestyle assumed its own, more flamboyant proportions as he emerged from the professional shadow of Greenwood, a churchman dedicated to the sanctity of his family life and purity in football.

What Moore regarded as an engaging lifestyle which promoted an irresistible team spirit, Greenwood suspected to be a social problem, rooted in drink and compounded by hangers-on.

Fans were only too aware that their most successful player and manager did not enjoy a happy bond. The complicated relationship between the two men had been allowed to fester for years and they never enjoyed the close connection that John Lyall later had with his skipper, Billy Bonds.

The frustration on Moore's part ran deep. He believed that Greenwood simply did not have the motivational skills and sheer determination to be a successful as well as principled manager. Greenwood's insensitivity often offended Moore. When asked if he was sorry to see the former England captain leave the club, Greenwood answered coldly, 'I'm sorry when all players leave the club.'

Ironically, Moore believed that nobody had more knowledge about football than Greenwood and despite their deep differences they usually presented a united front. A further nine years slipped away following the Cup Winners' Cup triumph in 1965, before Moore finally left Upton Park, years in which West Ham as a club began to lose its way.

The two men hardly spoke in the angry years which followed Moore's departure to Fulham in 1974 but before Moore died in 1993, Jeff Powell brokered a reunion – inviting both to 'a breakfast which lasted through an animated lunch into an emotional dinner'.

Jimmy Greaves was both a great friend of Moore and no fan of Greenwood. In *Don't Shoot the Manager: The Revealing Story of England's Soccer Bosses* he wrote, '[I] was surprised to find out how much ice there was between Greenwood and Moore, and it reached iceberg proportions over the Blackpool Affair.

'But all this petty nonsense melted away when dear old Bobby succumbed to cancer in the winter of 1993, and Ron – always the gentleman – could not have been warmer with his tribute to his old skipper who served him so well. Time heals old wounds, and I know Bobby would have been the first to acknowledge that for all his difference with Greenwood he was, at his peak, a marvellous manager, just as Bobby was a marvellous player.'

Football historian David Goldblatt wrote in *The Game of our Lives: The Meaning and Making of English Football*, 'Remembrance of the dead and remembrance of time past became indissolubly linked in the collective football imagination. This connection was made again when, in 1993, Bobby Moore died at the age of 51. Remembered, above all, as the captain of the victorious 1966 World Cup team his death was marked in rituals of public mourning at West Ham and across the football world. *The Guardian* described the feel of the moment: it was "another kind of mourning; for a world, as it seems looking back, when sometimes things used to go right". It was a time when England won the World Cup and heroes were kept unblemished; when a working-class boy could metaphorically become a gentleman, when the captain wiped the mud from his hands before shaking the Queen's.'

In his memoir, *The Last Game,* Jason Cowley, whose day job was editor of *The New Statesman,* wrote, 'One of my father's happiest memories was of a day he met Moore and his then wife, Tina, on a long flight back from Hong Kong. Moore had taken it on himself to act as a cocktail-fixer in the upper-deck bar of a jumbo jet.'

Ramsey and Moore

Alf Ramsey also recognised in Moore that calm, almost regal nature that distinguished him from other players. Yet theirs, as Moore's with Greenwood, was to be a purely professional relationship based solely on mutual respect and not on any deeper friendship.

And there were to be times over the first three years of Ramsey's England reign when Moore's behaviour off the field would lead him to re-examine his decision to make him captain.

Before an international against Portugal in 1964, prior to a trip to New York, seven players, including Moore, Jimmy Greaves and Johnny Byrne, broke curfew to go drinking in London's West End. When they got back to their hotel that night all found their passports lying on their pillows.

Ramsey deliberately waited a few days before confronting them and then gave, according to Byrne, 'the most severe and punishing reprimand' he had ever experienced. All seven would play against Portugal but Ramsey had made his point. He was the boss. Ramsey told them that if he had another seven players to fill their boots, he would have sent the drinkers home.

However, Moore was unimpressed, and in New York ten days later he and a group of others ignored Ramsey's threats and again went out for a drink. Ramsey was furious and confronted Moore, telling him that any drinking would be done as a squad and under his supervision. The confrontation strained their relationship for years afterwards, and it would not be until the immediate build-up to the World Cup finals that the strong bond between these two very different sons of east London would be forged once and for all.

The former quartermaster was a strict disciplinarian and did not want anyone stepping out of line on his parade ground. After his run-ins with Moore and Greaves, who like Moore didn't mind a pint and had the sort of troublesome, rebellious streak Ramsey found difficult to cope with, he was quick to lay down the law to newcomers to the squad.

Moore may have thought it all good fun but eventually Ramsey had had enough. On a trip to Northern Ireland in October 1964 they had what might be termed 'showdown talks' as Ramsey was worried that splits were building up between the London lads and some of the other players. The misbehaviour of Moore, Greaves and Byrne was beginning to affect morale. Cliques were forming and the captain was not setting the right example, so Ramsey decided to crack down.

When it came to the opening international of the following season, against Wales in Cardiff, he delayed choosing Moore as the captain until the last possible moment. He reminded Moore of his responsibilities and the need for greater trust between manager and his on-pitch leader. The captain respected the straight talk, and it was a critical juncture on the road to 1966.

According to Geoffrey Green of *The Times*, 'Up until then Moore had tended, with one or two others, to go his own way. A splinter group was developing within the team at the top. But the split was mended in time by Ramsey's firm action. The manager, after one year in the saddle, made it abundantly clear who was to be the boss, and duly the deviationists were brought to heel.'

Ramsey, like Greenwood, was an intensely private man; Moore positively revelled in the social opportunities now open to a football star. While Ramsey rarely drank, and rarely visited pubs or bars, for Moore drinking establishments were a second home. He would enjoy his fame, while Ramsey hated the limelight.

Moore wrote, 'Despite what the outside world thought, I would never regard myself as being the same as Alf. Not at all alike. The only Alf I knew was the football manager. We were together maybe a total of a month or two out of every year.

That didn't mean I knew the person. Alf never drew me into his social company.

It became clear to me that Alf and I were different personalities outside our working relationship. Apart from football, Alf would never talk in depth about anything at all. In company the conversation might flit across the usual small talk, but it would invariably settle on football. Alf had just two worlds, his players and his home. And they were kept strictly apart.'

He could have been talking about his club boss, as much as his national one.

There is seemingly a paradox between Moore the outstanding skipper and Moore the errant drinker. The contradiction certainly existed, and was touched on in a Ramsey quote about Moore, 'He was my captain and my right-hand man. Bobby was the heartbeat of the England team, the king of the castle, my representative on the field. He made things work on the pitch. I had the deepest trust in him as a man, as a captain, as a confidant … I could easily overlook his indiscretions, his thirst for the good life, because he was the supreme professional, the best I ever worked with.'

That was said when Ramsey could afford to reflect generously on all Moore's qualities but, through 1963 and 1964, those 'indiscretions' drove him to fury. When training started, Moore's focus could not be doubted. Ramsey, like Greenwood, saw the unquestionable logic of building a defence around Moore's anticipation and composure on the ball.

But away from the practice pitch, Moore was always drawn to the irreverent bunch, smirking at the back of the class with Byrne and Greaves. 'Bob was not Mr Perfect. He always lived with a bit of danger,' Greaves wrote. 'I think we were good for each other, Bob and me. I'm not sure Alf would have thought that.'

Moore's dry sense of humour was also beginning to take on a sharp, cynical edge. Legend has it that Ramsey was of traveller origin, a connection which made him extremely sensitive. The story is told of Moore making a joke when passing some travellers' caravans on a Balkans tour along the lines that the manager should drop in and see his relatives. Ramsey seethed at the slight. Ramsey's accent, and the rumour of him having taken elocution lessons, was a source of endless mirth.

Journalist Ken Jones said, 'I think it got to the stage that Bobby realised he was going too far and if he wasn't careful, he wouldn't go any further. He had to be careful with all that nonsense.'

That 'nonsense' would never quite be eradicated. Matt Dickinson wrote in his biography of Moore, *Bobby Moore: The Man in Full*, 'Perhaps the biggest difference was the streak of cynicism that lay at the heart of Bobby Moore, something that Alf utterly lacked. Naïve and earnest, Alf clung to the values of the era into which he had been born. He was no moraliser and was capable of deceit and ruthlessness but in his old-fashioned, often derided way, he strove to be an English gentleman.

'Bobby was far more worldly, more irreverent. Keenly aware of his status, he was capable of inflicting humiliation on others, often through a barbed comment or a withering look. It is one of the paradoxes of this golden era in English football that Moore is seen as the shining light, the epitome of English decency and warmth whereas Alf is so often regarded as the iron-hearted pragmatist.

'Moore, behind his front of charm, was calculating, cold, even cruel at times. When he was secretly conducting the affair which ultimately ended his marriage in the early 1980s, his wife Tina, unaware of his infidelity but disturbed by his indifference, asked him why she always seemed to come second to football. "What makes you think you're as high as second?" replied Moore.'

Greenwood wrote of Moore, 'I even wanted to sack him at one point and our relationship became unhappy and strained. He was very aloof, locked in a world of his own. He even started to give the impression that he was ignoring me at team-talks. He would glance around with a blasé look on his face, eyes glazed in a way that suggested he had nothing to learn. It was impossible to get close to him. There was a big corner of himself that would not or could not give. It hurt that he could be so cold to someone who cared about him.'

Jeff Powell of the *Daily Mail,* who was probably closer to Moore than anyone else in football, says that the player's early experiences at West Ham under Ted Fenton bred in him a contempt for all managers, a pattern that led to an artificial relationship with Ramsey. And according to renowned journalist Hugh McIlvanney, 'There was always a distance. You felt there was always another door inside him that you could never reach.'

In the weeks leading up to the World Cup finals, Ramsey had even given the impression that he was planning to drop Moore, not just from the England captaincy but even from the national team. His trust in Moore had been badly undermined by the pre-Portugal events of 1964 and he did not forgive or forget.

By the beginning of 1966, Moore was slipping back into his old ways of cockiness and complacency, especially when in the company of his old east London drinking partner, Jimmy Greaves.

Like Greenwood, Ramsey was also disturbed by the high priority Moore attached to his own monetary value. Every year, Moore was the last member of the West Ham squad to sign his annual contract, a form of financial pressure that ensured he received the largest possible salary increase.

One unwanted problem for England in 1966 was Moore's long-running dispute with West Ham. England's captain was out of contract with the club and therefore not officially an FA-registered player. As FIFA were technically obliged to bar him from England's squad, Ramsey summoned Greenwood to Hendon Hall, where he was put into a room with the captain. They emerged moments later with Moore clutching a contract to cover him for the month of July, enabling him to play in the World Cup.

Geoff Hurst wrote in *My Autobiography: 1966 and All That*, 'History could have recorded a very different chapter in the Bobby Moore story. None of us at the time realised just how close he was to losing his place in the team. Bobby was England's greatest captain, much admired by Alf Ramsey, but it now seems that at one point the manager contemplated the unthinkable – dropping his captain from the World Cup Final team.'

Right-back George Cohen claimed to have overheard a conversation between Ramsey, coach Les Coker and assistant manager Harold Shepherdson when they were discussing whether to drop Moore for the final in favour of Norman Hunter.

Hurst had found his introduction to the full England team in 1966 intimidating, 'Bobby Moore and I, although we were at West Ham, were never close socially. He was slightly older than me. I found it quite hard to settle into the England side at first. I didn't know anybody apart from Bobby. He wasn't a great help.'

In an earlier autobiography, *The World Game*, Hurst described his England boss as 'something of a mystery man even among the players he led to such tremendous success. Can you imagine spending the most important seven weeks in your life in the close company of a man and ending up not even being able to find out whether he enjoyed a quiet cigarette?

'Remote is a word that always occurs when people are talking about the England chief. And I suppose it is a fair description. For after knowing him for three years I still couldn't say if he drives a car, whether he like meat better than fish.'

Comparing Greenwood and Ramsey, Hurst added, 'As men the England manager and the coach who has created West Ham as a thinking club, Ron Greenwood, are very different. Yet it is in the many ways that they are so similar I believe the importance lies.

'They both have a towering ability to get the best of even ordinary players, of persuading their teams that no task is beyond them, of giving players an ambition and a target … and convincing them that it can be reached.

'They have both a fantastic knowledge of the game, an ability to pick out essential points from a mass of conflicting detail and opinion and conveying the essentials to the players they control.

'They are both quiet men, more given to reasoned argument than passionate speeches. And both are a bit nutty about football, regarding it not just as a sport or even a way of making a living but something more; a part of their lives to which they devote most of their time and all of their thinking.

'Now the differences. First is discipline. England players are kept on a tight rein. Ramsey is the boss. But West Ham work on the trust or honour system. I doubt if there is a club in the country that has fewer rules and regulations to control their players' lives.'

And therein lay the basis of many of the problems experienced at West Ham.

But Moore did not change his ways. During the Mexico World Cup in 1970 players were only allowed brief spells of sunbathing by the pool; they would lie on one side for 15 minutes, then Shepherdson would blow a whistle, and they would turn over and lie on the other.

Liverpool winger Peter Thompson once went up on the roof of the hotel for some illicit sunbathing, only to find Moore up there showing his customary indifference to Alf's injunction.

And neither did Moore forgive Ramsey for what he saw as being abandoned in Bogotá prior to the tournament to face the music alone over the stolen bracelet incident.

Moore regarded his national manager's demise in 1974 as inevitable, 'Football has a habit of running in ten-year cycles and when you come to the end of that period it takes a very flexible and adaptable man to move out of that pattern which has been successful for him. The cycle turned against Alf.'

Like Greenwood, Ramsey remained obsessively loyal to the players who had brought him success in the past. Rather than experiment, he preferred to surround himself with those he trusted. This inability to rebuild, to create a long-term culture of continuing success, was one of his weaknesses as a manager. It had happened at Ipswich, and following the shock 1970 quarter-final exit in León, the same process started to happen with England, just as it had with West Ham after 1965.

13

Appointment

BY THE mid-1970s Ron Greenwood had become very disenchanted with professional football. He admitted that this was partly a problem of his own making, harking back to his decision to hand over control of the West Ham team to John Lyall in 1974. He needed close contact with players and after becoming general manager, he was divorced from the one aspect of the game that really mattered to him.

Even when West Ham won the FA Cup in 1975, he stayed at his home in Brighton on the Sunday morning instead of joining in the celebrations. Lyall didn't want it this way; it was Greenwood's own choice to cut himself off.

He needed something to fire his enthusiasm again, and it came when he accompanied Walter Winterbottom on a trip to the first World Youth Championship in Tunisia in 1977 as a member of FIFA's Technical Committee. 'I thoroughly enjoyed it,' he said. 'I saw some marvellous youngsters in action, full of skill and adventure and I drew great hope from them.' Working with FIFA, he was mixing with the best of the international coaches who admired his work and passion for the game. 'I could feel the fire rising in me again,' Greenwood explained. 'I hoped my ideas might be suited to the international game and I was going to help restore faith and dignity in our game and prove to the world we could play a bit.'

Arguably the reputation of England's football team had reached the lowest point in its history by 1977. Not only was the side on the verge of not qualifying for the 1978 World Cup, but manager Don Revie took ignominious flight to the Middle East for the money. What was once a great footballing nation, feared and admired in equal measure around the world, had become a laughing stock. Even England's reputation for integrity and fair play had been sullied by the grubby skulduggery of Revie's departure. Not only were England a poor football team, but their manager was also apparently prouder of the size of his pay packet than the honour of leading his country. English football craved the return of stability and integrity.

Greenwood was called by the West Ham chairman Reg Pratt, who told him that Harold Thompson, the chairman of the FA, wanted to speak to him urgently. 'I think they're in trouble after Revie,' said Pratt. 'And if they want you to help them that's all right with us.'

Thompson then called Greenwood to tell him the FA would like him to stand in with England until they made a new appointment. Greenwood told him that there was no problem with that but would give a definite answer when he got back from West Ham's pre-season tour of Majorca.

It was what Thompson termed 'a bit of a situation'. Thompson was passing on to Greenwood an invitation to become England's team manager – but on a caretaker basis. On a hot summer's day in July 1977 Thompson was sitting with Greenwood in a noisy basement in Whites Hotel, near the FA headquarters at Lancaster Gate. Thompson was wary of being spotted by the press and also did not want to pay for a meeting room. He said to Greenwood, 'The image of the game is all wrong. We need a firm, stable hand immediately and we are wondering if you could take over as caretaker manager of England for a while.

'We're going to advertise the job, so no promises. See what you can do.'

Greenwood, then aged 55, was to admit later that he felt he was being sized up for the job largely because he was one of the few men available. With the 1977/78 season on the horizon, there could be no question of the FA risking accusations of trying to poach a boss from one of the clubs but Greenwood, it would appear, was not really seen as more than a stop-gap appointment. Indeed, when the news broke, it was officially announced that he would 'act as team manager for the next three internationals, until December'.

For a man hardly over-enamoured at the way the game itself was going, Greenwood happily jumped at the opportunity to show the world that England's team 'could still play a bit'. And he was keen 'to help restore faith and dignity in our game'.

Seventeen years before, Winterbottom had asked Greenwood if he was interested in taking the England job, but he thought it was too soon. Now was a much better time, though part of Greenwood wished he had been approached instead of Revie in 1974. By 1977 he was looked upon as the equivalent to a professor in football, with a worldwide reputation. After giving the job to the wrong person, the FA wanted a decent man who took the opposite approach, a Corinthian with high values. Greenwood soon accepted the invitation. Nevertheless, he later wrote, 'It occurred to me that I was the only man available.'

The formal announcement followed on 17 August 1977, reading, 'The Football Association has invited Mr. R. Greenwood of West Ham United Football Club to act as team manager for the next three internationals, until December next, and subject to the agreement of his board of directors he has accepted the invitation.'

Journalist Brian Glanville, who had personally witnessed every England manager since Winterbottom come and go, wrote in his 2008 history of the job, *England Managers: The Toughest Job in Football*, 'With Revie gone, Harold Thompson searched for an antidote, and the chosen antidote would be Ron Greenwood. Thompson, the *faute de mieux* kingmaker, picked him with idealism rather than objectivity. After the subterfuge and greed of Revie's going, Thompson wanted a manager who would be a symbol of probity. It seemed plain enough that he chose Greenwood because he had for many years been the inspiration of West Ham United's admired academy of football arts and sciences than because he had known him previously as the coach to an Oxford University football team over which he himself autocratically presided.'

Thompson was one of the most powerful figures in 1970s football, known to his enemies as the 'Atom Bomb'. The FA's new chairman wore his learning heavily – he was a former professor of chemistry at Oxford University, and had taught Margaret Thatcher – and was described as a man you did not want standing behind you with a cheese knife.

The normally restrained Alan Odell, secretary of the FA's international section, said, 'Harold Thompson was a bastard. He was a brilliant man, but as a person I could not stand him. He was one of the very few people I have met in my life that I detested. He treated the staff like shit.' As well as being pompous, Thompson had an appalling reputation for sexually harassing women.

In his biography of Alf Ramsey, Leo McKinstry described the 1970s as a dark decade for English football, beset by problems such as hooliganism, dirty play, lack of cash and woeful performances by the national side. 'But one of the most powerful malignancies lurked within the Football Association itself, in the person of Professor Sir Harold Thompson, who was the main force behind the sacking of Alf Ramsey, a manager who refused to kowtow to the Professor,' McKinstry wrote.

By 1977, Thompson was building up a fine collection of managerial scalps. Having already played Brutus to Ramsey's Caesar, he now led the campaign to destroy Revie's reputation. But there was little danger of any nuclear fall-outs between Thompson and Greenwood. The two men were old allies from Oxford University, where Greenwood had coached the Dark Blues in the late 1950s.

Malcolm Allison wrote in his autobiography, *Colours of My Life*, 'I was invited to take over Pegasus, the combined Cambridge and Oxford team. The offer was made by "Tommy" Thompson [Sir Harold's nickname], the scientist-football fanatic who was knighted and was to emerge as such a powerful figure along the corridors of the FA at the time of Alf Ramsey's sacking in 1974. But the offer, which on the face of it, was a great honour, had unacceptable strings. Thompson boomed at me, "You will train the players, Allison, and I will pick the team." I do not warm to people who address me by my surname, and I was even less disposed towards being ordered around by a man who, for all his intellect, was very much the football amateur. I told Thompson to, in effect, stuff Pegasus.'

If England were going to take a gamble on the mercurial, charismatic, hare-brained genius that was Brian Clough, this, surely, would have been the moment to do so. But Thompson was not a man who approved of insolence or flippancy – two qualities for which Clough was famed. Greenwood was far more his glass of port, being the nearest thing to a don that English football had yet produced.

In one of the many books bearing his name, Jimmy Greaves in *Don't Shoot the Manager: The Revealing Story of England's Soccer Bosses,* wrote, 'It is one of the scandals of English international football that the man best suited to the job of managing the team was never given a chance. I refer, of course, to the old bulldog Brian Clough, who, at his peak, would have made the perfect England boss. But the duffers who run our game were frightened of his bite … There is no question that the people's choice as successor to Revie would have been Brian Clough. If Cloughie had got the top job he would have swept the hangers-on and the busybodies out of his way at a rate of knots, and this I feel sure is what the FA feared.

'I believe the FA officials were frightened of him. They had already been burned by Revie, and they sensed they would have found Clough too hot to handle.'

World Cup winner and successful club manager Jack Charlton wrote to the FA in 1977 to apply for the job after Revie resigned. The FA never even had the courtesy to reply to an England great. The suspicion must be that he was seen as too closely associated with his old Leeds manager.

Greaves could not be described as a fan of Greenwood. 'It was like inviting a village vicar to take over from a foot-in-the-door salesman,' was his take on the contrast between 'Reverend Ron' Greenwood and 'Don the Deserter' Revie.

Greaves also suggested that Greenwood was the right man for the job at the wrong time, 'To the players he was selecting he was not far off a grandfatherly figure.' He did, however, admit that when he set out to research his book, 'Some of the built-in prejudices I had against the managers gave way to sympathy as I began to get some idea of the pressure they have faced.' He had played for Greenwood at under-23 level for England and then for West Ham when 'we had a bit of a bust-up'.

Greaves added, 'I have personal reasons why Greenwood was not my favourite person in football, but I will not allow this to cloud my judgement of him. My honest assessment is that he was an exceptional coach of players with tactical awareness, and a good but not outstanding manager. He lacked the will to win of a Revie, the steel of a Ramsey, the charisma of a Mercer, and the dynamism of a Clough, but he had a deep sincerity about him that appealed to many players who swore loyalty to him. The one area in which he was tops was that nobody could match his knowledge of international football. The England job suited him better than club football, but it had come at least ten years later than was ideal. Ron is a nice man – a very, very nice man – but nice men rarely come first.

'Greenwood was so enmeshed in the theory of the game that I always got the impression he would have been happy to have supervised his football in an empty stadium without the intrusion of a crowd or media. Football to Ron was almost like a game of chess, and he would see depths and subtleties in every match that escaped the notice of all but committed theorists and tacticians.'

Trevor Brooking had spent much of his career playing under Greenwood, and no doubt hoped to prolong his England career with him, and took a much more sympathetic view of his appointment. In his first autobiography, published in 1981, he wrote, 'Being appointed England manager in 1977 revived his career. He had become very disillusioned about the way English football was going. He thought it was too defensive, too physical and was not producing enough skilful players to compete with the best continental and South American players. He thought the emphasis in the clubs was too much geared towards competition and pressure instead of technique. Ball-winning and closing down space were looked on as finer virtues than controlling the ball and passing it properly. He felt there was a harsh tone about our game which put us out of step with the rest of the world. He did not belittle the competitiveness of our players. "If we had more of the continentals' skill added to our competitiveness, we'd beat everyone," he said.

'Taking over from Don Revie, who in many ways was the opposite of him, gave Greenwood the chance to change things, to put the smile back on the face of English football.

'I believe the period 1977–80 was the happiest period of his working life. Working with the country's best players comes easier to him than the day-to-day involvement with players at a club.'

Geoff Hurst wrote in his 2005 book, *My Autobiography: 1966 and All That*, 'All England coaches have to learn the importance of keeping their feet on the ground, and to be a bit shrewder tactically than the club coach. The international coach must improvise and bring together unfamiliar players within a team framework.

'Ron could do all of these things. In fact, I think he filled the criteria perfectly. He certainly worked with the players far more than Alf did during my time in the squad. Alf wasn't a coach in the way Ron was. He stood on the sidelines assessing the form of players. He could coach of course but it wasn't his forte. Ron, on the other hand, was a creator, a teacher, and an innovator. He devised strategies and then went on the pitch with the players to see whether his plan would work. When he pulled on a tracksuit he blossomed as a personality. Football was his whole world and at 55 he had the maturity to do the job in a relaxed, stimulating way that appealed to young players. He restored the faith of the players and public at a time when the game's popularity was at a low point.'

Greenwood and Revie had different ideas about the game and a personal relationship that could best be described as frosty. There was no love lost between them.

In November 1966 West Ham beat Leeds 7-0 in a League Cup tie at Upton Park. At the end of the match Revie went to their dressing room to congratulate the winners. He told Greenwood his team had been world-beaters, but Ron, who could be a bit pompous when he wanted, simply said, 'Thanks.' Revie went back to the Leeds dressing room and allegedly told his players, 'You will never lose to that man's team again.'

Greenwood would maintain it was a victory West Ham paid for, 'Leeds were as cold as ice, a team and a club without heart or mercy, when we played them over the next few years. They always saved up something special for us and even carried the cold war into the boardroom. I would go in after a game and immediately their directors would start chipping away. "Thought you played reasonably well," they'd say with little smiles, "but, you know, perhaps you're not quite ..." They would leave me to complete the thought. I hated it.

'We did not beat Leeds again until 1972, when a Clyde Best header in extra time put them out of the League Cup in a replay. It was at Elland Road, too, and in the boardroom afterwards I wasn't very charitable myself. "This time," I said, "it's somebody else's ... turn to be polite."'

Perhaps the real sequel to that famous win over Leeds came after Revie's appointment as England manager. He called the country's top players together – West Ham were the best represented with eight out of the 60 included – and then he toured the clubs to have a chat with the managers.

Greenwood's turn came, and Revie opened the conversation by saying, 'We've never really talked, have we?'

'I don't know why not,' Greenwood replied. 'I'll tell you,' said Revie. 'Remember when you beat us 7-0, well we were demoralised but I still went into your dressing room afterwards to congratulate you. You were over by the radiator and I came over and said, "Marvellous. Miraculous. What a game you played." And you looked at me and all you said was, "Thank you very much." I felt snubbed and I went back to our dressing room and told my players, "We never lose to that man's bloody team ever again."'

But it wasn't just about a difference in temperaments. Revie was appointed on 4 July 1974, a date when English football took the wrong fork in the road. FA secretary Ted Croker even admitted that he didn't know Revie too well, but such was his footballing reputation that no one else was interviewed and the FA blundered into swift action without much thought.

Football League secretary Alan Hardaker, a man who hated Revie, warned Croker that his candidate ought not to be considered because of his bungs and other excesses. Hardaker told Croker, 'You must be off your heads.' Six months later Croker admitted that Hardaker was right. Even his own brother warned Croker he was making a big error. Three years later most people realised it was a calamitous mistake.

Revie's successful record as a club manager persuaded everyone to take him on as England's third full-time manager irrespective of his excesses. He was not even a holder of the full coaching badge, which made a mockery of the FA's coaching system. Revie had the ruthlessness to succeed at club level, but different qualities were needed at international level. He didn't have them.

For in Revie's background there were already a number of shady transactions and events which someone on the FA should have known of and warned the decision-makers about. Some people knew him as 'Don Readies', a devious man who would cheat to become a winner and stay one.

As far back as 1962 it was alleged that Revie attempted to bribe Bury manager Bob Stokoe with an offer of £500 for his team to forfeit the match in Leeds's favour.

This was only the first in a series of similar allegation, made by the *Daily Mirror* in September 1977, claiming Revie had, on several occasions, tried to fix crucial matches for his team with the offer of financial inducements to opposing players. He denied all of them, though while he initiated proceedings for libel, he never went to court to clear his name.

Away to Newcastle in 1964 he had supposedly offered the home players £10 each to throw a match Leeds won 1-0.

Frank McLintock, Arsenal's double-winning captain, waited for nearly 40 years and used his book *True Grit* to reveal his account of the way Revie tried to bribe him before the Gunners hosted Leeds on 7 May 1968. 'He was a flawed man in flawed times,' was McLintock's description.

In 1972 the *Sunday People* alleged that Revie offered bribes of £1,000 to Wolves players to throw a match Leeds needed to win to secure that year's First Division championship.

The last thing Revie's Leeds could be accused of was innocence. It was curious that Revie, who professed high soccer ideals, and whose play could be characterised by cerebral elegance, should have bred a side that was to employ every tactic in the rule book, and several outside it, in its unswerving quest to gain an advantage. Foul play and various strains of gamesmanship became synonymous with the club. Revie was the father of Leeds's vigorous, physical style, which, judged by results alone, had every justification. He had created the will to win and there was little evidence of him seeking to curb the excesses on the field of his talented envoys.

There was no doubt that as the England manager, Revie missed his beloved Leeds and despised the FA. The only thing that Revie and Thompson shared was a mutual loathing. The FA chairman's condescension towards the working-class Revie was vintage Thompson. 'He and Thompson hated each other from first sight,' said Revie's son Duncan. 'That didn't help. Professor Sir Harold Thompson was very much "these people are serfs, they work for me", bowing and scraping and tugging the forelock.'

But it should be stressed that Revie's appointment was backed by Thompson, initially. He wanted a new start under a younger, more enthusiastic manager who could handle the press, qualities noticeably lacking in Alf Ramsey.

In his biography of Bobby Moore, *Bobby Moore: The Life and Times of a Sporting Hero*, Jeff Powell quotes his subject as saying to Revie, 'If I'd been at Leeds instead of West Ham there would have been no ordinary matches. Every game would have been a big game. Every game might have meant a championship medal. I'd have given you a Wembley performance every game.'

Which rather implies he was not giving such performances to West Ham, and that Greenwood was correct in his negative assessment of Moore's attitude after 1966.

* * *

After Greenwood's appointment, there were only three weeks until the next England game, a friendly at home to Switzerland, leaving him with little time to settle into the job.

Greenwood's first move as caretaker manager was to visit Anfield on the opening day of the new season, a place that had produced more England internationals than anywhere else at a time when Liverpool were newly crowned European Cup winners for the first time.

He talked to Reds manager Bob Paisley, the man who had reluctantly taken over from Bill Shankly. Like Greenwood, Paisley had regarded himself as 'a buffer' when handed the job; now England's caretaker boss was turning to Liverpool for their players, with half a dozen – plus Kevin Keegan, recently departed to Hamburg – chosen for the Switzerland fixture.

With so little time to promote his own football philosophy, Greenwood was looking to medal-winning players who already understood each other's game.

They may have all been winners but still spoke of how, at times, playing at Wembley for England was not an enjoyable experience, in front of a baying crowd that became impatient too quickly. Greenwood visited more teams across the country and a picture started to emerge of a lost spirit when playing for their country. Playing for England was starting to become a chore instead of the defining moment in their careers that it should have been. Another suggestion was that the link between the players and coaching staff had been allowed to grow too big and therefore it had become much harder to communicate across a large age gap. It was with this in mind that meant Greenwood turned to one of his own, Geoff Hurst.

Hurst would be the first to admit he owed his glittering career to Greenwood. Yet he was taken completely by surprise when contacted by his old boss in the summer of 1977.

'Your country needs you,' he told the World Cup winner. 'Again?' Hurst responded. 'Yes,' Greenwood said 'Well, to be honest, I need you. I feel there's a big age gap between me and the players. I want you to help me communicate with them.'

It had been five years since the two men had worked together at West Ham, but Hurst felt he needed a model, a demonstrator, someone to go on the training pitch and show the England players what he wanted from them. 'I was very familiar with his language, his coaching practices, and I was still fit enough at least to go through the motions on the pitch with the players,' Hurst would say.

But there was no place in the new coaching setup for his old club skipper, Bobby Moore. Journalist Jeff Powell campaigned for many years on behalf of the former England captain, and said, 'The game never made use of Bobby's great intelligence. He should have been England's defensive coach, not wandering off to manage Southend.'

Powell also pushed the case for the former England captain's early mentor, Malcolm Allison: 'The game never made the most of Malcolm's tactical and technical knowledge. It saw him as one of the great entertainers and didn't understand his influence on the game.'

Perhaps in the case of Moore, there were just too many ill feelings still between the two men for him to be brought into the England fold.

When Greenwood chose his first team to play Switzerland, it was replete with seven Liverpool players, including Ian Callaghan, once a right-winger who had been discarded at the 1966 World Cup by Ramsey.

Interviewed in the *Liverpool Echo* after Greenwood's death in 2006, Callaghan recalled his call-up, 11 years after the last, 'It really did come as a complete surprise. We were playing at Middlesbrough when Ronnie Moran said the new England boss wanted to talk to a few of us. I replied "well he won't want to be talking to me" – and it was only when the letters dropped the following week that I believed it.

'He really was a true gentleman who never seemed to lose his temper or get riled. And he earned me a place in the record books. I think I still have the longest gap between caps for any England player.'

Unfortunately it was an England team that floundered without inspiration in a frustrating 0-0 draw. England, by comparison with the Swiss, simply looked clumsy, their three-man midfield lacking pace and flair. As to the defence, Greenwood himself was obliged to confess that on a couple of occasions, players were going for the same opponent.

There were still five Liverpool players in the side for Greenwood's second game, a World Cup qualifier in Luxembourg. It was another poor match and England laboured to a 2-0 win against a team that were essentially amateurs.

If the fixture itself had been boring, the same could not be said for what happened in the streets of the tiny Duchy as England's hooligans again went on the rampage.

Back on home soil Revie had seemingly given up the ghost when it came to taking England to the finals of the World Cup in Argentina in 1978, but his defection didn't mean that qualification was all over bar the recriminations.

The final match of Greenwood's three came in November and could keep the impossible dream alive as victory over Italy would still leave the *Azzurri* with a final match in Rome, against Luxembourg, that they needed to win. Greenwood selected a team more in tune with his own predilections, with Keegan and Brooking, while the obsession with Liverpool players was at an end. Greenwood had traditionally believed in wingers and against Italy he picked two genuine ones in Steve Coppell and Peter Barnes; in front of a 90,000 crowd the more adventurous line-up produced a 2-0 win.

England won with two excellent goals, Keegan in the first half, and Brooking in the second and the victory was inspiring, bringing the two nations level on goal difference. Italy then beat Luxembourg 3-0 in Rome, finishing level on ten points with England but with a goal total of 18 scored and four conceded to England's 15 and four. The painful truth was that, as in 1974, England had fallen on the road to the World Cup finals. But at least there was, at long last, cause for optimism after the Revie years.

After the match, Greenwood sat down with the players and staff at the dinner table and told them, 'Perhaps this isn't the Last Supper after all.'

He later said, 'The players said it was nice to be cheered off the Wembley pitch. We set out to restore pride and respect in our football and we got the verdict from the crowd at the end.'

14

1977–1982

RON GREENWOOD'S three-match reign had come to an unbeaten conclusion, so the question now was who should be given the chance to take England through to the European Championship in Italy in 1980?

The Italy result had certainly boosted Greenwood's prospects of landing the job on a permanent basis. Greenwood had been close to the job 15 years earlier when his coaching mentor Walter Winterbottom approached the young West Ham manager about succeeding him. The plan hinged on Winterbottom being appointed FA secretary as successor to Sir Stanley Rous, but he missed out, and the move collapsed.

The FA settled on a shortlist of five in addition to Greenwood: club managers Brian Clough, Bobby Robson and Lawrie McMenemy, plus their own director of coaching Allen Wade and national coach Charles Hughes.

Each man was spoken to for 45 minutes at Lancaster Gate on 4 December 1977. FA secretary Ted Croker reckoned that the charismatic Clough was better than anyone, including Bob Paisley and Bill Shankly. But Clough's lack of diplomacy ruled him out, although his interview was impressive and even [chairman Harold] Thompson warmed to him, although the feeling was not mutual. Clough would later recall, '[I] didn't relish sharing the same room with Thompson. He was a stroppy, know-all bugger who in my view knew nothing about my game.'

Clough was easily the nation's choice and bookmakers' favourite for the job but, with the exception of Manchester City chairman Peter Swales, the other members of the panel were sceptical of his handling of star players, and also his press relations.

Clough emerged from Lancaster Gate to tell reporters that he had enjoyed 'a magnificent interview'. Greenwood was in the room for half an hour but had no idea that he had landed the post until a few days later when he heard the news on his car radio. He had just had lunch with wife Lucy in their favourite restaurant in Alfriston, Sussex, and was sitting in his car when the news came on the radio that he was the man. That was the first time he heard; another example of the FA's poor communication management.

Clough's reaction to his rejection was predictable, 'The entire bloody process was a sham and a sop to the public. They gave it to the manager who couldn't make up his mind which should be the very first name on the team sheet. Ron Greenwood didn't know who the best goalkeeper was. What chance has he got of coming up with the right combination all the way through to 11? Don't get me wrong – Ron was an accomplished manager, highly respected within the game among fellow professionals and in Europe.'

Clough was right. It would appear there was never a realistic chance of him being appointed England manager. In an interview in *The Times* on 21 March 2009, promoting a TV documentary on the subject, it was claimed that Clough had been the victim of a sham despite being the popular choice for the post.

Glen Kirton, FA press officer in the 1970s and who subsequently became the governing body's commercial direction and team administrator, working closely with Greenwood, claimed that Clough's interview *was* a sop to that public opinion. 'The decision had already been made that Ron Greenwood was the preferred candidate. There wasn't a vote. Sir Harold Thompson would have said "I want to appoint Ron Greenwood" and the panel would have agreed. The decision was made beforehand. Ron Greenwood was not even on the candidate list,' said Kirton.

And there was residual ill feeling between the two men. In the final days of Greenwood's reign at West Ham, Clough had tapped up Bobby Moore, and later asked Greenwood if he could buy Moore and Trevor Brooking. 'No chance,' was the curt response.

It says much for Greenwood that he could still offer Clough joint-managership of the England youth team.

For all the other candidates' pros and cons, it was probably Greenwood's style and overall compatibility that won the day.

On 12 December 1977, the FA held a press conference and as expected, Greenwood was bombarded by journalists wanting to know just what they could expect to see over the coming months and how he would use his philosophical manner in the dressing room. He merely assured them that all he wanted was common sense and good players. Greenwood was also questioned about whether he had been given too short a time to rebuild a team. He replied, 'Time doesn't worry me. I told them I didn't want a contract. They need not have made a specific time. I want to be a part of something which is going to make England successful. Two and a half years is time to set a pattern.'

The seven-man committee had voted unanimously in favour of Greenwood to continue the work he had already started, although the FA had to act quickly to quell suggestions that not all seven were completely convinced by the appointment.

Although Thompson stressed that there was nothing binding about the date, he gave July 1980 as the end of the contract, 'This will give Mr Greenwood time to take England into the European Championship finals competition in Italy that year.' It would also possibly allow the FA to reconsider should he fail. The FA were still hedging their bets going forward, not wanting to get burnt twice.

All club ties and duties with West Ham were now severed, and the job that Greenwood had secretly doted on for so long was now his. Seeing off the challenge of Clough, the 'people's choice', was not lost on him. He knew that should he fail he could be replaced as easily as hired.

Though there was approval from his star pupil Bobby Moore, 'Ron has certain beliefs about how the game should be played, and constant criticism of certain aspects of what he is doing upsets him. His attitude is, "Let me get on with the job, and if I don't succeed, fire as many bullets as you want."'

One item that Greenwood wanted to address was that of the team being more aggressive in its football. He had been encouraged by more teams at club level being more adventurous, starting to throw off the shackles of more defensive-minded approaches. This also had a reflection in the way the national team played, 'There are emerging now people with courage to take us back to positive football.'

Reflecting on his past talks with the players he had worked with in his tenure as caretaker boss, Greenwood knew that the players would work and play more efficiently if they were allowed more freedom. Gone were the days of rigid reporting for international duty, where the Revie era had them reporting to a hotel a weekend before a midweek game. 'I would prefer to have them in a happy frame of mind,' said the new man.

One of Greenwood's earliest and best ideas was to urge the FA to set up a chain of command and they agreed to nine more appointments: Bill Taylor and Geoff Hurst as coaches to help him with the senior side; Bobby Robson as manager of the B side with Don Howe as coach; Dave Sexton as manager of the under-21s with Terry Venables as coach; and Brian Clough, Peter Taylor and the FA's Ken Burton as joint managers of the youth team. Except for Taylor, they were all Winterbottom graduates from the coaching scheme.

Greenwood wanted to put in place a coaching structure that was based on what Helmut Schön had done in Germany and would serve England in the years that followed.

The Clough–Taylor experiment soon blew up. Their first trip was to Las Palmas where Clough upset the FA officials, who almost outnumbered the players. The unfortunate Burton was the first to resign, telling Greenwood, 'I can't put up with that.' The joint managers lasted a year before resigning, Clough summing up his relationship with the FA selectors thus, 'They rejected me because they were scared stiff. They wanted a diplomat, and I wasn't one. It was the worst decision they ever made.'

Asked by reporters to whom he was accountable as England manager, Greenwood replied, 'The whole country.' He knew that years of failure followed by the Revie scandal had increased the pressure on the incumbent to unprecedented levels.

'I was fully aware of all the press criticism that would come with the job if things went badly, as well as the high expectations in the country at large,' he recalled. 'For me it was a question of getting a group of good people together, and I was lucky to have Bobby Robson and Don Howe in the setup. After Don Revie had gone overseas, there was even greater interest in the position, but we just got stuck into the job and tried to forget about the pressure. But I enjoyed it from the beginning. It was an enormous challenge, and I was happy to get back on the training field again. I'd been with the youth team and the under-23s, so I just tried to see it as a continuation of that.'

* * *

Greenwood relished the next two friendlies: West Germany in Munich in February 1978 and Brazil at Wembley in April, both World Cup winners of recent vintage. 'The two games that followed my confirmation as England manager were the finest tests available. They might have been arranged in heaven,' he said. Yet England lost 2-1 in the Munich snow – 'A beautiful defeat,' said Italian manager Enzo Bearzot. 'To say that the English lost unjustly is the best compliment you can pay to Greenwood' – and a depleted side held Brazil 1-1. 'Not very impressive on the face of it but those two games were an important part of our education,' Greenwood would later write.

Greenwood derived even greater satisfaction from beating the Hungarians 4-1 at Wembley before they left for the 1978 World Cup in Argentina. One of the visitors' coaches reportedly told Sir Stanley Rous, 'England played like Hungary at their best.'

Brian Glanville wrote of the West Germany fixture, 'Ron was once again blessedly following his own instincts. It was a game which showed us that the reports of the death of English football had been greatly exaggerated. It showed that Greenwood's new regime had brought optimism and good humour into an ambience soured by the fear-ridden attitudes of Don Revie.'

Results for the rest of that 1977/78 season continued to be satisfactory, with wins in all three British Home Championship games following that 4-1 dismissal of Hungary.

Greenwood was nevertheless all too aware that one of the big problems facing him when he took over the England job was the variety of football styles in the domestic league. Whereas there was a certain conformity to the continental game in which teams built their attacks from the back, patiently keeping possession until movement off the ball created an opening, English football was a boiling pot of different styles. Some teams played with wingers, some relied on the long ball, some, like Liverpool and Forest, played a passing game at pace – all of which made it difficult for the new manager to establish a pattern of play his players felt comfortable with.

* * *

On 20 September 1978 England played their first qualifier for the European Championship in Italy two years hence. The points gained from a 4-3 victory were to be appreciated, but in terms of technique the match was a disaster with poor defences seemingly intent on surpassing each other in ineptitude.

A nasty side-issue was the scene of some fans causing chaos at refreshment kiosks, which was followed by ugly scenes on the terraces.

Greenwood came away from the ensuing qualifier with a 1-1 draw in Dublin against the Republic of Ireland. The defence this time had given away only one goal but never at any time, gambling again with a midfield that had no ball-winner, did they remotely subdue the most influential player on the pitch, Liam Brady.

Czechoslovakia came to Wembley the following month for a friendly and this time the English defence at last managed a clean sheet with a 1-0 win. The debut of Nottingham Forest's right-back Viv Anderson at least gave the match some historic significance when he became the first black player to play for the senior England side. Greenwood was thus maintaining a long-held 'colour-blind' policy of selecting black players.

The significance of the achievement didn't go unnoticed. The media seemed to regard it as part historic event and part novelty, and in the run-up to the game Anderson received telegrams from Queen Elizabeth II and Elton John. Television reporters visited his parents' home in Nottingham and broadcast a feature to mark the historic event.

When they played Northern Ireland at Wembley the following February, before the second consecutive 92,000 crowd, England brushed their opponents aside 4-0. Greenwood opined that teamwork and understanding were at the root of England's positive run but admitted that some problems still needed to be solved.

Bulgaria were beaten 3-0 in the one game of the summer tour which really counted, the European qualifier in Sofia, and Sweden, held 0-0 in a Stockholm friendly, couldn't breach England's defence either. But then Austria, surprisingly, scored four times in Vienna when the rearguard seemed to crumble. Attempting to put a brave face on such a defeat amid such shaky defending, Greenwood still insisted, 'We certainly proved that we are a team with plenty of character and spirit and there is enough evidence to suggest that we are progressing along the right lines.'

* * *

The opening international of the 1979/80 season witnessed a meagre 1-0 win at Wembley in a qualifier against Denmark. The following month, England overwhelmed Northern Ireland 5-1 in Belfast.

Even arch critic Brian Glanville conceded, 'Credit where credit was due, Greenwood, after a timorous and uncertain start in which he seemed reluctant to follow his true promptings, had lifted the miasma of fear, foreboding and negativity which was the relic of the Revie years. People wanted to play for him, and they wanted above all to play football.'

England then won the return against Bulgaria at Wembley 2-0 with the second goal being scored by debutant Glenn Hoddle. Even so, Greenwood would drop him from the next match with the bizarre excuse that 'disappointment is part of football'.

The fixture had been postponed for 24 hours because of fog, and Greenwood was not alone in thinking the crowd would be a smallish one for a game played on a Thursday evening, but all the fans were there again as 71,000 turned out, and the manager saw this a good sign: 'We had gone a long, long way to restoring faith in our national side. The way we were playing and winning counted once more. England mattered.'

Nevertheless, the media fuss over Hoddle would not go away. The player himself would tell journalist Henry Winter, '[I] played really well, scored a really good goal, made the other goal and had a great game … But I played that Bulgaria game, and then didn't play for three games which was really frustrating … I played mostly on the right wing which really did frustrate me.'

For his part, Greenwood believed the player was never properly fit, that he floated into poor positions and was not as commanding as he should have been. He also considered Hoddle obsessed with the long ball, as Johnny Haynes was. As a player Greenwood had witnessed the manner in which Haynes was indulged at the expense of the Fulham team.

Greenwood was also being criticised for not having settled on tactics and a core team. He was accused of recalling players who had been given chances but not made the grade, while leaving out those who clearly had.

Then, as if to answer his critics, in March Spain were well beaten 2-0 in Barcelona, with a performance of such virtuosity that one Spanish newspaper described their play as 'out of this world' and suggested that the country's footballers should go to England to finish their education.

England would beat world champions Argentina 3-1 at Wembley in May, though they were never able to contain a dazzling Diego Maradona. But their form deserted them in the first two matches of the British Home Championship. A 4-1 defeat by Wales was not the best result to improve a team's self-esteem. A 1-1 draw against Northern Ireland followed, and when England arrived in Glasgow for their final match they were presented with a giant wooden spoon. The gift was handed back the next day as

Greenwood's side silenced 80,000 Scots at Hampden Park with goals from Brooking and Coppell.

A trip to play Australia in Sydney climaxed what must have been one of the happiest periods of Greenwood's managerial life. With only three defeats in the team's first 29 matches under his stewardship, 20 of which were won, England were in good shape ahead of the 1980 European Championship. They had qualified after all by dropping only one point from a group comprising Bulgaria, Denmark, Northern Ireland and the Republic. Eight players played in six of the eight matches, a marked contrast with Revie's constant chopping and changing. While sticking with a fairly experienced group of players during the qualifiers, he also gave youth its chance to impress by handing debuts to Hoddle, Bryan Robson and Kenny Sansom, all of whom would have significant England careers.

Greenwood maintained that the format was simple but adaptable, 'We were solid at the back, an area which never lost me any sleep. There was variety and enterprise in the middle and going forward we had width and pace. The side was experienced too and could adjust and improvise to meet the unexpected.'

Greenwood could justifiably claim to have successfully restored England to the top tier of world football. As a consequence, he found himself welcomed by the nation's sports writers who, after years of embarrassments, were happy finally to be reporting some good news. The players, too, were happy with the more relaxed regime off the pitch which allowed them to have a pint or three in the evening rather than don plastic smiles as the carpet bowls were brought out. 'If players like to relax by having a drink, why stop them? They're grown men,' said Greenwood.

According to Trevor Brooking, the boss succeeded in quickly restoring morale: 'Under Ron, there was a much happier, more relaxed atmosphere in the squad, and that was reflected on the pitch. There was less of the tension which had built up under Don Revie.'

However, like all his predecessors, Greenwood was frustrated by the small amount of time the Football League were prepared to yield to the national side, 'It's completely different from managing a club side because you are only with the players a short time. It's not like being with them every day. The one thing I tried to establish was some continuity whereby whenever we met, we felt as if we had never been apart. I tried to create a club atmosphere with all my staff and players.'

Greenwood's transformation of the England team also drew a wave of plaudits from across the continent. 'He thinks European,' said Germany's manager Helmut Schön. 'Unlike a lot of people in English football, he can see beyond Dover.'

Brooking spent the majority of his career playing under Greenwood at West Ham and England. He later wrote, 'Working with the country's best players comes easier to him than the day-to-day involvement with players at a club. If Ron had a weakness, I would say it is in handling players, or man management, at club level. Not every player in a club responds the same way to the manager, and during his 16 years at Upton Park Ron had his problems with one or two players. At club level it is not easy for the manager to move dissident players out quickly. At international level it is simple: you do not invite them back for the next match. Ron Greenwood liked being England manager more than being a club manager because his strength is the football and coaching side and working with the players. The other side, the arguing with players about money and contracts, was less appealing to him.'

* * *

In *Who Dares Wins: Britain: 1979–1982*, the historian Dominic Sandbrook wrote, 'With the winds of recession whipping through the factories of industrial Britain, the prospect of victory in the Italian sunshine came as a welcome tonic. Even the manager, Ron Greenwood, seemed a throwback to a vanished age.'

And as Greenwood prepared to lead his men to take on the continent's finest in the 1980 European Championship, the *Daily Express*'s David Miller joined many of his fellow writers in predicting that the manager's 'lonely crusade to change the face of English football' would end in triumph. 'By that achievement, with the style Greenwood has promoted,' he wrote, 'England would have done more for the world of football than any team other than Hungary, Brazil or Holland.'

Viscount Montgomery, probably the most well-known of Britain's Second World War generals, once told Greenwood, 'Any leader has to have luck in his rucksack,' and he admitted he had had plenty. But in the weeks before the tournament Greenwood was running short of it. Trevor Francis snapped an Achilles tendon and Kevin Keegan was suffering from a long season with Hamburg. These two had been the team's most potent attackers. But their lack of fitness was not the reason England failed.

Former prime minister Harold Wilson had started the habit of putting himself before the cameras with the England football squad to court support and even current incumbent Margaret Thatcher did the same in 1980. After a cocktail party at 10 Downing Street the team flew out to their base at Asti, near Turin. With an excellent record under Greenwood they were considered to have as good a chance as anyone of being crowned champions of Europe three weeks later.

After a week together, the players and staff flew out to Italy on the Tuesday, just two days before their opening game against Belgium. Euro '80 was the first to contain eight countries, a move away from the previous format of four teams playing a straight knockout tournament. The eight sides – Greece, England, the Netherlands, Czechoslovakia, Spain, Belgium, West Germany and hosts Italy – were placed in two groups of four, with both group winners contesting the final, and the runners-up meeting in a seemingly pointless third-place play-off.

Greenwood was optimistic without being overly confident and viewed the tournament as another stepping stone in the bigger pond of world football.

He wrote, 'The European Nations Championship reflected all that's good in football during the Belgrade final matches in 1976. I only hope that when we reflect on this next championship, we will be able to say that England have contributed to another fine tournament in which the standards of the game can again be held as an example to the world.'

On paper, the biggest obstacle to English hopes appeared to be Italy, the host nation. Yet their opponents in the opening group match proved to be the surprise package of the tournament. Belgium had qualified by winning a group that contained Scotland, Austria, Portugal and Norway. And they had won seven games in a row leading up to the finals.

'You would be very silly to underestimate us,' said manager Guy Thys before the tournament. 'People talk as if Italy and England are the only teams in our group. Of course, I am concerned with them. But they worry me far less than West Germany or Holland would.'

English eyes were more focused on their own team. 'Today England will begin to learn the true currency of the recovery which has been achieved under the direction of Ron Greenwood over the last three years,' wrote David Lacey in his preview of the Belgium match for *The Guardian*. Not quite a nation expects, more a case of cautious optimism after the years of drought.

Hooliganism was a growing problem in England, and it was tarnishing the country's reputation abroad. Riots involving Spurs fans at the 1974 UEFA Cup Final, Leeds supporters at the 1975 European Cup Final, and England followers in Luxembourg in 1977 were just a few examples of an issue that would become known as 'the English disease'. The night before England's opening match in Turin, police arrested 36 English supporters.

So, in the early evening of 12 June and with millions watching at home, England's finest walked out into the sunshine in Turin for their opening match against the unfancied Belgians, whom Greenwood had watched five times. Ray Wilkins beat the persistent offside trap and scored with a lovely lob, but deplorable defending allowed Jan Ceulemans to equalise within minutes and suddenly fighting broke out among a section of the England supporters. The Italian police used their batons and fired tear gas. This started spreading towards the pitch and Greenwood persuaded the referee to stop play so that goalkeeper Ray Clemence and other England players could be treated for sore eyes.

England's first game in a finals tournament for a decade finished 1-1 and Greenwood, finally losing his composure, said angrily in a BBC interview, 'In ten minutes these imbeciles have ruined it for us. They should be put on a boat, and halfway across someone should pull out the plug.' UEFA arranged an emergency meeting to discuss the violent scenes, with a points deduction or even expulsion mooted as possible punishments. The resulting £8,000 fine was seen as lenient, with FA chairman Harold Thompson admitting, 'It could have been a lot more serious for us. But it is a pity we have to pay for the actions of those sewer rats.'

Yet again, now on the crumbling terraces of Turin's Stadio Comunale where a paltry 15,186 fans had paid to see the game, came bedlam. Journalist Frank McGhee wrote, 'The louts and drunks who defile the Union Jack they wrap around themselves immediately started hitting out at any neutral who happened to be handy.'

At half-time, with running battles continuing in the stands, an official read a message from Greenwood over the public address system, 'You are doing the chances of the England team and the reputation of England no good at all. Please, please behave yourselves.'

Greenwood said he felt ashamed of his own supporters. 'We have done everything to create the right impression here, then these bastards let you down,' he said bluntly.

The manager was also incensed by the disallowing of what seemed a perfectly legitimate goal by Tony Woodcock, but it was the behaviour of England's fans, again, which generated the biggest headlines on the back and front pages. 'We are ashamed of people like this – the Italians must think we are idiots,' said Greenwood.

Mrs Thatcher, who was in Venice for a Common Market Summit, added to the increasing volume of dissenting voices, 'The behaviour of some British supporters in Turin was disgraceful. When they come here, they are ambassadors and should show the best of Britain. It was a very dark day.'

But 24 hours is a long time in football, long enough to calm down and perhaps regret some outlandish remarks. Greenwood was the first to admit that his comment of taking unwanted followers on to a boat and pulling out the plug was harsh, but it was a general feeling in the heat of the moment. It took a lot to get Greenwood so riled up, but in this case, he was seeing years of hard work suddenly extinguished through no fault of his own, or of his players.

England's next game was against Italy three days later at the same venue, but this time with 60,000 spectators packed in, most of them fervently behind the hosts. Everyone was worried about further disturbances, and there were reportedly more than 1,500 policemen on duty. Perhaps this gave the English yobs second thoughts, and there were no arrests.

The Italians had not been beaten on their own territory in ten years and a tight encounter was settled by a Marco Tardelli goal, ending England's hopes of reaching the final.

A 2-1 victory over Spain in Naples kept alive hopes of making the third-place match, but, perhaps thankfully, a 0-0 draw between Italy and Belgium ended England's campaign after three matches.

Against Spain, Greenwood profitably used Keegan as a striker, with plenty of evidence of Hoddle's potential at this level in midfield. Brooking and Woodcock scored; Dani replied from a penalty.

Once it was confirmed that England would not be in the play-off, the BBC replaced live coverage of the match with the Tommy Steele film *Half a Sixpence*. If ever one decision summed up the lack of enthusiasm for Euro '80 and football in general in the country, then this was it. Italy against Czechoslovakia would hardly have been a ratings winner, but the lack of interest showed just how apathetic the country was to the game at the time.

* * *

Greenwood's luck had been miniscule. Still, it did him no credit to lament England's poor fortune when they had laboured miserably against Belgium, could have given four goals away to Italy and were unconvincing winners against Spain. It was a less than distinguished contribution by England and their unruly followers.

Greenwood had used 19 of the 22 players during the tournament, a sign that after three years in charge he still didn't know his best team.

He also allowed himself to be upset about the way he was criticised by the ITV panel. Ted Croker said in his book, *The First Voice You Will Hear Is*, 'He suffered from it but was a master of disguising his feelings. One of the few times I saw him really annoyed was when he had been criticised or misinterpreted in the press. That was his one weakness, if it could be called a weakness, he tended to be over-sensitive in the face of criticism.

'None of us really like being told we are wrong, and the manager of the national football team is told by more people than most. It needs a strong personality to withstand such criticism.'

'There is nothing I can think of that I would have done differently,' said Greenwood defiantly as the team prepared to pack up and leave Italy. There was the inevitable talk that he might be pushed out before having a chance to lead his team into the World Cup qualifying games, something his captain couldn't understand. 'We feel, as players, that we have let him down. The bottom would fall out of our lives if he were to go,' said Keegan. *The Sun*, nevertheless, made its feelings plain with a headline simply reading 'For God's Sake Go'.

Reflecting a few years later on the tournament, Greenwood still thought that the finals should have been 'a showpiece for football but they proved to be perfectly in tune with the modern game. They were dull, wretchedly supported, and coldly undermined by live football. We travelled in high hope and returned with empty hearts.

'The football was functional at best and instantly forgettable at most other times. There was a chronic shortage of originality which depressed me because it seemed to be a signpost to the future. The matches were an indictment of the game rather than a celebration of it. Football is what men choose to make of it and Europe's best players made a pig's ear of the tournament.

'I did not conjure up any excuses or hard luck stories about England's modest achievements in Italy because in a short, high-pressure tournament like this a side either gets it right or it doesn't. Every nation has its problems, but winners patch them up and still manage to peak. I thought we did everything we could to prepare our players for the job, and our build-up, organisation and spirit were right on cue. But when we came to it, we could not make good the loss of Trevor Francis or a Kevin Keegan below his best.'

The 1980 tournament was described as 'leaden, negative and lacking in outstanding players' and hardly a rip-roaring success.

Attendances were low for matches not featuring Italy; there were only 7,614 fans in Rome's Stadio Olimpico for the group game between Greece and Czechoslovakia, and the final was not even a sell-out. The *Daily Mirror*'s McGhee described the whole affair as 'a morass of mediocrity'. England's tournament seemed to sum up the situation neatly: not a complete embarrassment, but hardly exciting.

Come the end of it all there was a familiar outcome as West Germany beat Belgium in the final. Although England failed to make an impact, they had at least returned to the top table in Europe. It was just a shame that, when they got there, the behaviour of their fans dominated the headlines.

* * *

The draw for the qualifying rounds for the 1982 World Cup provided England with what seemed a relatively straightforward passage to the finals in Spain. In a group of five from which two teams would go through, their opponents were Norway, Romania, Hungary and Switzerland – reasonable teams all of them but not exactly world-beaters.

Greenwood attempted to provide a note of caution. 'There are no easy internationals these days,' he quipped when the draw was concluded.

The national press adopted the opposite way of thinking. They thought the draw was as good as printing the flight tickets, booking the hotels and slapping on the suntan lotion. 'If England fail to qualify for the 1982 World Cup finals, they should be retired forever to a shelf in the British Museum,' wrote David Miller of the *Daily Express*.

First up, at Wembley in early September, were Norway, where England triumphed by the handsome margin of 4-0.

The first away qualifier was in Bucharest against Romania. After a sobering 2-1 defeat, Greenwood had to admit, 'Romania were an awkward side, Latin-European in style, technically sharp and good spoilers. We lacked real craft in midfield and found difficulty in breaking them down. We did not deserve more than a draw, but we did deserve that on our second half performance.'

A 2-1 victory against Switzerland the following month at Wembley at least maintained hopes of qualifying. Before the game, Greenwood plaintively appealed for people to stop denigrating his team and encourage it instead. That may be why, despite a plodding performance, the 70,000 spectators restrained the slow handclap until the 90th minute, greeting the final whistle with an outburst of booing.

In March 1981, at the third time of asking, Spain finally got the better of England at Wembley by a 2-1 margin in a friendly, but qualifying fixtures were back at the end of April 1981 with the return match with Romania, and again England were firing blanks in a 0-0 scoreline.

Just to rub things in, Paul Breitner, the ever-contentious and quotable West Germany left-back, dismissed English football as 'stupid', lacking subtlety, relying for goals on mere pressure.

There then followed a further three matches at Wembley, two of which were lost – to Brazil in a friendly and Scotland in the British Home Championship, with only a draw against Wales breaking the rot – and without a goal scored.

As if Greenwood didn't have enough problems, on the morning of that Scotland defeat newspapers were claiming that the manager had bowed to player power in dropping Peter Barnes. Greenwood was understandably annoyed at the suggestion, and Trevor Brooking would later claim that no such discussions had taken place among the players.

But with the results being what they were, the press were only too happy to seek out any opportunity to put the knife in.

The criticism that followed England's exit in Italy was relatively mild, but by the same time the following year the press was clamouring for Greenwood's head following an astonishing slump in form. England were clearly struggling to find their rhythm and confidence as they suffered their worst ever sequence of results at Wembley.

Greenwood grew used to the chants of 'What a load of rubbish!' echoing around the ground as he made the long walk back to face a group of journalists who were becoming increasingly hostile with every match. The tabloid newspapers of the period make for uncomfortable reading for those, like Greenwood, of a sensitive nature. Such was the directness and intensity of the attacks that the mild-mannered Greenwood exploded at the press conference after the Scotland match.

Subeditors at *The Sun*, the most unforgiving and unrestrained of the tabloids in the 1980s, showed an especially vicious wit in their headlines. After the goalless draw with Wales in May the back page read 'WALK SMALL', and Frank Clough, the chief football writer, warmed up for what would become an all-out assault in the coming weeks. 'The worry lines are back and biting deeply into Ron Greenwood's brow … Not to beat about the bush, England were pathetic.'

Greenwood was starting to experience the massive difference between managing a club and managing a country. 'If West Ham or Preston lose, only the people of West Ham and Preston are upset, but if England lose it's a national disaster,' he wrote. In his autobiography, Greenwood put the experience more poetically, 'Victory is a slice of heaven and defeat is a step towards the fire below.'

But there was much worse to come. On the day of the Scotland defeat, 23 May, *The Sun* ran the headline 'FOR PETE'S SAKE'. In his report Clough claimed that Greenwood had been pressured by the players to drop Barnes. After the 1-0 loss a thunder-faced Greenwood marched into the press conference and flew at the massed ranks of raincoats and notepads ranged before him. He said, 'To all of you a big thank you. I have been stabbed in the back. The prefabricated messages that went out today about my speaking to the players was the biggest load of journalistic licence I have ever read.' And with that he turned on his heel and stormed from the room.

The papers clearly enjoyed the confrontation. 'RON HITS ROCK BOTTOM' ran the headline in the *Sunday Mirror*. In his report, Ken Montgomery showed his quarry little mercy, 'England's goalless, guileless, soccer squad head for Switzerland and Hungary on Thursday – facing the worst results sequence in their 109-year history. Don Revie had a run of six winless games in 1977 – and that signalled his departure. Incredibly, Greenwood still has the backing of the FA.'

Greenwood would claim that he never let the press criticism get to him, 'I just ignored the headlines. You appreciated that they had a job to do but what you had to do was try and win them over by getting close to them and letting them know what's going on and not trying to keep anything secret. You wanted to get them on your side, and that was the main thing. I found it easy to relax after games because I went home to a strong family, to people not connected with the job, and so I could shut it out of my mind.'

At the end of May, England travelled to Basel for the return qualifier against Switzerland and fell to yet another 2-1 defeat.

Brian Glanville called the result 'humiliating', suggesting, 'With his tactics, Ron Greenwood looked a busted flush. How obscure it was that the FA should persevere with a team manager who had long since lost all direction, consistency and coherence.'

Elsewhere, the flak was becoming more personal with *The Sun* outdoing its rival the *Daily Mirror* with more and more damning headlines such as 'For God's Sake, Ron, Pack Up'. Greenwood said, 'People were looking on me as though I had committed some crime. I was hurt, and I had a feeling of shame.' As if a defeat and the attendant abuse wasn't bad enough, pot-bellied hooligans wearing T-shirts with the words 'Battle of Turin' resumed the hooligan war, smashing up the centre of Basel, and then turning on the football stadium. Greenwood felt sick to the bottom of his stomach. *The Mirror*'s front page captured the mood, 'A stab in the back for Britain!'

The so-called 'Battle of Basel' was a genuinely shameful moment for English football. Only 2,000 fans had travelled to Switzerland, yet they caused mayhem.

'The Union Jack,' said *The Express,* had become a 'flag of shame' while *The Guardian*'s Patrick Barclay opined, 'The events in Turin and Basel … verged on international incidents which went beyond football.'

Greenwood could not be blamed for thinking of quitting and within a minute or two of the final whistle against Switzerland he had decided to retire. Two days later, he told Dick Wragg, his immediate boss, and FA secretary Ted Croker, 'Not resign, just retire. This will leave you with room to bring in someone in good time for Spain.'

'Don't be daft,' said Wragg. The three men decided to keep the news quiet until the second game on the summer tour of 1981, against Hungary in Budapest.

Michael Hart, a long-time close friend of Greenwood's who covered England matches for the *Evening Standard*, said, 'It wasn't pressure from the media that made him feel like resigning though. What was written about him and his team was water off a duck's back to him and he didn't feel pressure in that sense.

'He found the baggage that came with a few of the players a bit distasteful, but it was a feeling that he was no longer the right man for the job that made him want to stand down. When Ron handed over to John Lyall at West Ham, he'd become a little bit cynical about the game. He felt that perhaps he should have been given the chance to manage England a little earlier, at the time Don Revie got the job.'

For England to retain any chance of reaching the World Cup finals, victory in Budapest was essential. And they achieved it, on a ground where they had not won since 1909, and where indeed they had been thrashed 7-1 in 1953. Finally Greenwood had triumphed, and in a nation whose football had always meant so much to him.

However welcome, the 3-1 win did not change the manager's decision to retire. Post-match, journalists must have been taken aback by his brief summary. 'I'd like to thank you for your support over the years,' he said. 'Our win was a good one, well deserved, and it's given me great pleasure to beat the Hungarians. I don't want to answer any questions. Thank you.' At that he left the room. None of them seemed to realise the real meaning of his words.

On the flight back to Luton Airport, Greenwood finally told the players it had been his last game in charge. He looked emotional and the squad were stunned. 'You're out of order,' said Keegan. Mick Mills allegedly told him, 'If you retire, I'll never speak to you again.' The journalists sitting at the back of the plane knew nothing of the drama being played out. On the ground, the players were still in groups discussing what should happen as they waited for their luggage. Dick Wragg, who had returned to London earlier, was going to make the announcement inside the main hall. Suddenly, Greenwood, almost overcome by the emotion of the players' reaction, told the squad, 'Okay then. I'll tell Mr Wragg I won't resign. I'll give it until after the World Cup.' Greenwood gave the news to Wragg, who said, 'I was going to have another go to change your mind, but you've saved me the trouble.'

Yet there still wasn't a hint in the papers the next day that Greenwood was on his way out of football. It was remarkable, in a sport where the slightest whiff of a rumour can produce a back-page story after someone has added two and two and come up with five.

Greenwood later remembered the occasion well, 'I was very moved by their support. I had begun to feel very downhearted, but it was touching that they still believed in what we were doing. We had built up that kind of spirit in the squad despite the run of bad results.'

Bryon Butler, who co-wrote Greenwood's autobiography, believes the relationship between the England setup and the press changed beyond all recognition at the start of the 1980s, 'The thicker the skin an England manager can get hold of these days the better. Now the media coverage has become an absolute circus. Even at the beginning of Greenwood's time in charge there was still a manageable amount of media. There was a chap from each of the main papers and that was that.

On the day after the match about half a dozen of us would go and have breakfast with Ron and discuss the game. We would all be there for up to a couple of hours just chatting about the match. It was all very friendly.

'After a while, other TV companies and radio stations started to say, "Why can't we come along?" So the FA started to hire a room in the hotel and there would be about 12 or 15 reporters there. But it was still nothing compared to recent years. Now radio people queue, TV people queue and then there are all the papers who want it carved up for themselves. The amount of media attention on the England setup is monumental now.

'For the last 20 years or so the manager has become part of a circulation war or the victim of an editor or journalist trying to establish his reputation. They're trying to outdo each other at the England manager's expense. There was always aggro in Revie's time, but it got really nasty in the Greenwood era. The problem is the increasing number of media organisations, which has brought more competition and a hardening of attitudes.'

Greenwood had been talked out of resigning by his players, with Keegan to the fore. Two decades later Keegan himself was the England manager. After a miserable 1-0 defeat to Germany in a World Cup qualifier at Wembley, he too was serenaded by cries of 'What a load of rubbish'. He too told the players he was resigning, echoing Greenwood. But Keegan stuck to his guns and walked away from the impossible job.

* * *

England had scored no fewer than four goals on each of their five previous encounters with Norway, and they travelled to Oslo in September 1981 in the knowledge that anything less than a victory would, barring the unexpected, mean they would not be going to Spain.

Norway, then still relative minnows in international football, pulled off probably the greatest result in their history as England slumped to a 2-1 defeat, the first time they had lost to the Scandinavians.

As events unfolded in front of him, Greenwood must surely have pondered upon the wisdom of not sticking to his decision to retire after the Hungary victory because after having taken the lead in Oslo, England fell apart as their opponents scored twice before half-time.

Predictably, the criticism of Greenwood and his team rained in from all directions back home; the matter of England's evident decline as a footballing power even provoked a debate in the House of Commons.

'I felt like public enemy number one,' said Greenwood. And he probably was.

In a broadcast that has become part of football folklore in both countries, Norwegian commentator Bjørge Lillelien exploded in a frenzy of nationalistic pride at the final whistle for state broadcaster NRK.

'We have beaten England! England, birthplace of giants. Lord Nelson! Lord Beaverbrook! Winston Churchill! Henry Cooper! Clement Attlee! Anthony Eden! Lady Diana! Der stod them all! Der stod them all! Maggie Thatcher can you hear me?

Can you hear me Maggie? Your boys took one hell of a beating tonight!'

Lillelien's tirade was voted the greatest piece of football commentary in *Observer Sport Monthly* magazine in 2002.

This outburst was later chosen by the Norwegian Arts Council to represent their country's contribution to mankind's cultural heritage.

'Will you get the sack tomorrow?' Greenwood was asked by a Norwegian TV commentator. 'Will you get the sack tomorrow?' he replied. 'I don't know,' was the confused response. 'And neither do I. Next question please.' England's manager was not in a jovial mood.

Outside the plate glass window of the room where Greenwood was giving his press conference, a disgusted young fan was mouthing inaudible insults, finally tearing off his England scarf and stamping on it.

Yet somehow, Greenwood's men managed to scrape through the group, while Norway would finish bottom as football has a habit of throwing up the most extraordinary results, not least on 10 October 1981. When Greenwood took his seat at Maine Road for the second half of the Manchester derby it was with a sly grin across his face as Switzerland had won 2-1 in Romania.

Ridiculed for his optimism when all others were writing his football obituary, he could now feel a little justified. Perhaps the luck Montgomery said he needed had finally made an appearance.

Romania and Hungary had been the favourites to go through – until Switzerland, the no-hopers in the group, came to England's rescue by beating Romania in Bucharest and then holding them to a goalless draw in Berne.

The latter game was played on 11 November 1981 – Greenwood's 60th birthday. Quite the unexpected present.

A month after the defeat in Norway, in an unprecedented move, Football League secretary Graham Kelly had agreed to postpone games the Saturday before the final qualifier at Wembley against Hungary.

With the excitement and anticipation building the 18 November encounter was officially declared a sell-out. The sale of tickets had risen sharply after Switzerland's win in Romania had opened the door again. England were now ready to push through it with 92,000 braced to watch first-hand.

England may now have needed only a draw at home to Hungary but nevertheless, it was a situation which prompted discomforting parallels with the match against Poland eight years earlier that had cost Alf Ramsey's men a place in West Germany. And the tabloids were not letting up. On the day of the match, stories appeared on their front pages reporting that Glenn Hoddle and others had been on a drinking binge the night before.

Hungary themselves were already certain of qualification, so there would be no pressure on them at Wembley, and Greenwood was encouraged sufficiently to tell his players that they had been given a 'kiss of life'.

Meditating nostalgically before the game, Greenwood reflected, 'Football's emotional, it's involved, it stirs everybody's imagination. That's why it's such a beautiful game; there are so many opinions.'

In the event, the match was scarcely remarkable for drama, while one goal, from Paul Mariner, was enough to ensure an unconvincing England victory. Naturally, Greenwood's wife

Lucy was there in the stands. She had still to see England lose at Wembley.

It meant England qualified as runners-up in Group 4 for the 1982 World Cup in Spain, their first appearance on that stage since 1970.

As Greenwood strolled, head up, back to the tunnel, 92,000 voices boomed out a rendition of 'You'll Never Walk Alone'. England and Greenwood had pulled off what one paper called 'The Great Escape'.

For the whole week after the match the England manager wore the tie he had bought in Switzerland.

England then beat Northern Ireland 4-0 at Wembley in February and won 1-0 in Wales at the end of April in the British Home Championship, before playing twice late in May – beating the Netherlands at home in a friendly then returning to the British competition for a 1-0 win at Hampden against Scotland.

For the latter two games, Greenwood was without his Tottenham players, who were preparing for the FA Cup Final, and his Aston Villa players, who were in Rotterdam winning the European Cup Final, so he must have been delighted with the two victories. Having suffered that embarrassing defeat to Norway six months earlier, Greenwood's team had now won five games in a row. Things were looking up.

England had another warm-up match scheduled for Thursday, 3 June, in Helsinki to mark the 75th anniversary of the Finnish FA. England had also organised to play a B international in Iceland the night before the Finland friendly, but it was assumed the majority of players picked for this fixture would not be boarding the plane to Spain for the World Cup.

With England facing two games in two countries in two days, Greenwood divided the 32-man group in half, with 16 players going to Reykjavík and 16 going to Helsinki. 'It should not be taken as read that the 16 players going to Finland can assume they are automatically in the final squad of 22,' said Greenwood, although it was hard not to arrive at this conclusion.

Greenwood was not in attendance in Iceland, but he was determined that the match would not be dismissed as a pointless exercise and even appealed to the FA's International Committee that the game be awarded full international status. 'A team of such strength deserves caps,' he said, even though the match would be widely reported as a B international or Iceland v an England XI.

There was very little hype surrounding the game, and the blustery conditions and poor playing surface did little to encourage free-flowing football. The press dedicated very few words to the 1-1 draw in Reykjavík, concentrating instead on the game in Finland. *The Guardian* had described the situation as 'Possibles tonight, Probables tomorrow' in its preview of the Iceland fixture. 'Goddard saves England's face' declared the headline in the same paper in reference to West Ham striker Paul Goddard scoring his team's only goal, as the tabloids praised Hoddle.

England had played half a dozen matches before departing for Spain. All were won except for that weakened team drawing in Iceland. Clean sheets were kept in four of the games. Perhaps now that qualification had been secured there was less pressure on players who had struggled in Oslo and Berne.

* * *

It was a long 12 years since England had reached the World Cup finals and their emergence in 1982 was dogged by political considerations. The Falklands War was going on in the spring and though the FA wanted the team to still go to Spain, there was a lot of pressure on them to withdraw England.

There was even discussion as to if any of the home countries should be prepared to participate in a tournament which included Argentina – who had invaded the Falkland Islands and thus started a war with Britain. There was a threat from FIFA that the home countries risked being fined, should they pull out, but fortunately the conflict was settled just as the tournament kicked off. Britain had won the war and it was decided that Greenwood and his men could win football matches in Spain as well.

The draw for the finals, on paper at least, was good to England, pitching them in a relatively easy-looking group with France, Czechoslovakia and Kuwait, and basing them in the northern coastal town of Bilbao. But given England's problems qualifying from an 'easy' group nobody in the party was taking anything for granted, not least the manager.

Greenwood had spared no detail in his preparations for England's first appearance in a World Cup since 1970. Accompanied by the FA's administration officer, Alan Odell, he went on a reconnaissance mission to test everything from the firmness of mattresses in hotels to the security and cooking arrangements.

Security worries were heightened by the threat from ETA, the Basque separatist group that was still active and killing people in the Basque region.

The San Mamés Stadium, known locally as 'The Cathedral', was similar to English grounds in its design with the crowd pressed right up against the pitch. There were understandable fears among Bilbao's 600,000-strong population in the industrial port that England's notorious hooligans would cause mayhem, but a few months before the finals Greenwood struck a diplomatic blow for the country when he took over an England XI to play Athletic Bilbao in a testimonial match that drew a crowd of 40,000 and finished in a 1-1 draw.

There was another much less welcome innovation – the arrival of 'The Rottweilers'. The FA's Glen Kirton explained, 'With hooliganism rearing its head, the newspapers sent news reporters to follow England as well as the usual sports journalists. They were known as "The Rottweilers". Their job was to dig out tasty stories for the front pages and some of them were pretty upsetting.

'Ron didn't like what appeared, but you had to grin and bear it. At the end of the tournament, the regular journalists chipped in to pay for an expensive watch for Ron when he retired, with an engraved message of thanks. Ron also got on well with the sports writers, although one or two papers used to annoy him. There was one who got up his nose, the freelance Andrew Warshaw. He used to keep asking infuriating questions, like about his cream cake consumption.'

Another smart move by Greenwood to win over the locals in Bilbao was to invite on board an old playing opponent, Ronnie Allen, the former West Bromwich and England forward who had once managed Athletic Bilbao. Allen spoke fluent Spanish and was used as an interpreter and advisor.

By the time England arrived in Bilbao, they had put together a run of seven matches without defeat, and they tackled France in their opening group game only 24 hours after the Falklands War had ended. Only 27 seconds had been played when Bryan Robson scored the fastest goal in the history of the competition. While France equalised, Robson struck again and Mariner made it 3-1 to get the team off to a good start.

After their well-deserved victory against the French, in oppressive summer heat, England would meet a Czech team who had laboured in their opening match against Kuwait. Goals from Mariner and Trevor Francis did the trick, and England topped their group.

Kevin Keegan and Trevor Brooking, who were unfit when they arrived in Spain, were still short of fitness and Greenwood was also worried about Keegan's hyperactivity. Keegan kept complaining about the state of his back, although the team doctor Vernon Edwards told Greenwood that in his view there was nothing wrong with it. Keegan came to Greenwood with an astonishing request. 'I'm still not right,' he said. 'I've got a specialist in Hamburg who treated my back. Do you think I ought to see him?' Greenwood said, 'Well, it's pointless you staying in Spain if you don't think you'll be fit.' So he agreed to a bizarre plan. It was almost midnight. 'How are you going to Hamburg?' asked Greenwood. 'I'll drive to Madrid and catch a flight,' said Keegan.

Keegan set off, alone, on a 250-mile drive. The next day the press naturally wanted to know where he was and Greenwood kept saying, 'He's visiting his specialist.' Which, of course, was true, except that the specialist was in Germany. Four days later, Keegan turned up and declared himself fit.

Having beaten the Czechs, England gave a strangely strangulated performance against Kuwait in a laborious 1-0 win. Francis got the only goal, but England's performance level dropped, being caught offside 20 times, much to the annoyance of Greenwood. He must have been tempted to recall both Brooking and Keegan. He didn't, mainly because if either of them broke down it would ruin the team's chances in the later stages.

This result gave England a 100 per cent record and comfortable qualification from their group, which put them into Group 2 with West Germany and Spain. These were mini-leagues, with no knockout ties until the semi-final stage.

The match against the Germans, in Madrid, was one of drab sterility. The Germans played it tight, and there wasn't a goal in sight. Perhaps it needed a Keegan and a Brooking to break the stalemate, but a cautious Greenwood left them on the bench.

There had been bigger news the day prior to the game as it had been announced that Bobby Robson had been named as his successor, to take over at the end of the World Cup.

Hopes of qualification hinged upon the outcome of Spain's games against England and the Germans, and the latter scored a 2-1 win against the host nation. In the final analysis England would have to master the Spaniards 2-0 or 3-2. Spain had one thing going for them, though; they would be playing in front of 75,000 home fans at Real Madrid's Santiago Bernabéu Stadium. And the atmosphere and support appeared to have stiffened the resolve of England's opponents, who held firm even if they were unable to score themselves. After 63 minutes Greenwood sent on Brooking and Keegan for their only World Cup appearances. Both would miss good chances. The scoreless result meant that England were out, even though they remained undefeated after five matches in which they had conceded just a single goal.

There were tears in the dressing room afterwards, but Greenwood told his players, 'You've done your best. None of you have let your country down. Things just didn't go for you.' As the team coach drove off, a brick was hurled into a window, narrowly missing Greenwood and his coach Don Howe. It was the first time in the tournament there was no police escort. Losers didn't have protection. That was reserved for winners.

Reflecting on the tournament in his autobiography four years later, Greenwood wrote, 'We did not fail but we were stopped one place short of the semi-finals, which would have been happily acknowledged by everyone as success, because we lacked a quality which always separates the winners from the rest at this level. We lacked someone who could provide a flash of brilliance, a player who could suddenly do better than his best and find within himself a moment of rare inspiration or invention. We did not have a killer.

'We have no complaints. We didn't lose a game, so it wasn't so much a moral defeat as a factual defeat. I would like to go on record and thank all the coaches who have helped me, especially Don Howe. Yes, it's been a marvellous five years.'

Now it was the time for Greenwood to go, and he was able to retire with dignity and honour. He had done the job after Don Revie's defection, and he had rightly earned a vote of genuine appreciation from his bosses.

England could consider themselves unfortunate, but at least Greenwood could now retire from football knowing that his reputation as one of the country's best coaches had been restored following the ferocious battering he had suffered in the press 12 months earlier.

He was always a champion of decency, sportsmanship and positive, attractive football. After the disgrace of Revie's departure, he brought dignity back to the number one job. If his chance had come ten years earlier, he might have proved himself to be the greatest manager of all time. He gave Bobby Robson a tough act to follow.

After he arrived home, Greenwood, ever the private man, told the FA that he didn't want his telephone number to be passed on. He wanted to be left alone.

'The impossible job,' he had called his position. The 1982 World Cup was the end for Greenwood, but at least it was a humane end. Greenwood was able to retire to his seaside retreat in Brighton with dignity intact. His influence over English football had been beneficial, in style if not necessarily results.

He watched the 1982 World Cup Final on television at his home, 700 miles from the colour and passion of the Bernabéu, with his wife Lucy, a cup of tea and that little word 'if' to keep him company. He was a former manager of England.

15

Retirement

IN HIS autobiography *Yours Sincerely*, published in 1984, Ron Greenwood described retirement as coming 'at me like a crafty opponent on the blind side. It had come and gone before I realised it.'

He briefly became a director of his local club, Brighton & Hove Albion, as well as a regular analyst on the BBC's radio coverage, reporting on the Mexico World Cup in 1986 and the European Championship in Germany two years later. Journalist and friend Michael Hart recalled how the experience of being 'on the other side' gave Greenwood a greater understanding of the media, 'Ron spent quite a lot of time with the press and came to understand us a bit more. In Mexico, we stayed in the same hotel as the England team and although he was quite close to Bobby Robson, Ron deliberately kept out of the way of him and his players. He didn't feel it was his place to get involved.'

Having already served as a technical adviser to FIFA at the 1966 and 1970 World Cups, in 1988 Greenwood sat on a committee charged with improving the English game. Typically, he argued that greed had hijacked the game he loved. For him, football was always more important than money.

Trevor Brooking expressed disappointment that the FA didn't tap into Greenwood's wealth of knowledge after his retirement but not everyone turned their back on him. Very public recognition came with the award of a CBE in 1981. There was recognition too from the Football Writers' Association, who in 1983 presented him with a tribute award for his outstanding service to the game. Greenwood also received a PFA Merit Award in 1985 and in October 2006 he was posthumously inducted into the FA's Hall of Fame. He is also a member of the League Managers' Association Hall of Fame, one of only 20 managers to be so honoured.

The town council of Loughton, where Greenwood lived during his time as West Ham manager, erected a blue plaque to his memory on one of his former houses in the town, 22 Brooklyn Avenue. It was unveiled by Brooking and the town's mayor, Chris Pond, on 28 October 2008. The Heritage Foundation charity erected a blue plaque in Greenwood's memory at West Ham's Upton Park, which was unveiled by his family on 21 January 2007.

Ron's son Neil, interviewed in Tony McDonald's *West Ham United: The Managers*, maintained that football had always consumed his dad's life. 'Mum ran the house – she had to. This hit home later in life when he had nothing else to occupy him, and he suffered from Alzheimer's. After he resigned from the England job and retired from football, that was it. He had lived and breathed football all his life and had no time for hobbies whatsoever. The only other sports he took a slight interest in were rugby league, which he watched on TV, and cricket. Mum and Dad lived in a nice flat at Hove overlooking the Sussex cricket club ground, so he'd sit out on the balcony and watch play from there. It was after they moved, from Loughton down to Brighton, that his health started to deteriorate. I think the first real indication that something wasn't quite right with him was the day he drove into Brighton and briefly forgot the way home to their flat.'

Not that Neil feels aggrieved by the fact that football appeared to have turned its back on his father, 'Dad had finished with football, he wasn't quoted in the press or pursued by them for years. He retreated to a private life, which is how he wanted it to be.'

After Brighton, Ron and Lucy moved to Sudbury, Suffolk, to be nearer their daughter Carole Johnson. Then, when Ron became too ill for Lucy to cope with on their own, he was admitted to The Beeches Residential Home at Ixworth, near Bury St Edmunds, where he spent the last 14 months of his life.

Ron died aged 84 on the morning of Wednesday, 8 February 2006 from a heart attack, after a prolonged struggle with Alzheimer's disease. He was survived by his widow, Lucy, two children, five grandchildren and four great-grandchildren. He is buried in the Town Cemetery at Sudbury in Suffolk, fittingly, only 20 miles from Alf Ramsey's grave in the Old Cemetery at Ipswich.

Alas, the powers-that-be at the FA did not see fit to show respect for the man who led England to the 1982 World Cup. There was no minute's silence at football grounds, unlike for George Best who had several, but before the England v Uruguay friendly on 1 March the organisation relented. On the day that Peter Osgood died at the age of 59 from a heart attack, they gave the order for a minute's silence for these two very different but much-admired men. It was totally respected. General Douglas MacArthur once famously said, 'Old soldiers never die; they just fade away.' The general was 84 when he died. Ron died at the same age, and his family requested a private funeral.

When West Ham played Birmingham City in a Premier League fixture on 13 February 2006, a minute's silence was held in Greenwood's memory. The Irons duly won the game 3-0.

Yet West Ham had not always been appreciative of the man who had put the club on the world football map. Harry Redknapp, one of Greenwood's successors and a former Hammers player, once revealed how during his days in charge, 'Ron Greenwood turned up for one of our games, and visited me in my little office. He was talking about walking down Green Street through the crowd, and I asked him why he hadn't driven here. He said he had. "Then where have you parked?" I asked. "Up past the station," said Ron. They couldn't get him a car park ticket apparently. Ron Greenwood, the greatest manager West Ham ever had, the man that cemented the principles that are at the heart of the club – stuck down a side street past Upton Park station because they couldn't make room for him in the car park.'

Nevertheless, Greenwood made contact with then-West Ham chairman Len Cearns in January 1990 to arrange to sell his holding of ten club shares to him for £1,000 each. Greenwood had just been approached by rivals of the Cearns family, urging him to sell to them, but the former manager demonstrated unreciprocated loyalty to his former employers by giving them first option, which they were eager to take up.

Although he didn't become a recluse, Greenwood was happy to withdraw from football, which by then had lost the values which characterised his own career in the game. However, he did keep in regular touch with his successor John Lyall and returned to Upton Park a few times in the early 1990s to lend Billy Bonds some words of support.

Bonds said, 'Ron would come to the games and pop his head inside the dressing room. He'd come into the manager's office with his grandson, but he never interfered or told me if I was doing anything wrong. I'm sure he would love to have got involved but it just wasn't his style.'

Suitably, Greenwood's last appearance on the Upton Park turf would be immediately prior to West Ham's match against Wolves in March 1993, when he, along with Geoff Hurst and Martin Peters, laid a wreath in the centre circle on the day the club paid tribute to its most famous son, Bobby Moore.

Lyall, a man who always acknowledged the positive influences of his predecessor, would pass away from a heart attack just two months after his mentor. He was only 66.

16

Legacy

IN 2017, journalist Henry Winter published *Fifty Years of Hurt,* an account of 'the second most important job in England' since 1966. Ron Greenwood was England manager for five of those years, yet his reign merited only a favourable quote from Peter Shilton, a total of 31 words.

In December 2017 an online piece was headed 'Ron Greenwood – England's "Forgotten Manager"'. It read, 'The basic fact he wasn't Clough, the people's choice, would forever make it difficult for Greenwood to capture the public imagination and shake off the perception that he was the safe rather than sexy option. While his death in 2006 did not pass unnoticed, there did not seem to be anything like the same widespread mourning as when his successor Sir Bobby Robson died in 2009.'

The piece mentioned a BBC documentary, *Three Lions,* in which Greenwood got the briefest of mentions while all other England managers since 1966 were duly accorded more space. Another programme, *Tina and Bobby,* drew a picture of Greenwood as unlikeable and even unpatriotic, suggesting that as West Ham boss he had been obstructive to Bobby Moore.

Greenwood would never have recognised himself as a 'man of the people' as Brian Clough did, but even those such as Jimmy Greaves who confessed their lack of respect for him as a manager were open in their admiration for him as a coach and footballing brain. And there is no doubt that he wanted England to succeed, or that he would be disappointed when he failed.

'To listen to him talk about football was both a pleasure and an education,' wrote BBC commentator Barry Davies in his autobiography. Trevor Brooking, in his own autobiography, said, 'Even today, England players of that era will tell you how much they thought of him. The Liverpool lads of the time were playing for the best, most successful club in Europe and they thought he was terrific to work with.'

Greenwood was first and foremost a football man rather than a celebrity, so unlike Clough he was not likely to be in demand to appear in front of the cameras on shows such as *Parkinson*. But within the game his views and ideas were highly respected. As with Ramsey before him he was a player's manager. Somehow as England boss he never seemed to quite register in the public consciousness in the same way that many of his predecessors and successors have. He was a man who deliberately kept a lower profile than others and once he retired, he went out of his way not to interfere with those who followed in the role.

With the exception of Sir Alf Ramsey, most England reigns are primarily defined by how they end. Greenwood's retirement in 1982 was amicable and he left amid neither national joy nor humiliation at the World Cup in Spain. He had realistically reached par with England effectively back as quarter-final losers.

He bucked the national trend and ushered in the emergence of black players in the English game – having earlier given Clyde Best his chance at West Ham – as Viv Anderson, Laurie Cunningham and Cyrille Regis were all handed their England debuts. 'Yellow, purple or black. If they're good enough I'll pick them,' he declared ahead of Anderson winning his first cap against Czechoslovakia in 1978.

Greenwood had long preached his purist beliefs about how to play, rather than how to win, going on record as saying, 'I cared more about the purity and finer values of football than I did about winning for winning's sake – and if that is a sin then I am a sinner. Football should be about taking risks.' And yet the game against West Germany at the 1982 World Cup seemed to go against everything he stood for as England played out a cagey 0-0 draw that smacked of a fear of losing rather than a belief they could win.

Davies wrote of Greenwood, 'He had left his club position at West Ham much too soon, to give his protégé John Lyall his chance. He came to the England helm a little too late and was probably too influenced by the eager, and from a fitness point of view too demanding, coach Don Howe.'

In tributes after his death his footballing philosophy was lauded, but his England reign was remembered more as a moderate success. Brian Glanville wrote in Greenwood's obituary in *The Guardian*, 'It was an irony that he probably did more for the England team that won the 1966 World Cup by helping the development of Bobby Moore, Geoff Hurst and Martin Peters than he did as manager in the 1982 World Cup in Spain.' His reign seemed to mainly be regarded as a solid, if unspectacular, work. Ivan Ponting in *The Independent* described him as 'having done an honourable and competent job without ever capturing the imagination of the public'.

David Lacey, also in *The Guardian*, wrote that Greenwood 'represented everything that football could be but has infrequently achieved. Throughout his career, as player, coach and manager, he strove to emphasise the game's aesthetic qualities and became disillusioned when the need to win forced teams to compromise those beliefs.'

To put these remarks in a more modern context, Arsène Wenger's Arsenal would certainly have appealed more to Greenwood than José Mourinho's Chelsea. Something else that he shared with the Frenchman was the accusation that they stayed at their respective clubs too long.

Like Wenger, Greenwood did not accept pragmatism without style, but strove for football that engaged the full range of senses, and if he lost to Liverpool or Manchester United the way that Wenger's Arsenal would lose to Chelsea's more functional football, it would only make him more determined to coach the game his way.

His approach to the game was particularly valuable at a time when the Football Association had a director of coaching, Charles Hughes, who espoused a doctrine of one-dimensional 'direct football'.

Greenwood did not believe that British was best and was convinced that British insularity was an obstacle to progress. He was critical of those players who refused to practise either to improve skills or to eliminate weaknesses. He liked to think of football as a battle of wits and disliked the British tendency to reduce it to a conflict of speed and aggression. To him it was a game of risk and teams should gamble, but with intelligence and skill.

Jeff Powell, a close friend of Bobby Moore and no apologist for Greenwood in life, wrote after his death, 'Call him Professor now, in memory of this keeper of every football-loving youngster's most precious dream. The Professor Emeritus of the West Ham Academy, that priceless font of learning back when a working man's game was struggling to emerge from its industrial age.

'A Professor who taught one truth above all others, "Football is a simple game. The enemy of the young footballer is the coach who complicates the game to try to make himself look clever. Football is about the space between two players." About that and – though he refrained from saying so – about the space between the ears of the men we refer to as managers. About that and about refusing to betray a pure philosophy no matter how heavily it was buffeted by the win-at-any-cost merchants.

'Without those principles, without that unwavering conviction, England would not have won the World Cup. There would have been no Bobby Moore collecting the Jules Rimet Trophy from Her Majesty. No Geoff Hurst scoring the only hat-trick in a World Cup Final. No Martin Peters ten years ahead of his time. No knighthood for Sir Alf Ramsey.

'And 1966 is only part of the debt this nation owes Ron Greenwood. Post-match he dispensed glasses of sherry and bucket-loads of wisdom to a room crowded with friends, admirers, football men and a few privileged reporters.

'Greenwood was the first European thinker – long before Wenger, [Gérard] Houllier, Mourinho and Rafa Benítez – to manage (sorry, teach) an English team. His legacy is seen in the Premiership today.'

Another journalist, James Lawton, elaborated:

'At the height of his glory Ron Greenwood dispensed post-match sherry and football advice in his little office at West Ham United. The talk stretched late into the night. The sherry more often than not was Bristol Cream. The talk was always golden.

'If all the chairs were taken, you sat on the floor and you listened. However imperious his manner – and it could often be at least that – everyone hung on his words, even the most self-opinionated man in English football, Sir Alf Ramsey.'

Michael Hart was probably the journalist closest to Greenwood. He wrote, 'As a schoolboy I loved watching West Ham and as a young reporter I established a rapport with Greenwood that was to last a lifetime. In the days when reporters and club managers spoke regularly and trusted each other, he taught me more about football than anyone else.

'Norman Giller was sports editor of the local newspaper in the early days of Greenwood's reign at Upton Park, and he says he learnt more about the game listening to Greenwood during weekly two-hour meetings than from anybody else he has ever met in football. Norman also used to attend Greenwood's famous after-match talk-ins when Ron would hold court in his Upton Park office while pouring sherry and analysing the game. He says that he had never met anybody to match Ron for being able to assess and dissect a game. But speaking as a player who had to carry out his orders, I have to say that for many footballers he made a simple game seem complicated.'

West Ham were fond of thinking of themselves as somehow a different club to others. That claim stems from the early 1960s when Greenwood introduced techniques unprecedented in English football. Greenwood believed that as leagues could only have one winner, clubs should look beyond success. 'Our fans,' he often claimed, 'would rather we lost an entertaining match 5-4 than won a dreary one 1-0.' Along with Greenwood's insistence on clean play, honed technique and upright discipline, this became the essence of West Ham's identity.

Which, in turn, would become the problem. When West Ham won two cups in the mid-1960s and three of their men starred in England's 1966 World Cup-winning side, Greenwood's ethos seemed on the point of vindication. It appeared that by the mid-60s the east London club had the advantages any outfit wanting to dominate English football would kill for: a thriving youth policy; directors who never interfered; stable finances; and a huge, locally focused fan base.

The trouble was that the club did not want to do anything except be itself. By the time John Lyall succeeded Greenwood as manager in the mid-1970s, West Ham's brand of football could rarely win matches, let alone trophies. Nonetheless, the scouting network continued to churn out nice young men who rather liked five-year contracts and entertaining rather than battling. When other clubs started building private boxes, West Ham swore they never would and, as football gradually opened up to the media, Lyall boasted of never having gone to lunch with a journalist.

As they passed through lesser hands, Greenwood's ideals turned insular and soft. Dominant characters and stars skipped training, while discipline, according to one former player, was nonexistent, training 'aimless' and fitness a matter of 'a coach deciding if you looked fit'.

Probably the people most familiar with Greenwood were of course his players, and it is fair to say he provoked a wide range of opinions.

Clive Charles admitted that he really did not know Greenwood, 'He was a bit aloof, and, though a great coach had his weaknesses as a man-manager. Not a lot of people got close to Greenwood.'

His brother John spent most of his career playing under Greenwood and was quite clear about his relationship with the manager, 'Greenwood was a bit careful, maybe sly even. For instance, he'd just leave you out and not tell you. I hardly ever spoke to him, as it happens, no one did really.'

However Clyde Best, who had lodged with the Charles brothers for much of his early West Ham career, said that Greenwood became a father figure to him, particularly after he received a letter in 1970 saying acid would be thrown in his face when he took the field. To him Greenwood was just a fantastic human being who understood the mentality of his players and instilled in them the way he wanted them to play.

Roger Cross would become a coach and it was no accident that when he signed as a pro Greenwood would put him in local schools to coach in the afternoons. This encouraged him to think about the game from a young age, and it was no coincidence that so many players from that era went on to coach, because it was basically ingrained in them from the moment they joined the club.

Ronnie Boyce was the heartbeat of the FA Cup-winning side, and he described Greenwood as a training ground manager who was very good at putting his ideas across and explaining the reasons behind them. He acknowledged that his man-management could be a problem, though he never had an issue with it himself.

Another stalwart, Frank Lampard, offered high praise for the man who gave him his first chance in football, 'Ron Greenwood was the Bobby Moore of the coaching world.'

Mick McGiven probably had more success as a coach than as a player and declared, 'Ron was a football genius. I remember seeing Ruud Gullit playing for Holland against England and putting in a cross with the outside of his foot for [Marco] van Basten to head in at the near post. They had been doing that at West Ham since the '60s and we used to practise it every Thursday when I was a player in the early '70s.'

Peter Brabrook signed for West Ham from Chelsea and later reflected, 'Ron was far in advance of anyone else as a manager and when I came from Chelsea it was an entirely different ball game. The coaching at Chelsea was nowhere near the same quality as that at West Ham ... he baffled me a little bit because he was so far advanced. It was unbelievable really, and things he used to do back then are even being done at West Ham now. That's how far-sighted he was.'

According to Johnny Byrne, 'The way Ron wanted us to play did take a bit of getting used to ... more for some than others though. And there were a few who expressed their doubts in no uncertain terms. And Ron's way was if you didn't want to play his way, you didn't have to and you got dropped. He was a gentle, calm man, but he could be ruthless if pushed. If you didn't understand his ways, he sometimes came across like a bit of an assassin.'

The mid-1960s were West Ham's peak years, but they were unable to sustain their success. For Byrne this was due to a combination of factors, one being that this young and boisterous team could not be controlled by Greenwood. He admitted, 'We needed someone a lot stronger who could keep us in check. He could do nothing to stop us, and we went completely berserk, living it up, day in and day out.'

But chasing players was not Greenwood's way. He wanted them to act like adults and thought the only way that would happen was if they were treated and trusted like adults. He believed that they had to take responsibility for themselves and deal with the consequences.

Harry Redknapp, in *My Autobiography*, relayed a comment from Bobby Moore, 'Do you know, Harry, that in all my time with West Ham Ron never said "well done" or "well played" to me. Not once.' That was Moore's big regret. Greenwood didn't show his feelings.

Redknapp admitted, 'Ron Greenwood had a big influence on me. He was West Ham manager when I arrived at Upton Park in 1963 and he was a fantastic coach. Every day in training was different, he could see things in a game that no one else could. He was miles ahead of anyone.

'But I think Ron had it tough handling the West Ham lads in those days. Speaking as a manager now, there's no way I would stand for some of the things Ron had to tolerate. Drink was the single biggest problem.'

Trevor Brooking's career took in the last decade of Greenwood's time at Upton Park. He reflected, 'Ron Greenwood is totally involved in football. He will talk about it for hours and no other subject will intrude. I have known him for 16 years and yet if someone asked me what his hobbies were outside football I do not know ... Away from the game he is a private person, a family man and a church man.'

According to Brooking, Greenwood didn't like confrontation, particularly when it came to his established big-name players. When they lost, he found it easier to leave out the younger players if he wanted to make changes. Picking centre-half Tommy Taylor in midfield at the start of the 1971/72 season was seen as another example of the manager's reluctance to upset his big-name signings.

John Bond said in Brian Belton's *They Nearly Reached the Sky: West Ham United in Europe*, 'When Greenwood came to West Ham and got the club into Europe, he had the chance to put into practice all the things that he'd got into his head. A lot of players had trouble understanding some of it though, but if you stuck with it, persisted, it made sense. Although he wasn't a people person – that was his biggest weakness – he was quite schoolteacher-like, not that everyone warmed to that. He got over that eventually, I think, when he managed England.'

When the Hammers had come back from playing international opposition in the USA a couple of years earlier, Greenwood had called it a new era for the club – and he had been right. He saw that West Ham's success was founded on a belief by everyone in the club, and it was this that had to be built upon. It had caused a team of great style to be developed in London's East End.

According to Ronnie Boyce, 'Football was for him, at its best, a battle of wits. He viewed any match on a slightly higher plane than most other managers.'

In Bond's opinion, Greenwood was a paradox, 'He was often accused of being a blackboard theorist, and that, to some extent, was true, but there was never a more practical manager than Ron

Greenwood. But for Ron, the person wasn't central. Sometimes, I think, on some level, he thought people just got in the way of football.

'Greenwood, quite rightly, got a lot of credit for what happened at West Ham in the mid-60s. However, you've got to remember that when he arrived at Upton Park, the place had a way of doing things that did not really change when Ron came along, but he built and strengthened the structure. What happened in 1964 and 1965 wasn't just the result of one mind or person, with a number of other folks just following instructions. Dozens of people were involved, all pulling together, handing on and working on ideas and moves over many years, from the late 50s in fact.

'Ron had players who believed in what he believed in. It's no good if a manager says what he wants, and the players don't believe in it. We gelled together. Ron developed his ideas with the players – that is, he didn't just come to transplant a way of doing things, although in the first instance I think he had a notion of creating a kind of "Arsenal lite". What was produced was something quite unique, and I think even he was surprised.

'The Cup Winners' Cup win was the perfect example of how he wanted the game thought about and performed. I don't know if it ever happened for him again. Maybe that would have been the best time for him to have left the club. It's difficult to build on something that has already reached your ideal. It's got to be all downhill when you've come to the top of the mountain, hasn't it? A Malcolm Allison coming in at that time would have driven West Ham on to bigger and better things, and a move to somewhere like Arsenal or Chelsea would have given Ron a more comfortable situation in terms of his personality.'

* * *

Ron Greenwood's legacy is both tangible and intangible. Winning two major trophies at a relatively modest club cements his place in the history books. However, it's the pioneering philosophies that ensure his fingerprints will remain on West Ham's history forever, long after the move from Upton Park to Stratford.

Aside from his impact at the Boleyn, Greenwood's influence on English football as a whole is almost immeasurable. Having already helped develop some of England's World Cup-winning stars during his time running the Three Lions' youth setup, the West Ham boss instilled a winning mentality into three of 1966's most iconic stars.

He additionally helped rewrite the managerial rulebook, particularly during those West Ham days, by building an attacking team despite actively working around the qualities of a talented defender. Similarly, while he wasn't the first or only person to do it, a conscious decision to incorporate the same blueprint from youth level through to senior football would have a telling impact on the future of English management.

Managers such as Ken Brown, John Bond, John Lyall and Harry Redknapp all graduated from his academy, while West Ham men such as Tony Carr, whom Greenwood once coached, were behind one of the richest production lines in English football: Frank Lampard, Joe Cole and Rio Ferdinand among others. His desire for continuity at England level was a by-product of his stewardship – Bobby Robson, Terry Venables and Howard Wilkinson were all part of his team.

He might not have enjoyed the same affection from players and fans as Sir Matt Busby and Bill Shankly, but his integrity, knowledge and dedication invariably commanded respect.

West Ham were among the 'entertainers' of the English game in the 1960s. Unfortunately, Greenwood's style was also widely seen as a soft touch for the ever growing 'professionalism' of other teams in the league. While his knowledge of the game and purist style gained many admirers, some of his players in later years described him as not a people person who was aloof in many ways.

But Geoff Hurst was more complimentary in his autobiography and wrote, 'Much of what I learned from him in those days is still relevant today. When I am watching games, situations arise on the pitch that often make me think of the things he used to tell us. For every tactical problem he had an answer. When I see a team with a problem, I still think to myself, Ron would solve it this way or that way. For instance, a team may be having difficulty in bypassing opposing defenders. Ron taught us to create what he called "two against one" situations all over the pitch. The object was to bypass defenders with a forward pass rather than a square one across the field. It was really the essence of West Ham's one-touch game and was dependent on the sharpness, vision and movement of our players. Too often today players accept second best with a square pass or high ball over the top of defenders simply because they have never been taught a passing strategy that carries them through the heart of the opposing team.'

Through good seasons and bad, Greenwood always stood by his West Ham style and he always thought there was a magical missing link that would take the team to the heights of English football. He never found it and his purist ideals also led to players being sent out to play with strict instructions that they were not to 'hurt' opposition players. These were forefront in his mind when he said the most disappointing thing that happened in the 1968/69 season was Redknapp getting sent off at Leeds. There seemed to be a theme, especially from northern teams back in those days, that they would openly applaud West Ham's style by saying 'they let you play'. It was really a backhanded compliment in many ways as their more unscrupulous tactics often won the day.

Greenwood will always be remembered as a great West Ham manager, playing the game the traditional 'West Ham Way'.

Much of Sir Alf Ramsey's success was due to Greenwood's vision. It was Greenwood who converted Hurst from half-back to striker; it was Greenwood – a centre-half as a player – who helped mould the young Bobby Moore into an imperious defender; and it was Greenwood who persuaded Ramsey to employ the talents of Martin Peters, the player Ramsey would later describe as 'ten years ahead of his time'.

It was Greenwood, too, who perfected the art of the cross to the near post – perhaps his major contribution to coaching – used to stunning effect by Hurst, Peters and Moore during England's 1966 campaign.

The website Footballwhispers claimed, 'Quite simply, Greenwood is the finest manager to occupy the home dugout in West Ham's 112 years at the Boleyn. When supplemented by his role in building England's 1966 heroes, he is the tenth best manager that the country has ever produced.'

'Yes, I suppose you could call me a tracksuit manager,' he once replied immediately in an interview to what was probably intended as a criticism. Greenwood's humility and openness with reporters led, perhaps unfairly, to him being the inspiration for *Private Eye* magazine's spoof manager of Neasden FC, Ron Knee.

Let the final verdict be Greenwood's own, 'The game goes on though, and I am still part of it; but I know now what the real prizes in life are. Cups and medals are important, but football offers nothing more precious than true friends. A warm handshake and a shared memory, such simple things, mean more than a line in the record books. It is a lesson only time teaches.

'The memories and friendships endure, and so will football. It is a game, but it can be more than a game. It is what we choose to make it.'

Appendix

England under-23 manager: October 1958–March 1961

- 15 October 1958: England 3 Czechoslovakia 0
- 19 March 1959: France 1 England 1
- 7 May 1959: Italy 0 England 3
- 10 May 1959: West Germany 2 England 2
- 23 September 1959: England 0 Hungary 1
- 11 November 1959: England 2 France 0
- 2 March 1960: Scotland 4 England 4
- 16 March 1960: England 5 Netherlands 2
- 15 May 1960: German Democratic Republic 1 England 4
- 18 May 1960: Poland 2 England 3
- 22 May 1960: Israel 4 England 0
- 2 November 1960: England 1 Italy 1
- 8 February 1961: England 2 Wales 0
- 1 March 1961: England 0 Scotland 1
- 15 March 1961: England 4 West Germany 1

West Ham manager: season by season
1960/61 First Division
Played: 4
Won: 0
Drew: 3
Lost: 1
For: 5
Against: 6
Points: 3

1961/62 First Division
Played: 42
Won: 17
Drew: 10
Lost: 15
For: 76
Against: 82
Points: 44
Position: 8/22

League Cup
1: Plymouth A (H) W 3-2
2: Aston Villa (H) L 1-3

FA Cup
3: Plymouth A (A) L 0-3

1962/63 First Division
Played: 42
Won: 14

Drew: 12

Lost: 16

For: 73

Against: 69

Points: 40

Position: 12/22

League Cup

1: Plymouth A (H) W 6-0

2: Rotherham United (A) L 1-3

FA Cup

3: Fulham (H) D 0-0

3R: Fulham (A) W 2-1

4: Swansea Town (H) W 1-0

5: Everton (H) W 1-0

QF: Liverpool (A) L 0-1

American Soccer League in New York, Detroit and Chicago

1963	Kilmarnock (Scotland)	3-3
1963	Mantova (Italy)	2-4
1963	Preussen Munster (West Germany)	2-0
1963	Valenciennes (France)	3-1
1963	Oro (Mexico)	3-1
1963	Recife (Brazil)	1-1
1963	Górnik Zabrze (Poland)	1-1
1963	Górnik Zabrze (Poland)	1-0

Challenge Cup Final in New York

1963	Dukla Prague (Czechoslovakia)	0-1
1963	Dukla Prague (Czechoslovakia)	1-1

1963/64 First Division

Played: 42

Won: 14

Drew: 12

Lost: 16

For: 69

Against: 74

Points: 40

Position: 14/22

League Cup

2: Leyton Orient (H) W 2-1

3: Aston Villa (A) W 2-0

4: Swindon Town (A) D 3-3

4R: Swindon Town (H) W 4-1

5: Workington (H) W 6-0

SF1: Leicester City (A) L 1-4

SF2: Leicester City (H) L 0-2

FA Cup

3: Charlton (H) W 3-0

4: Leyton Orient (A) D 1-1

4R: Leyton Orient (H) W 3-0

5: Swindon Town (A) W 3-1

QF: Burnley (H) W 3-2

SF: Manchester United (Hillsborough) W 3-1

F: Preston North End (Wembley) W 3-2

1964/65 First Division

Played: 42

Won: 19

Drew: 4

Lost: 19

For: 83

Against: 71

Points: 42

Position: 9/22

Charity Shield

Liverpool (A) D 2-2

League Cup

2: Sunderland (A) L 1-4

FA Cup

3: Birmingham City (H) W 4-2

4: Chelsea (H) L 0-1

European Cup Winners' Cup

1L1: La Gantoise (A) W 1-0

1L2: La Gantoise (H) D 1-1

2L1: Spartak Sokolovo (H) W 2-0

2L2: Spartak Sokolovo (A) L 1-2

3L1: Lausanne-Sport (A) W 2-1

3L2: Lausanne Sport (H) W 4-3

SF1: Real Zaragoza (H) W 2-1

SF2: Real Zaragoza (A) D 1-1

F: 1860 Munich (Wembley) W 2-0

1965/66 First Division

Played: 42

Won: 15

Drew: 9

Lost: 18

For: 70

Against: 83

Points: 39

Position: 12/22

League Cup

2: Bristol Rovers (A) D 3-3

2R: Bristol Rovers (H) W 3-2

3: Mansfield Town (H) W 4-0

4: Rotherham United (A) W 2-1

5: Grimsby Town (A) D 2-2

5: Grimsby Town (H) W 1-0

SF1: Cardiff City (H) W 5-2

SF2: Cardiff City (A) W 5-1

F1: West Bromwich Albion (H) W 2-1

F2: West Bromwich Albion (A) L 1-4

FA Cup

3: Oldham Athletic (A) D 2-2

3R: Oldham Athletic (H) W 2-1

4: Blackburn Rovers (H) D 3-3

4: Blackburn Rovers (A) L 1-4

European Cup Winners' Cup

2L1: Olympiakos (H) W 4-0

2L2: Olympiakos (A) D 2-2

3L1: FC Magdeburg (H) W 1-0

3L2: FC Magdeburg (A) D 1-1

SF1: Borussia Dortmund (H) L 1-2

SF2: Borussia Dortmund (A) L 1-3

1966/67 First Division

Played: 42

Won: 14

Drew: 8

Lost: 20

For: 80

Against: 84

Points: 36

Position: 16/22

League Cup

2: Tottenham Hotspur (H) W 1-0

3: Arsenal (A) W 3-1

4: Leeds United (H) W 7-0

5: Blackpool (A) W 3-1

SF1: West Bromwich Albion (A) L 0-4

SF2: West Bromwich Albion (D) 2-2

FA Cup

3: Swindon Town (H) D 3-3

3R: Swindon Town (A) L 1-3

1967/68 First Division

Played: 42

Won: 14

Drew: 10

Lost: 18

For: 73

Against: 69

Points: 38

Position: 12/22

League Cup

2: Walsall (A) W 5-1

3: Bolton Wanderers (H) W 4-1

4: Huddersfield Town (A) L 0-2

FA Cup

3: Burnley (A) W 3-1

4: Stoke City (A) W 3-0

5: Sheffield United (H) L 1-2

1968/69 First Division

Played: 42

Won: 13

Drew: 18

Lost: 11

For: 66

Against: 50

Points: 44

Position: 8/22

League Cup

2: Bolton Wanderers (H) W 7-2

3: Coventry City (H) D 0-0

3R: Coventry City (A) L 2-3

FA Cup

3: Bristol City (H) W 3-2

4: Huddersfield Town (A) W 2-0

5: Mansfield Town (A) L 0-3

1969/70 First Division

Played: 42

Won: 12

Drew: 12

Lost: 18

For: 51

Against: 60

Points: 36

Position: 17/22

League Cup

2: Halifax Town (H) W 4-2

3: Nottingham Forest (A) L 0-1

FA Cup

3: Middlesbrough (A) L 1-2

1970/71 First Division

Played: 42

Won: 10

Drew: 14

Lost: 18

For: 47

Against: 60

Points: 34

Position: 20/22

League Cup

2: Hull City (H) W 1-0

3: Coventry City (A) L 1-3

FA Cup

3: Blackpool (A) L 0-4

1971/72 First Division

Played: 42

Won: 12

Drew: 12

Lost: 18

For: 47

Against: 51

Points: 36

Position: 14/22

League Cup

2: Cardiff City (H) D 1-1

2R: Cardiff City (A) W 2-1

3: Leeds United (H) D 0-0

3R: Leeds United (A) W 1-0

4: Liverpool (H) W 1-0

5: Sheffield United (H) W 5-0

SF1: Stoke City (A) W 2-1

SF2: Stoke City (H) L 1-0

SFR1: Stoke City (Hillsborough) D 0-0

SFR2: Stoke City (Old Trafford) L 3-2

FA Cup

3: Luton Town (H) W 2-1

4: Hereford United (A) D 0-0

4R: Hereford United (H) W 3-1

5: Huddersfield Town (A) L 4-2

1972/73 First Division

Played: 42

Won: 17

Drew: 12

Lost: 13

For: 67

Against: 53

Points: 46

Position: 6/22

League Cup

2: Bristol City (H) W 2-1

3: Stockport County (A) L 0-1

FA Cup

3: Port Vale (A) W 1-0

4: Hull City (A) L 0-1

1973/74 First Division

Played: 42

Won: 11

Drew: 15

Lost: 16

For: 55

Against: 60

Points: 37

Position: 18/22

League Cup

2: Liverpool (H) D 2-2

2R: Liverpool (A) L 0-1

FA Cup

3: Hereford United (H) D 1-1

3R: Hereford United (A) L 1-2

1974/75 First Division

Played: 5

Won: 1

Drew: 1

Lost: 3

For: 4

Against: 9

Points: 3

Position 13/22

England

England 0 Switzerland 0 (Friendly)
7 September 1977
Wembley Stadium

Luxembourg 0 England 2 (World Cup qualifier)
12 October 1977
Stade Municipal, Luxembourg

England 2 Italy 0 (World Cup qualifier)
16 November 1977
Wembley Stadium

West Germany 2 England 1 (Friendly)
22 February 1978
Olympiastadion, Munich

England 1 Brazil 1 (Friendly)
19 April 1978
Wembley Stadium

Wales 1 England 3 (British Home Championship)
13 May 1978
Ninian Park, Cardiff

England 1 Northern Ireland 0 (British Home Championship)
16 May 1978
Wembley Stadium

Scotland 0 England 1 (British Home Championship)
20 May 1978
Hampden Park, Glasgow

England 4 Hungary 1 (Friendly)
24 May 1978
Wembley Stadium

Denmark 3 England 4 (European Championship qualifier)
20 September 1978
Idraetsparken, Copenhagen

Republic of Ireland 1 England 1 (European Championship qualifier)
25 October 1978
Lansdowne Road, Dublin

England 1 Czechoslovakia 0 (Friendly)
29 November 1978
Wembley Stadium

England 4 Northern Ireland 0 (European Championship qualifier)
7 February 1979
Wembley Stadium

Northern Ireland 0 England 2 (British Home Championship)
19 May 1979
Windsor Park, Belfast

England 0 Wales 0 (British Home Championship)
23 May 1979
Wembley Stadium

England 3 Scotland 1 (British Home Championship)
26 May 1979
Wembley Stadium

Bulgaria 0 England 3 (European Championship qualifier)
6 June 1979
Natsionalen Stadion Vasil Levski, Sofia

Sweden 0 England 0 (Friendly)
10 June 1979
Råsunda Fotbollsstadion, Solna

Austria 4 England 3 (Friendly)
13 June 1979
Praterstadion, Vienna

England 1 Denmark 0 (European Championship qualifier)
12 September 1979
Wembley Stadium

Northern Ireland 1 England 5 (European Championship qualifier)
17 October 1979
Windsor Park, Belfast

England 2 Bulgaria 0 (European Championship qualifier)
22 November 1979
Wembley Stadium

England 2 Republic of Ireland 0 (European Championship qualifier)
6 February 1980
Wembley Stadium

Spain 0 England 2 (Friendly)
26 March 1980
Camp Nou, Barcelona

England 3 Argentina 1 (Friendly)
13 May 1980
Wembley Stadium

Wales 4 England 1 (British Home Championship)
17 May 1980
Racecourse Ground, Wrexham

England 1 Northern Ireland 1 (British Home Championship)
20 May 1980
Wembley Stadium

Scotland 0 England 2 (British Home Championship)
24 May 1980
Hampden Park, Glasgow

Australia 1 England 2 (Friendly)
31 May 1980
Sydney Cricket Ground

England 1 Belgium 1 (European Championship finals)
12 June 1980
Stadio Comunale, Turin

England 0 Italy 1 (European Championship finals)
15 June 1980
Stadio Comunale, Turin

England 2 Spain 1 (European Championship finals)
18 June 1980
Stadio San Paolo, Naples

England 4 Norway 0 (World Cup qualifier)
10 September 1980
Wembley Stadium

Romania 2 England 1 (World Cup qualifier)
15 October 1980
Arena Naţională, Bucharest

England 1 Spain 2 (Friendly)
25 March 1981
Wembley Stadium

England 0 Romania 0 (World Cup qualifier)
29 April 1981
Wembley Stadium

England 0 Brazil 1 (Friendly)
12 May 1981
Wembley Stadium

England 0 Wales 0 (British Home Championship)
20 May 1981
Wembley Stadium

England 0 Scotland 1 (British Home Championship)
23 May 1981
Wembley Stadium

Switzerland 2 England 1 (World Cup qualifier)
30 May 1981
St Jakob-Park, Basel

Hungary 1 England 3 (World Cup qualifier)
6 June 1981
Népstadion, Budapest

Norway 2 England 1 (World Cup qualifier)
9 September 1981
Ullevaal Stadion, Oslo

England 1 Hungary 0 (World Cup qualifier)
18 November 1981
Wembley Stadium

England 4 Northern Ireland 0 (British Home Championship)
23 February 1982
Wembley Stadium

Wales 0 England 1 (British Home Championship)
27 April 1982
Ninian Park, Cardiff

England 2 Netherlands 0 (Friendly)
25 May 1982
Wembley Stadium

Scotland 0 England 1 (British Home Championship)
29 May 1982
Hampden Park, Glasgow

Iceland 1 England 1 (Friendly)
2 June 1982
Laugardalsvöllur, Reykjavík

Finland 1 England 4 (Friendly)
3 June 1982
Olympic Stadium, Helsinki

England 3 France 1 (World Cup finals)
16 June 1982
San Mamés Stadium, Bilbao

England 2 Czechoslovakia 0 (World Cup finals)
20 June 1982
San Mamés Stadium, Bilbao

England 1 Kuwait 0 (World Cup finals)
25 June 1982
San Mamés Stadium, Bilbao

England 0 West Germany 0 (World Cup finals)
29 June 1982
Santiago Bernabéu Stadium, Madrid

England 0 Spain 0 (World Cup finals)
5 July 1982
Santiago Bernabéu Stadium, Madrid

England Managerial Records – More Than 50 Matches

Manager	Played	Won	Drawn	Lost	Win %
Alf Ramsey	113	69	27	17	61.1%
Ron Greenwood	55	33	12	10	60%
Sven-Göran Eriksson	67	40	17	10	59.7%
Roy Hodgson	56	33	15	8	58.9%
Walter Winterbottom	139	78	33	28	56.1%
Bobby Robson	95	47	30	18	49.5%

Match Record – All Matches

Type	P	W	D	L	F	A	GD
Home	24	15	6	3	39	10	+29
Away	25	14	4	7	45	27	+18
Neutral	6	4	2	0	9	3	+6

Match Record – By Type of Match

Type	P	W	D	L	F	A	GD
World Cup Qualifier	10	6	1	3	17	8	+9
World Cup Finals	5	3	2	0	6	1	+5
World Cup – Total	15	9	3	3	23	9	+14
European Championship Qualifier	8	7	1	0	22	5	+17
European Championship Finals	3	1	1	1	3	3	=0
European Championship – Total	11	8	2	1	25	8	+17
British Championship	14	9	3	2	20	8	+12
Friendly	15	7	4	4	25	15	+10

Bibliography

Books:

Malcolm Allison, *Colours of My Life* (Everest Books, 1976)

Robert Banks, *An Irrational Hatred of Everything* (Biteback Publishing, 2018)

John Barnes, *The Autobiography* (Headline, 1999)

Brian Belton, *Burn Budgie Byrne* (Breedon Books, 2004)

Brian Belton, *Bubbles, Hammers & Dreams* (Breedon Books, 1997)

Brian Belton, *The Black Hammers* (Pennant Books, 2006)

Brian Belton, *They Nearly Reached the Sky: West Ham United in Europe* (Fonthill, 2017)

Brian Belton, *The First and Last Englishmen: West Ham United in the 1960s* (DB Publishing, 2013)

Clyde Best, *The Acid Test,* (deCoubertin, 2019)

Kirk Blows and Tony Hogg, *The Essential History of West Ham United* (Headline, 2000)

Simon Briggs, *Don't Mention the Score: A Masochists' History of the England Football Team* (Quercus, 2009)

Trevor Brooking, *An Autobiography* (Pelham Books, 1981)

Trevor Brooking, *My Life in Football* (Simon & Schuster, 2014)

Jason Cowley, *The Last Game* (Simon & Schuster, 2009)

Iain Dale, *West Ham: A Nostalgic Look at a Century of the Club* (Haynes Publishing, 2011)

Eric Dunning, Patrick Murphy and John Williams, *The Roots of Football Hooliganism: An Historical and Sociological Study* (Routledge and Kegan Paul, 1988)

Matt Dickinson, *Bobby Moore: The Man in Full* (Yellow Jersey Press, 2014)

Paul Dutton and Rick Glanvill, *Chelsea: The Complete Record* (deCoubertin, 2015)

David Edgerton, *The Rise and Fall of the British Nation* (Penguin Books, 2019)

Niall Edworthy, *The Second Most Important Job in the Country* (Virgin Publishing, 1999)

Ted Fenton, *At Home with the Hammers* (Nicholas Kaye, 1960)

Brian Glanville, *England Managers: The Toughest Job in Football* (Headline, 2008)

Rick Glanvill, *Chelsea: The Official Biography* (Headline, 2006)

David Goldblatt, *The Ball is Round: A Global History of Football* (Viking, 2006)

David Goldblatt, *The Game of our Lives: The Meaning and Making of English Football* (Viking, 2014)

Jimmy Greaves, *Don't Shoot the Manager: The Revealing Story of England's Soccer Bosses* (Boxtree, 1994)

Ron Greenwood, *Yours Sincerely* (Willow Books, 1984)

John Helliar and Clive Leatherdale, West *Ham United – the Elite Era: 1958–2009* (Desert Island Books, 2009)

Jimmy Hill, *The Jimmy Hill Story* (Hodder & Stoughton, 2016)

Tony Hogg and Tony McDonald, *Who's Who: A Player by Player Guide to West Ham United* (Independent UK Sports Publications, 1996)

Richard Holt, *Sport and the British* (Oxford University Press, 1989)

Arthur Hopcraft, *The Football Man* (Autumn Press, 2006)

Geoff Hurst, *The World Game* (Stanley Paul, 1967)

Geoff Hurst, *My Autobiography: 1966 and All That* (Headline, 2005)

Dennis Irving, *The West Ham United Football Book* (Stanley Paul, 1968)

Dennis Irving, *The West Ham United Football Book No. 2* (Stanley Paul, 1969)

Gary Jordan, *Out of the Shadows: The Story of the 1982 England World Cup Team* (Pitch Publishing, 2017)

Charles Korr, *West Ham United* (Duckworth, 1986)

Stan Liversedge, *This England Job* (Soccer Book Publishing, 1996)

John Lyall, *Just Like My Dreams: My Life with West Ham* (Viking, 1988)

Tony McDonald, *West Ham United: The Managers* (Football World, 2007)

Tony McDonald, *West Ham in My Day* (Football World, 2007)

Tony McDonald and Terry Roper, *West Ham in My Day, Volume 2* (Football World, 2008)

Leo McKinstry, *Sir Alf* (HarperSport, 2007)

Andrew Marr, *A History of Modern Britain* (Pan Books, 2008)

John Moynihan, *The West Ham Story* (Arthur Barker, 1984)

Graham Morse, *Sir Walter Winterbottom: The Father of English Football* (John Blake, 2016)

Andrew Mourant, *Don Revie: Portrait of a Footballing Enigma* (Mainstream, 1990)

John Northcutt and Steve Marsh, *West Ham United: The Complete Record* (deCoubertin, 2015)

John Northcutt and Roy Shoesmith, *West Ham United: An Illustrated History* (Breedon Books, 1998)

Emy Onuora, *Pitch Black* (Biteback Publishing, 2015)

Tony Pawson, *The Football Managers* (Eyre Methuen, 1973)

Martin Peters, *Martin Peters: The Ghost of '66* (Orion Books, 2006)

Jeff Powell, *Bobby Moore: The Life and Times of a Sporting Hero* (Robson Books, 1993)

J.B. Priestley, *English Journey* (William Heinemann, 1934)

Harry Redknapp, *My Autobiography* (CollinsWillow, 1998)

Harry Redknapp, *Harry: My Autobiography* (Ebury Press, 2013)

Harry Redknapp, *Harry: A Man Walks on to a Pitch* (Ebury Press, 2014)

Barney Ronay, *The Manager: The Absurd Ascent of the Most Important Man in Football* (Sphere, 2009)

Terry Roper, *West Ham in the Sixties: The Jack Burkett Story* (Football World, 2009)

Dominic Sandbrook, *White Heat: A History of Britain in the Swinging Sixties* (Abacus, 2007)

Dominic Sandbrook, *State of Emergency – The Way We Were: Britain 1970–74* (Allen Lane, 2010)

Dominic Sandbrook, *Seasons in the Sun: The Battle for Britain 1974–79* (Allen Lane, 2012)

Dominic Sandbrook, *Who Dares Wins: Britain 1979–1982* (Allen Lane, 2019)

Brian Scovell, *Bill Nicholson: Football's Perfectionist* (John Blake, 2011)

Brian Scovell, *The England Managers: The Impossible Job* (Tempus Publishing, 2006)

Phil Stevens, *John Lyall: A Life in Football* (Apex Publishing, 2015)

Steve Tongue, *Turf Wars: A History of London Football* (Pitch Publishing, 2016)

David Tossell, *Big Mal: The High Life and Hard Times of Malcolm Allison, Football Legend* (Mainstream, 2008)

David Tossell, *Natural: The Jimmy Greaves Story* (Pitch Publishing, 2019)

Adam Ward, *The Official History of West Ham United: 1895–1999* (Hamlyn, 1999)

Eric White, *100 Years of Brentford* (publisher unknown, 1989)

Henry Winter, *Fifty Years of Hurt* (Black Swan, 2017)

Magazines:
Ex Magazine
Soccer Star
When Saturday Comes
World Soccer
The Blizzard

BIBLIOGRAPHY

Newspapers:
The Guardian
The Independent
Daily Telegraph
The Times
Daily Mail
Daily Mirror
The Sun
Ilford Recorder
Newham Recorder

Websites:
https://en.wikipedia.org/wiki/Ron_Greenwood
https://www.theguardian.com/football/2006/feb/09/sportobituaries
https://www.independent.co.uk/news/obituaries/ron-greenwood-6109500.
    html
news.bbc.co.uk/sport1/hi/front_page/1447218.stm
https://www.wsc.co.uk/the-archive/32-Managers/1355-thinking-mans-
    manager
https://www.telegraph.co.uk/news/obituaries/1510087/Ron-
    Greenwood.html
www.leaguemanagers.com/managers/ron-greenwood-cbe/
https://www.flickr.com/photos/norfolkodyssey/18151828055
www.theyflysohigh.co.uk
www.whu-programmes.co.uk
www.westhamstats.info/
www.kumb.com
www.westhamtillidie.com/
https://www.whufc.com/club/history/managers/ron-greenwood
https://www.11v11.com/
https://www.nationalfootballmuseum.com/explore-the-museum/hall-
    of-fame/about-the-hall-of-fame/
https://www.bbc.co.uk/sport/football

european-football-statistics.co.uk/

fchd.info

https://www.fulhamweb.co.uk/player/319/ronald-greenwood.aspx

www.englandfootballonline.com/Seas1946-60/1951-52/
    M0269bNed1952.html

www.englandfootballonline.com/teammgr/Mgr_Greenwood.html

https://englandmemories.com/2017/12/19/ron-greenwood-englands-
    forgotten-manager/

https://en.wikipedia.org/wiki/Belfast_Celtic_F.C.

https://en.wikipedia.org/wiki/Bradford_(Park_Avenue)_A.F.C.

https://web.archive.org/web/20120320161613/http://bpafc.com/wp-
    content/uploads/2010/07/Bradford-Park-Avenue-History-Long1.
    pdf

https://bpafc.com/club/history/

https://www.chelseafc.com/

Podcasts:

Coming in from the Cold